PALEOLITHIC
TYPOLOGY

HANDBOOK OF
PALEOLITHIC
TYPOLOGY

VOLUME ONE: LOWER AND MIDDLE PALEOLITHIC OF EUROPE

André Debénath & Harold L. Dibble

Editing
Publications Division, The University Museum

Design, production
Bagnell & Socha

Printing
Cypher Press

Library of Congress Cataloging-in-Publication Data

Debénath, André
Handbook of paleolithic typology / André Debénath, Harold L. Dibble.
      p. cm.
Includes bibliographical references (v. 1, p.   ) and index.
Contents: v. 1. Lower and middle paleolithic of Europe.
ISBN 0-924171-23-5
1. Paleolithic period—Europe. 2. Stone implements—Europe—Classification.
3. Tools, Prehistoric—Europe—Classification. 4. Europe—Antiquities. I.
Dibble, Harold Lewis. II. Title.
GN772.2.A1D43 1993
936—dc20   93-12451
     CIP

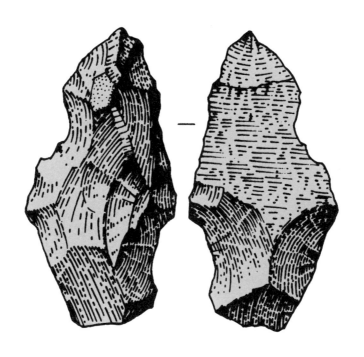

T o

L e e   a n d   G e n e v i è v e

CONTENTS

FOREWORD

THIS VOLUME CONSTITUTES A MOST USEFUL, INFORMATIVE, AND WELCOME aid to workers and students in paleoanthropology. It presents thorough discussion and substantial illustration of the technical and typological aspects of the lithic components of the European Lower and Middle Paleolithic. It is based on the system of typology developed and refined over a period of years, through analysis of artifact collections and his own exceptional

skill at replicating such artifacts, by the late Prof. François Bordes. The typology, its basis and criteria for delineation of major categories and specific types, was published and illustrated *in extenso* (in French) by him in two large-format volumes in 1961, reissued in 1967 and 1979, and subsequently republished in 1981 as the initial volume of the series, *Cahiers du Quaternaire*, under the auspices of the Centre National de la Recherche Scientifique, Paris.

Since the initial publication some thirty years ago, these volumes have constituted the fundamental resource and guide for prehistoric archaeologists in their concern with the analysis, description, and comparison of assemblages of Lower and Middle Paleolithic lithic artifacts. Ultimately, this approach to artifactual analysis and categorization, and overall characterization of lithic assemblage structure and diversity, was to be adopted, in whole or in large part, and with attendant modifications and additions as necessary of distinctive, unrecognized types or subtypes, throughout Europe, including the former Soviet Union, and in countries of western Asia. The impact was extensive and profound; it afforded great impetus to efforts at systematization of analytical and descriptive procedures and enabled, for the first time, quantitative and other comparative studies previously hindered by the absence of consistent terminology and/or the idiosyncratic perspectives of individual investigators. Moreover, for well over twenty years the Institut de Préhistoire, at Université de Bordeaux, was to serve as a focus for the exposition of *la Système Bordes* to innumerable Paleolithic archaeologists from throughout the world.

My own first direct exposure to this approach resulted from an opportunity to participate in the initial field season (1953) of excavations at the Abri Pataud (Dordogne), under the direction of H. L. Movius, Jr., at which time I also met both Profs. F. and D. Bordes, and had an opportunity to work briefly at Pech de l'Azé. A rather deeper immersion followed in 1956, in Paris at the Institut de Paléontologie Humaine. However, this was well prior to the initial and full publication of the *Typologie* in 1961. Thus, when (1957–1958) it became necessary

to deal with the typological diversity of the Acheulian assemblages from Isimila (Tanzania) it was incumbent on my colleagues (Glen Cole and Maxine Kleindienst) and me to devise, from a diversity of published sources, a suitable set of categories and denominations to facilitate assemblage analyses there, and subsequently at other East African localities (e.g., Kariandusi, Olorgesailie, etc.) that had yielded important Acheulian assemblages. This effort was elaborated and systematized, and duly published by Kleindienst (1961, 1962), based on her doctoral dissertation, and was subsequently modified and substantially expanded, in association with the researches at Kalambo Falls, by J. D. Clark and Kleindienst (1974). It is worth mentioning that F. Bordes was in residence, as visiting professor of anthropology, at the University of Chicago in autumn of 1959, on the occasion also of the Darwin centennial celebration, and had substantial input into our then on-going efforts on the excavated assemblages from the Isimila locality (now housed at the Field Museum of Natural History, Chicago). He then also illustrated for us a substantial number, and some diversity of types from that locality (mostly excepting small tools, many of which are made on quartz, a new material largely unfamiliar to Bordes at that time).

Bordes visited for several days the on-going excavations at the Torralba and Ambrona (Spain) Lower Paleolithic localities in the summer of 1963. We then had the advantage of his published *Typologie*, which we found to be broadly appropriate, with some modifications and additions, to the Acheulian assemblages from these localities. Moreover, our assessments and attributions were very largely supported by him in the course of his own examination of the lithic collections stemming from the three field seasons at the sites. L. G. Freeman had also worked for some time, earlier that year, in the Bordeaux laboratory as part of his doctoral research on the Mousterian of Cantabrian Spain.

In the spring of 1964, Bordes, Movius, and I were together in Hungary for some weeks, at the invitation of Laszlo Vértes and Miklos Kretzoi and under the auspices of the Hungarian Academy of Sciences. The occasion was the recent discovery and then on-going excavations at the site of Vértesszölös, which, along with various other sites and geological sections, we were able to visit. Each of us, because of our then prevailing interests, concentrated our study opportunities on different aspects of the available Paleolithic record in Hungary. Movius concentrated on the Upper Paleolithic, Bordes on the Middle, and I on the Lower (namely, Vértesszölös). Thus, in a way, my observations on the Vértesszölös assemblage reflect a composite and consensus perspective of the three of us. Later that summer, in the course of a study trip lasting over several months in Europe (including England), I was able to work again on assorted, often excavated Lower Paleolithic assemblages; in the Bordeaux laboratory, most time was devoted to the Cagny-la-Garenne collections, again with much interaction with F. Bordes. The latter, and the previous experience with Vértesszölös, brought home to me most forcefully the importance of raw material resources as a significant factor in aspects of assemblage structure.

The following academic year, in the course of my own visiting professorship at the University of Chicago, F. and D. Bordes were visitors in the spring term. At that time much photographic footage was expended in recording his (and also Don Crabtree's) efforts in producing a diversity of Paleolithic artifacts. Only a very limited amount of this footage was subsequently employed in the production of *Early Stone Tools*, a brief twenty-minute educational film of the University of Chicago Extension Media Center, which I reviewed and found inadequate and disappointing in its pedagogical intent.

These fragments of historical incidents are recorded from the perspective of one peripherally rather than centrally involved with in-depth description and analysis of Paleolithic lithic residues. My own research program was always more broadly concerned with major aspects of hominid biological evolution and adaptation, and the concern with such lithic (and other) products of human activities, with their organic associates, was conceived as an adjunct toward insight into the former domain. Nonetheless, my experience forcefully brought to the fore both the practical utility of such analytical procedures as well as their limitations in particular site contexts with reference to local or more regional settings. It brought to mind, in fact, certain difficulties or problems which have since become, in the past decade or so, central foci for new sorts of research by a younger generation of investigators.

Much of the past concern with archaeological typology was motivated particularly by cultural-historical and developmental/evolutionary paradigms. The *fossile directeur* concept, now largely out of fashion, is reflective of that preoccupation which, frankly, has both a typological and antiquarian ring to it. The increasing attention focused on raw material variability, whether local or exotic, and on such resources and their exploitation within local and broader settings is an important and refreshing development. The processes of artifact production, expressed in delineation of *chaînes opératoires*, the recognition of reduction sequences, and investigation of artifact curation, discard, and utilization are now matters of enhanced and central concern. Similarly, conjoining/refitting studies are an integral aspect of assemblage analysis, as are studies of breakage patterns, and edge-damage and use-wear, the latter through replication and experimentation and the employment of microscopy. Such developments enable new insights, beyond mere inference and rank speculation, into the "life history" of artifacts, and have shifted in a substantial fashion prior concern with statics to an evaluation of dynamics within the context of site visitation, occupation, and utilization. Bordes' original concern with seeking comprehension and quantitative assessment of *assemblage* composition, variability, and structure, was, in its way, fundamental to these subsequent developments and current research concerns. It is critical always to bear in mind the source, composition, and idiosyncrasies of assemblages within the perspective of site structure, overall associations and distributions, and site-formation processes. The most elaborated typological analyses are largely for naught if these essential contextual aspects are absent or remain unevaluated.

For those not immediately concerned with the older phases of the Paleolithic there is, I feel, a kind of impenetrable *mystique* surrounding the recognition and assessment of those lithic products so critical in the life of ancient human groups. This volume should do much to dispel such reaction in the broader archaeological community, and at the same time serve as an invaluable resource, indeed a handbook, for those, professional and student alike, who seek to comprehend and evaluate a major body of evidence reflective of the human past.

F. Clark Howell
Laboratory for Human Evolutionary Studies
Department of Anthropology
University of California, Berkeley

June, 1991

ACKNOWLEDGMENTS

WE WOULD LIKE TO THANK ALL OF THOSE who have helped to make this Handbook possible. First, our utmost appreciation goes to all those who have willingly and graciously furnished drawings or material:

Prof. D. de Sonneville-Bordes	Prof. H. de Lumley
Mme. A. Thibault	M. Y. Pautrat
Prof. G. Bosinski	M. J.-L. Ricard
Dr. J. Combier	Dr. J.-Ph. Rigaud
Dr. J.-M. Geneste	Dr. J.-P. Texier
Mr. O. Jöris	Dr. J. Tixier
Dr. M. Lenoir	Dr. J. Tyldesley

and to Susan Trammell for the supplemental illustrations of the material from the collections of The University Museum. We would also like to thank the several colleagues and students who have made valuable comments, including Philip Chase, Simon Holdaway, Shannon McPherron, Helen Sanders, Gilliane Monnier, and Andrew Pelcin. It should be noted that all direct quotations from non-English publications were translated by the authors. We are grateful to the Publications Department of The University Museum for publishing this volume and in particular would like to acknowledge the efforts of the head of the department, Karen Vellucci, as well as Georgianna Grentzenberg and Toni Montague. Patricia Maddaloni was responsible for the design concept of the volume, and Bagnell & Socha for its design and production. Our single biggest debt, however, is to Helen Schenck, for her skillful editing of the text and meticulous handling of the many thousands of details that went into this publication.

PART
I

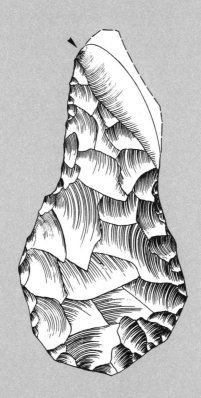

CHAPTER ONE

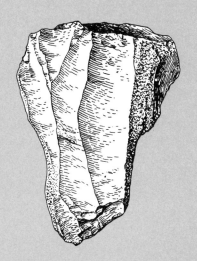

INTRODUCTION

Bordes' Typology of the Lower and Middle Paleolithic
Organization and Scope of the Handbook

TO UNDERSTAND THE ORIGINS AND evolution of hominids, there are two principal sources of evidence that must be examined and understood. First is the biological evidence, consisting primarily of skeletal remains of the hominids themselves. The second source of evidence is behavioral, consisting of the artifacts and other remains that directly reflect human activities. These include not only tools and weapons, but also faunal remains, habitation structures, and other features of human origin. Of these, probably the most important are lithic remains, that is, stone tools and the by-products of their manufacture. They are important not necessarily because they give the truest or most detailed picture of past behavior, but simply because they are the most common remains available to us. After all, they are virtually indestructible and so they remain preserved in the archaeological record the longest of any form of evidence.

The durability of lithic remains, coupled with the enormous span of time during which hominids made them, results in an almost staggering amount of potentially recoverable data. Imagine, for example, that during the time of the Acheulian in Europe, which lasted for at least 500,000 years, there was a constant population of 5,000 active tool makers. Imagine also that each of these flintknappers made only ten bifaces per year and perhaps 100 flake tools. Even with such conservative parameters (see Gould 1977; Hayden 1977, 1979; Luedtke 1984), this would have resulted in the production of 25,000,000,000 bifaces and 250,000,000,000 flake tools, of which only a miniscule proportion has been collected during the history of Paleolithic research.

Thus, there is surely not a scarcity of lithic data. Nonetheless, there are real problems in using those data to interpret the behavior of Paleolithic peoples. In large part these problems stem from the fact that lithic technologies such as those that existed in Paleolithic times have virtually disappeared from use. This means that it is impossible to study such technologies in the context of living societies that traditionally employ them. In turn, this lack of ethnographic analogies to Paleolithic lithic assemblages makes it much more difficult to understand the factors—social, cognitive, functional, and technological—that underlie Paleolithic lithic variability. It is not really a surprise then, that artifacts of Paleolithic age were not even recognized as being of human origin until the early part of the eighteenth century (see, for example, Daniel 1975). Even today it is mostly up to prehistorians themselves to rediscover certain techniques of manufacture and to experiment with possible functions of these kinds of tools in order to better understand and categorize them. Such categorizations take the form of typologies.

There is no question that typology is a major analytical tool for prehistoric research. However, there are several points that must be kept in mind about archaeological typologies, especially those dealing with prehistoric remains of such remote antiquity. Above all, it has to be remembered that typologies are constructed by modern archaeologists: it is difficult, if not impossible, to know how well they correspond to "native" classifications. In the American literature there has been some debate on whether or not such a correspondence is even important (see Ford 1954; Krieger 1944; Spaulding 1953; Bordes 1969; Semenov 1964, 1970; Whallon and Brown 1982). But, regardless of whether they do or do not reflect prehistoric categories, typologies serve two important purposes for archaeology. First, they impose an order on artifact variability, which facilitates the description of prehistoric objects among researchers. Second, the groupings defined in a typology represent analytical units that can be compared with other variables in an attempt to explain variability between those units. In other words, we can try to determine if certain of our types are associated with particular environmental conditions, temporal periods, geographic regions, activity areas, and so forth. In this way, typologies can be used analytically to interpret assemblages of artifacts in evolutionary, cultural-historical, and/or behavioral terms.

Thus, like all archaeological typologies, Paleolithic typologies constitute the basic analytical units both for reconstructing and interpreting human prehistory in the Pleistocene and for communicating these results to the scientific community. As a result, a thorough grounding in Paleolithic typology is essential to understand the nature of lithic variability during that time as well as to interpret what that variability means in terms of past human behavior.

BORDES' TYPOLOGY OF THE LOWER AND MIDDLE PALEOLITHIC

The aim of this book is to introduce some of the lithic types currently used for research in the Lower and Middle Paleolithic of Europe. The principal typology presented here is that of François Bordes (1961), though supplemented by a number of types defined by others. Why do we choose to present this typology? It is certainly not the only typology for Lower and/or Middle Paleolithic lithic industries, since the typology of Laplace-Jauretche (1957) is also used by some European archaeologists and the typologies of Clark and Kleindienst (1974) and Leakey (1971) are most often used for the earliest industries of Africa. Nor can it be demonstrated that Bordes' typology is the most accurate or even the most analytically useful. It is, however, the typology *most often* used by prehistorians in much of the Old World. Thus, it is important to learn this particular typology in order to understand and critically evaluate the results of much of current Lower and Middle Paleolithic archaeology.

Bordes' typology is, like most lithic typologies, primarily a morphological typology. That is, the overall form of the object and the location of retouch or modification are the principal criteria used in classification, although technological criteria (i.e., processes of manufacture) are considered to some extent. This emphasis on formal variation reflects the history of classification in Paleolithic research. But before Bordes, the description of lithic assemblages varied dramatically according to the individual excavators, which led to a great deal of confusion since the categories of one frequently did not correspond to the categories of another. Objects were most often given names that corresponded to perceived functions, some of which were understandable in a Paleolithic context, such as knives, axes, scrapers, points, etc., but some of which were not (Coon's [1951] class of "Screwdrivers," for example). In *all* cases, however, it was, and still is, completely unknown whether the objects were actually used for those purposes. Other types were named after similar-looking vegetation, such as *feuilles de laurier*, or "laurel leaves"; after animals, such as *limaces*, or "slugs"; or after various sites, towns, or regions.

But the names given to these types is not really the issue. Rather, the principal problem has always been a lack of consensus as to the exact morphological criteria corresponding to each type. One of the major contributions of Bordes' typology is that it provides standardization of the type definitions based on observable landmarks or features of the artifacts.

But in spite of the advance that Bordes' typology represented in terms of methodological rigor, there are a number of criticisms of it that can be made. First, it is somewhat subjective, in that some of the criteria employed are, in fact, judgments regarding the quality of manufacture ("typical" versus "atypical" types); interpretations of function (e.g., Mousterian points versus convergent scrapers); or presumed recognition of the intent of the prehistoric knapper (as in the "predetermination" of

Levallois flakes). This subjectivity decreases the reliability of the typology, which means that different typologists may classify the same assemblage somewhat differently.

A second criticism of Bordes' typology is that virtually none of the type categories have been demonstrated quantitatively to represent discrete modalities of variability among artifacts and may instead represent partitions along a continuum of variability. This criticism requires some clarification. As noted above, one of the principal goals of prehistorians has been to organize and classify lithic assemblages. In order to do this, it was necessary to give names to prehistoric objects. Beginning in the last century, and taking as their model the methods of other natural scientists, prehistorians established a classification system based on the notion of types, which Bordes himself retained. For most of them a "type" represented an ideal concept, which carried with it the assumption that most examples of a type will exhibit very similar patterns, with few cases exhibiting characters that are very different from the ideal. Unfortunately, variability of Lower and Middle Paleolithic lithic artifacts cannot be fully understood or presented according to such a concept. There is no such thing as an ideal sidescraper, for instance. There are no two sidescrapers exactly alike, and it is not yet clear that there are any real modalities in their overall morphologies. Thus, the variability inherent within a particular type may result in a continuous gradation into other types, with many intermediate examples. In such a case, it can be argued that the type boundaries as defined by the archaeologist are somewhat arbitrary.

A third criticism of Bordes' typology is that it is not consistent in terms of its application of particular criteria. For example, different types of scrapers are characterized by retouch on one or two lateral edges, on the distal edge, or on the distal and lateral edges; the retouch can be on the exterior, interior, or both surfaces; it can be flat, abrupt, or bifacial, etc. Virtually each unique combination of these attributes is designated as a different type, though we really have no idea whether such distinctions are warranted or not. On the other hand, a notch can be simple or complex, made on the interior or exterior surface, and located on almost any edge (except the distal end) and the type remains the same. Thus, the kinds of typological distinctions made for scrapers are not made for notches. Moreover, the typology is a rather uneven mix of the technology of blank production and the application of secondary modification, through retouch. Actually, some of the types (particularly types 46 through 50) do not reflect deliberate retouch at all, but rather post-depositional damage.

Part of this problem is that the meaning of each of these attributes is, at best, only poorly understood, and the same is true of the types themselves. We simply do not know which attributes or types are functional, stylistic, or related to some entirely different factor. Bordes' typology undoubtedly reflects several of these factors, which may lessen the interpretive potential of typological variability. This leads to a fourth criticism of Bordes' typology, namely, that because the exact meaning of these types (in either behavioral or cognitive terms) is not known, the typology is primarily descriptive and not analytically useful.

While such a criticism is valid to a point, it does ignore the fact that description was one of the principal goals of the typology's original formulation, which facilitated interassemblage comparisons and integrated a large body of material that had been collected and described according to a number of incompatible classificatory schemes. The result of this effort was the definition of the major assemblage groups that represent the basic industrial units of the Lower and Middle Paleolithic. This was clearly an important step in Paleolithic research. But, just as clearly, it represents only one step in the reconstruction and interpretation of hominid evolution and behavior during the Paleolithic. The ideal analogy here is the Linnaean system of biological taxonomy, developed in the mid-eighteenth century. This taxonomy was fundamental for development of Darwin's theory of evolution, even though at the time of Linnaeus these same taxa were offered as proof of the immutability of species. Thus, the interpretations of the taxa and their relationships changed completely, though their original definition was vital for the progress of science.

In a similar manner, the definition of lithic types is fundamental to understanding the nature of variability in Paleolithic assemblages. But this does not mean that typological description is, in itself, the goal of Paleolithic archaeology; rather it is a first, and fundamentally important, step. To go further, that is, to use these types analytically, we must better understand those factors, which include raw materials, technology, function, and style, that underlie lithic variability in general and which underlie the variability among these types in particular. Unfortunately, the types defined by Bordes often reflect several of these factors simultaneously, and isolating the contribution of any single one to interor intratype variability (between types or within a single type, respectively), and to assemblage variability in general, is difficult.

All of these problems lead to the possibility that Bordes' typology can be interpreted in different ways. Actually, the two authors of this Handbook have different views and assumptions concerning this typology (see Dibble and Debénath 1991). For Debénath, and for Bordes himself (Bordes 1965, 1969; Bordes and de Sonneville-Bordes 1970) most of these types are assumed to reflect intentional end-products that were behaviorally and cognitively meaningful, that is, what the prehistoric flintknapper wanted to make for specific purposes. In this view, variability within individual type categories is seen as deviations from a conscious norm, as errors, ad hoc accommodations to specific circumstances, such as blank morphology, or due to other outside factors, such as the use of raw materials with different flaking qualities. Variability between type categories, on the other hand, is thought to relate to differences in style (different peoples or cultures who make different desired endproducts because of choice) or to reflect different activities that required specific tools.

Dibble, on the other hand, takes the view that while most of the tools were deliberately retouched to achieve a desired working edge, variability in overall morphology among many of these types is more continuous in nature. He believes that the typology in general represents an arbitrary partitioning of that variability. Thus, for him, the types represent neither modal categories nor intentional endproducts, but more or less arbitrary categorizations of pieces that were reworked and rejuvenated until they were no longer useful or desired and then discarded. So, while the flakes were undoubtedly deliberately retouched to achieve a suitable working edge, the overall morphology of the final piece is not, in his view, intentional or necessarily desirable.

These are obviously quite different views concerning the interpretation of the typology and they do lead directly to differences in interpretation of assemblage variability. However, it is equally obvious that both of the authors use the same typology and believe it to be important for Paleolithic research. This is because without a standardized typelist, there is simply no possibility of comparing and integrating the material from sites that span such a wide geographical and temporal spread. A descriptive typology such as Bordes' addresses that need and so is useful to proponents of both views. Thus, while interpretations of the types may change significantly in the future, this does not in itself mean that the typology itself must be replaced, unless of course, the type distinctions are found to be either completely uninterpretable (in which case the typology may be producing only so much "noise"), or of little relevance to current theoretical problems. Hopefully, any such changes would, at the outset, be based on a more thorough understanding of the factors affecting lithic morphological and technological variability. Unfortunately, such an understanding has still to be achieved.

ORGANIZATION AND SCOPE OF THE HANDBOOK

This Handbook departs from Bordes' typology in a number of ways. In particular, it presents many additional types that have been defined by other authors, especially for some of the Central European material. While not every published type has been included here, an attempt has been made to describe the most commonly recognized ones.

A second, and more subtle, departure is in terms of how the types are presented. For each type, a more or less formal definition is presented, often the original type definition. But, as was discussed above, it sometimes seems that some of these Middle and Lower Paleolithic type categories reflect partitions along a continuum of variability, at least insofar as their morphologies are measured according to today's systematics. It is not enough to learn so many ideal forms, or "mental templates"; it is perhaps more important to learn the boundaries, or cutoffs, between types. These must be internalized to the point that newly encountered objects, each one unique in its morphology, can be correctly (or at least, consistently) classified. Therefore, the presentation of only a few "ideal" examples of each type is inappropriate. Instead, in this Handbook we try to present many examples of each type in order to give an idea of the kinds of intratype variability that one can and does encounter and we also try to offer some guide to the implicit type boundaries by contrasting easily confused types.

Unfortunately, Lower and Middle Paleolithic typology still remains subjective. There are no explicit, objective, or unambiguous criteria given here for differentiating convergent scrapers from Mousterian points, or for deciding whether a perçoir is typical or atypical. This is because such criteria do not yet exist. This may be confusing to the novice, but it is essential that he or she understands that these sorts of problems exist. And because of this subjectivity it cannot be claimed that this Handbook is anything more than a starting point for learning the typology. It still requires an enormous amount of experience with actual material to become proficient.

A third departure from Bordes' typology is that

this Handbook is not intended to be a defense of the "reality" or "accuracy" of the types presented here, but rather to be an introduction to the major aspects of lithic typological variability in the European Lower and Middle Paleolithic as it is currently recognized. Where relevant, an attempt is made to introduce students to the current debates over the interpretation of these types, though it is not our intention to argue for or against any particular position. Thus, while many interpretive issues are raised here, most are left unresolved. In large part, this only reflects the current state of Lower and Middle Paleolithic typology.

It is certain that debates over the meaning of Lower and Middle Paleolithic assemblage variability will continue for many years. To be most effective, however, the participants of these debates must all share a standard descriptive vocabulary. The typology represents a major part of this vocabulary and therefore something that must be learned by everyone concerned with these industries or the hominids responsible for them.

The Handbook is divided into two parts. The first, which begins with this Introduction, is intended to provide some background to the study of Paleolithic lithic assemblages. Thus, Chapter 2 presents an overview of how stone tools are made as well as some of the common terms that are used to describe both them and the by-products of their manufactures. Chapter 3 describes some of the techniques and technologies that are often recognized in Lower and Middle Paleolithic industries.

Part II is concerned with the presentation of actual named types, organized primarily according to major typological classes. Chapter 4 presents those types that have been defined not according to the type of retouch they exhibit but rather on the basis of the technology used to produce the blank. These include such types as Levallois flakes and naturally-backed knives. Chapters 5 through 9 cover the retouched flake tools, such as scrapers, notches, and points, as well as the various "Upper Paleolithic" types sometimes found in Lower and Middle Paleolithic contexts. Chapters 10 and 11 deal with core tools, such as choppers and bifaces.

There are two appendices. The first offers an overview of what has come to be known as the "Bordian Method" for presenting typological and technological descriptions of Lower and Middle Paleolithic assemblages. This includes not only the presentation of type counts but also the calculation of various indices as well. Appendix II is a listing of the sources and proveniences for each of the illustrated tools.

CHAPTER TWO

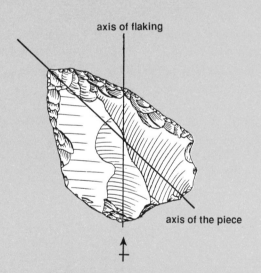

axis of flaking

axis of the piece

FUNDAMENTAL CONCEPTS AND TERMS

The Products of Flaking
Flake Landmarks
Measurements
Conventions of Lithic Illustration

ALL THREE OF THE BASIC ROCK TYPES (igneous, metamorphic, and sedimentary) were used to make artifacts during the Paleolithic, though in Europe primarily flint and other siliceous rocks are represented depending on local availability. The most important quality of such rocks is the fact that when struck they fracture conchoidally, which results in the removal of flakes. The term **raw material** is applied generally to all potentially flaked material as it exists in its natural state. Certain distinctions are made depending on the form of the stone. Flint and other fine-grained cherts normally occur either as more or less rounded stones (**nodules**), or as flattish **tablets**. Other raw material types are frequently found as squarish or angular **blocks**. When the stones have been heavily rounded due to river, marine, or glacial action, they are called **pebbles** or **cobbles**.

On nodules of flint there often exists a natural exterior surface, called **cortex**, which is more calcareous in composition than the highly siliceous interior flint. However, the term "cortex" is often applied to any natural surface of a rock, and may be due to several different weathering processes. **Patina** is another term used to describe surface weathering, but is usually applied only to an alteration of a surface of the rock after it has been flaked. A patinated surface is usually much lighter in color than the natural, unaltered flint.

The total of the various processes for the preparation of a flint nodule, the production of flakes, and their final retouching into finished tools is called a **reduction sequence**. The principal stages are the following (see Figure 2.1): flakes are removed by striking the material with a **hammer**, either of stone or, usually in later stages of reduction, a piece of antler or wood. The application of force initiates a **conchoidal fracture** that cleaves through the material until it intersects an exterior surface, thus producing a **flake**. The surface of the core that is struck is called the **striking platform** (or simply the platform) and is usually preserved on the flake.

The first flake removed from a piece of raw material, which will preserve cortex on its entire exterior surface, is called a cortical or **primary flake**. In French terminology, this first flake is also referred to as the *éclat d'épannelage* (de Heinzelin 1962), *éclat de décorticage* (Goury 1931), *calotte de préparation* (Eloy 1950), *éclat d'entame* (Tixier 1963), or an *éclat d'amorçage* (Leroi-Gourhan 1964). At this point, the stone from which this flake is removed is considered a **core**. If many such flakes are removed from the same core in such a way that they do not overlap each other (that is, they are all fully cortical), they are all still considered primary flakes. Their removal constitutes the initial preparation of the core. As further flakes are removed from the core they will show diminishing, though variable, amounts of cortex on their exterior surfaces because their exterior surfaces will be partially or completely composed of previous flake scars. These are often called **secondary flakes**.

Any of these flakes can be either used in their unfinished state or transformed further, through **retouching**, into various types of retouched pieces. Deliberately retouched flakes are generally considered **tools**. Flakes that are sufficiently large and/or have other necessary characteristics to be counted as potential tools are called **blanks**. Each of the stages of reduction results not only in classifiable pieces (blanks, cores, retouched tools), but also in a considerable amount of small **debris**.

Thus, the initial lump of raw material passes through a number of stages of transition. In the case of **flake tools**, i.e., those that are fashioned from a flake blank, there is the preparation of the core, the production of blanks, and then the retouching of these blanks into tools. In the case of **core tools** (i.e., finished tools that are fashioned by the removal of large flakes from a raw nodule, such as most bifaces, for example), they often go though a stage of preliminary roughing-out, or preforming, before they are further reduced to their final form. Other core tools, such as pebble tools, do not pass through any preforming stage and so preserve many of the aspects of the original piece of raw material.

However, the sequence shown in Figure 2.1 is perhaps too simple to describe the actual dynamics of lithic production, especially since it implies a strict linear sequence of events. In fact, depending on the technology employed and the circumstances present at the time, some of the various stages can either be eliminated or repeated, as shown in Figure 2.2. Thus, cores can be reused, or flake blanks can serve as cores (for the removal of smaller flakes, for example). Even a finished tool can later be remodified into an altogether different type, what Jelinek (1976) calls the "Frison effect," after the American archaeologist, George Frison, who clearly demonstrated this sort of process. Such continuous reworking and remodification of the various products during lithic reduction is a fundamental principal of lithic technology and one that differentiates it from other technologies, especially ceramics. Moreover, even after a tool is discarded, post-depositional factors such as crushing or rolling can result in features that can be mistaken for retouch. Thus, in a real sense, a lithic artifact is never "finished," until it is stored safely on a museum shelf.

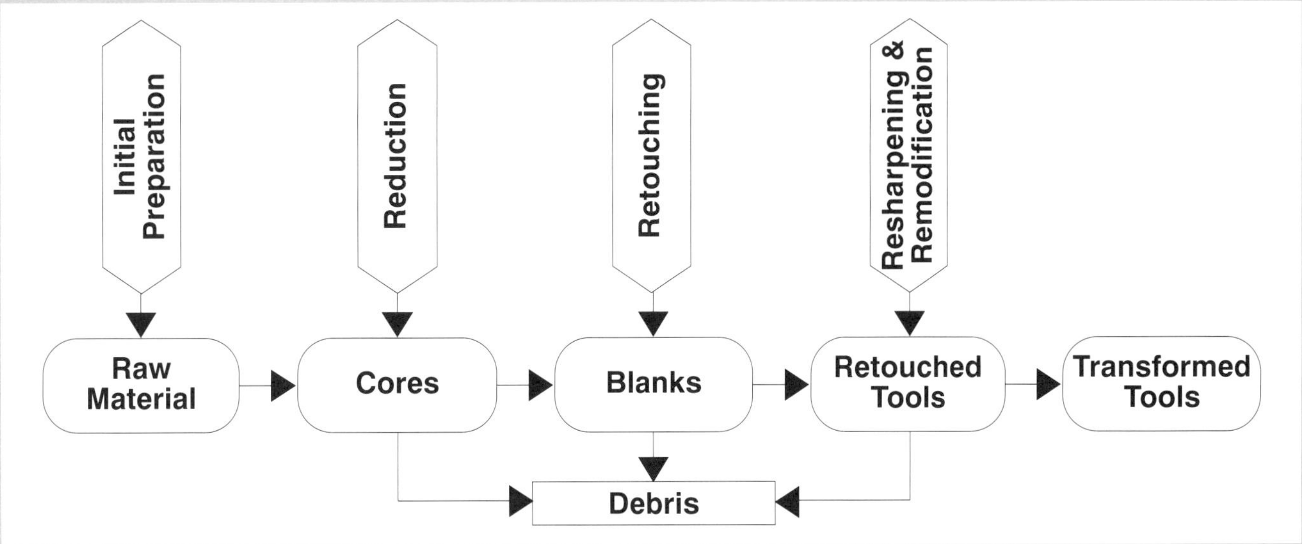

Figure 2.1 Lineal reduction sequence

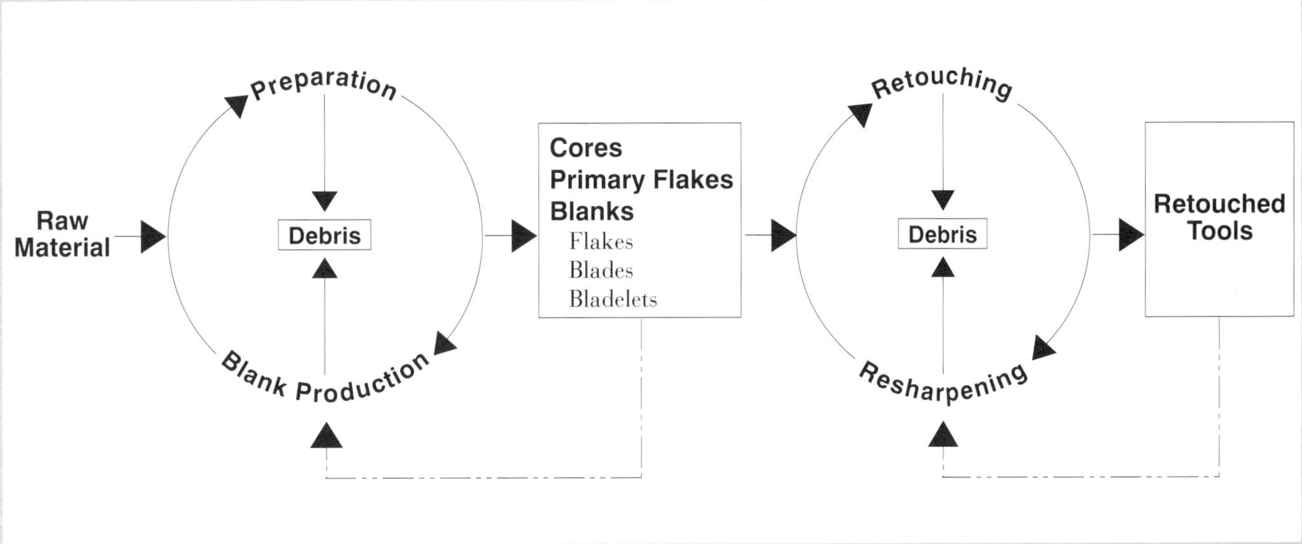

Figure 2.2 Dynamic reduction sequence

THE PRODUCTS OF FLAKING

FLAKES, BLADES, BLADELETS: In a broad sense, any piece struck conchoidally from a block of material is rightly called a flake. Some distinctions are made, however, on the basis of the form of the piece and its completeness.

Obviously, a **complete flake** is one that is whole—i.e., not broken—even if there are small nicks or damage along the edges. One rule of thumb is to consider a damaged piece complete if the damage would not seriously affect the taking of measurements. Although a retouched tool is, by definition, a flake that has had material removed, it is nonetheless considered complete if it has not been broken since the time of its manufacture. A partial flake or tool that retains the platform is referred to as **broken**, while medial and distal portions are called **fragments**. A flake sometimes shatters into angular chunks with no clear flake landmarks, which are considered generally as debris or **shatter**. Sometimes flakes that break longitudinally during manufacture are confused with burins (see Chapter 7).

The distinction between a flake and a **blade**, on the one hand, and between a blade and **bladelet** on the other, has been a source of confusion for some time. Many Old World researchers follow the definition given by Tixier (1963) for blades, which are flakes whose length is at least two times greater than their width. The distinction between blades and bladelets is based on absolute size: bladelets are smaller than 50 mm in length or 12 mm in width. Occasionally the term "bladey flake" or "flake blade" is applied to flakes whose length is between 1.5 and 2 times their width. Some archaeologists (e.g., Jelinek 1977) reserve the term "blade" for only those long flakes that have both parallel sides and parallel flake scars on their exterior surface, indicating they were made by a special technique.

CORES: For a number of reasons, cores are among the most difficult objects to classify in the Paleolithic industries—for example, Brézillon (1968) counts almost 50 different named types, differentiated on a variety of attributes. From a typological standpoint, the principal problem with cores stems from their variability: about the only consistent feature of cores is that they show one or more platform surfaces and one or more faces from which flakes were removed.

Often, core types are distinguished on the basis of technological considerations and not on overall form, for the reason that the shape of a core may change considerably as reduction continues. Thus, a core discarded early in a given sequence may differ significantly from a core abandoned late in the same sequence, even though the technology was the same. On the other hand, during a sequence of reduction, even the technology applied to a core may change considerably (see Baumler 1988). In this case only the last technology applied is preserved on the final, discarded core.

Another important problem is that the distinction between cores and other kinds of tools is somewhat arbitrary. For instance, there are problems in distinguishing between choppers/chopping-tools and cores (Chapter 10), and even some bifaces are very similar to cores (see Chapter 11). One way to approach this problem is to subjectively evaluate the flintknapper's intent: if the object is being flaked only to produce desired blanks, then it is a core; if the flakes are being removed to shape the object for an intended use, then it is a tool. But it is sometimes difficult to demonstrate intentionality and, in fact, the flintknapper's goals may change during a reduction sequence. In the Lower and Middle Paleolithic, for example, retouch flakes removed during the manufacture of a biface were often used as blanks for flake tools. This raises the question whether the primary intention was to produce blanks for tools (in which case the "biface" should really be considered a core) or to shape the core itself into a tool. Probably

both goals were in mind at the time, but the problem of classification of the piece as a core or core tool remains. The retouching of flakes presents related classificatory problems. In a sense, the modification of these results in "core tools" (since small flakes are removed during retouching), although the distinction comes from the fact that the original blank was a flake. But flake blanks were sometimes used as cores to produce other usable blanks (Newcomer and Hivernel-Guerre 1974) and perhaps this is true of one type of flake tool, namely truncated-faceted pieces (see Chapter 9). So even this distinction between flake tools and cores is not always reliable. The classification completely breaks down, however, when we consider the use of a spent core as a tool blank and retouched as if it were a flake (a denticulate or scraper made on a core, for example). In fact, most of the retouched types in Bordes' typelist of "flake tools," including all of the scrapers and denticulates, can be made on pebbles or cores. All of this just proves that it is virtually impossible to have too rigid a classification system for a process that is as dynamic as flintknapping, even at this very basic level of distinction.

FLAKE LANDMARKS

All complete flakes of human origin have certain characteristics and landmarks, many of which are important to typological classification (see Figure 2.3). Flakes have both an **interior** and **exterior** surface. The latter represents the exterior of the core before the flake was removed, while the former corresponds to the surface created by the fracture plane. These are also referred to by some authors as the **ventral** and **dorsal** surfaces, respectively.

The interior surface exhibits certain characteristics that are the result of fracture mechanics and which can be present in varying degrees. The exact point of impact on the platform immediately adjacent to the interior surface is the **point of percussion**, which is the origin of the **cone** and **bulb of percussion**, located on the interior surface. Often there are concentric **ripples** that radiate distally from the point of percussion along the bulb, whose concavity reflects the direction of the blow that removed the flake. These ripples are most pronounced on extremely fine-grained materials (especially obsidian and flint) and are virtually invisible on more heterogeneous materials such as quartzite or sandstone. Sometimes there are tiny cracks or **fissures** near or on the bulb, which are more or less parallel to the axis of force but converge toward the point of percussion. Thus, even in the absence of the

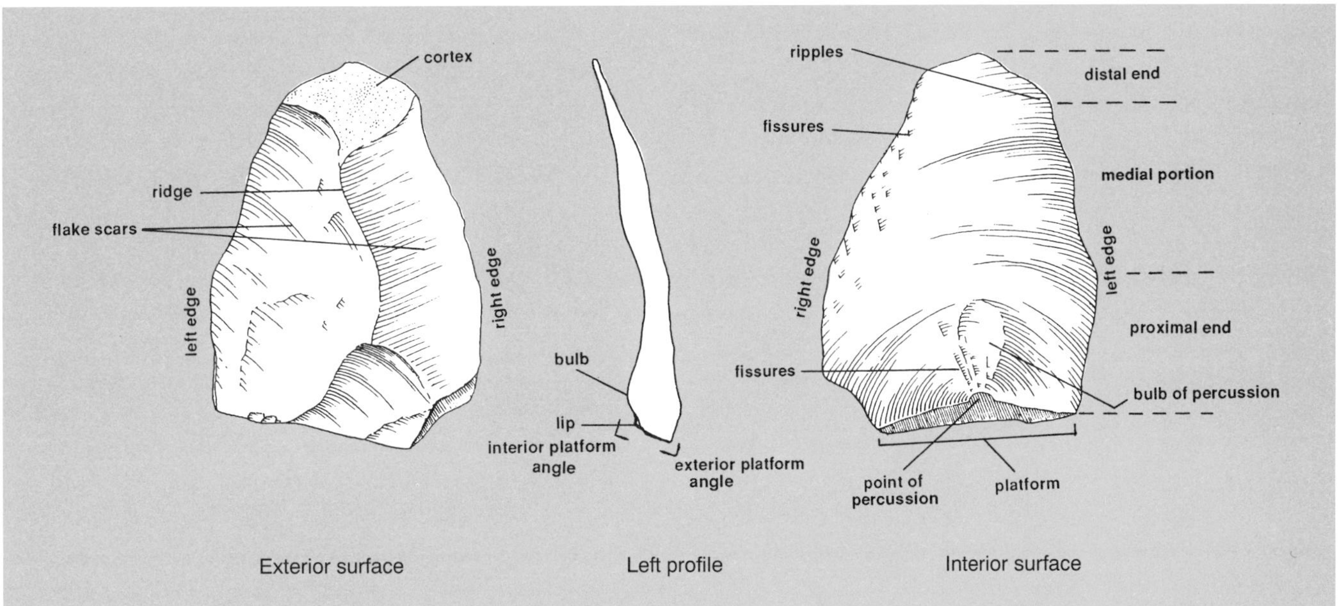

Figure 2.3 Flake landmarks

platform, the direction of force or at least the proximal and distal ends of the piece can usually be identified on the basis of these ripples and fissures. Sometimes too, a small, isolated flake scar, called an *éraillure* scar, appears near the bulb. Usually the interior surface of a flake is relatively flat, though it may sometimes be twisted laterally. Of course, the flake scars on cores share the same characteristics as the interior surfaces of flakes, except as negative impressions (e.g., of the bulb of percussion and ripples).

The exterior surface of a flake can be quite variable. It can exhibit full or partial remnants of the original cortex that was on the nodule, or traces of flakes that were removed previously. These previous flake removals are evidenced by negative **flake scars** with **ridges** between them.

The platform end is called the **proximal** end (also the **base** of the tool for retouched pieces), and the opposite end is the **distal** end. The **medial** portion is the region between the proximal and distal ends. The right and left **lateral** margins are as viewed from the exterior surface with the proximal end down.

The platform surface can be **cortical** (Figure 2.4), **plain** (Figure 2.5) (i.e., a smooth, previously flaked surface), or **prepared**. Platform preparation usually involves the removal of small flakes, or **facets**, from the exterior margin of the core along the platform surface before a flake is removed, and is often done to modify the angle of the platform or to strengthen the platform for flaking. Two major types

of prepared platforms are usually recognized for Paleolithic assemblages: a **dihedral** platform (Figure 2.6), where two facets intersect at a relatively sharp angle, and **faceted** platforms which exhibit three or more facets along the surface (Figure 2.7a–c). When viewed from the exterior surface of the flake, such platforms are usually moderately convex, but can also be straight or slightly concave. A special form of faceted platform is called a *chapeau de gendarme*, which has a surface that is markedly convex near the point of percussion and usually somewhat concave or straight near the lateral margins (Figure 2.8). A particular kind of platform preparation, or more correctly, rejuvenation, often occurs in Upper Paleolithic industries, where the entire platform surface is removed in one blow. The flake that is removed, called a **core tablet** (Figure 2.9), has as its exterior surface the core's entire original platform surface, and facets on its margins that are portions of previous flake scars of the core (and which can be confused with platform faceting).

The exterior margin of the platform can also exhibit preparation, either as **trimming** or **grinding**. In fact, it is not always possible to tell the difference between exterior platform trimming and true retouch that was produced after the flake was removed (as in the so-called *racloirs sur talon*—see Chapter 6). The distinction between platform preparation and retouch, then, is whether it occurred before or after the blank was removed, respectively. It is often stated that the use of a soft hammer (of wood, bone, or

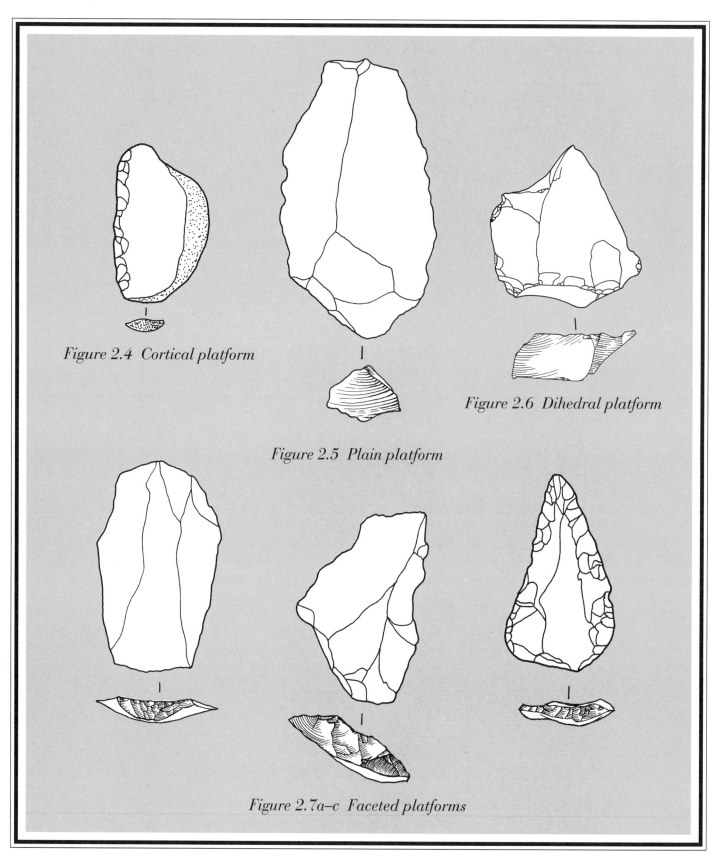

Figure 2.4 Cortical platform

Figure 2.5 Plain platform

Figure 2.6 Dihedral platform

Figure 2.7a–c Faceted platforms

antler) will produce a characteristic **lip** on the interior margin of the platform (Figure 2.10), though whether this is due to the density of the hammer or to platform preparation and how the flake was struck is open to dispute. Some flakes can exhibit an extremely narrow or small platform, called a **punctiform platform** (Figure 2.11). The angle formed between the platform surface and the interior surface of the flake is called the **interior platform angle**, while the angle between the platform surface and the exterior surface of the flake is called the **exterior platform angle** (see Figure 2.3).

The distal ends of flakes are characterized by the kinds of termination they present. A normal, or

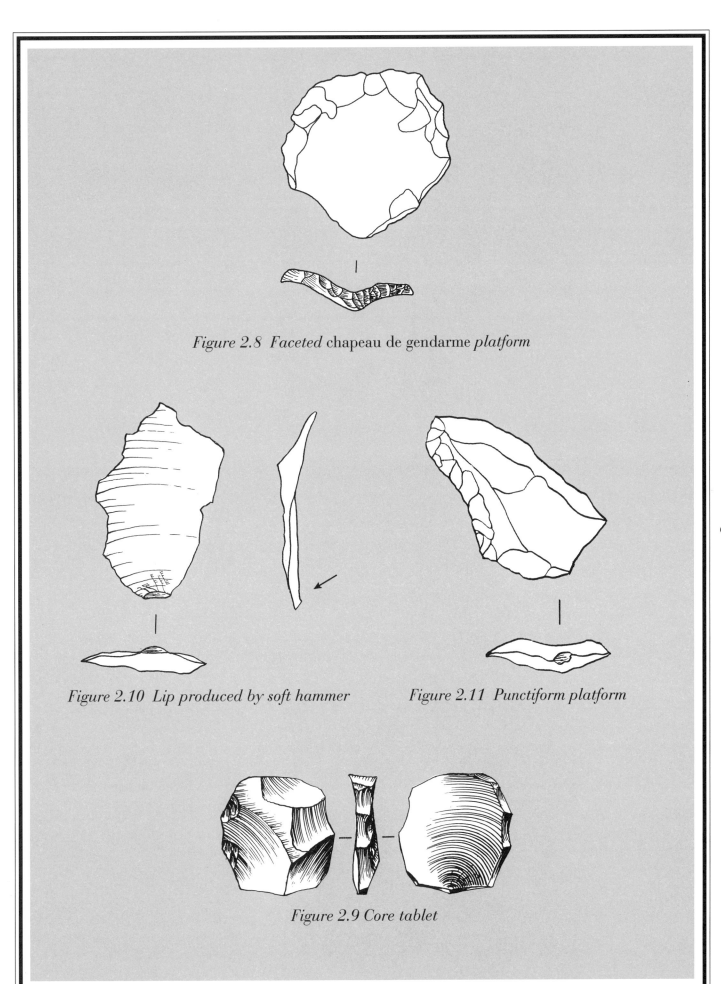

Figure 2.8 *Faceted* chapeau de gendarme *platform*

Chapter

2

Figure 2.10 *Lip produced by soft hammer*

Figure 2.11 *Punctiform platform*

Figure 2.9 *Core tablet*

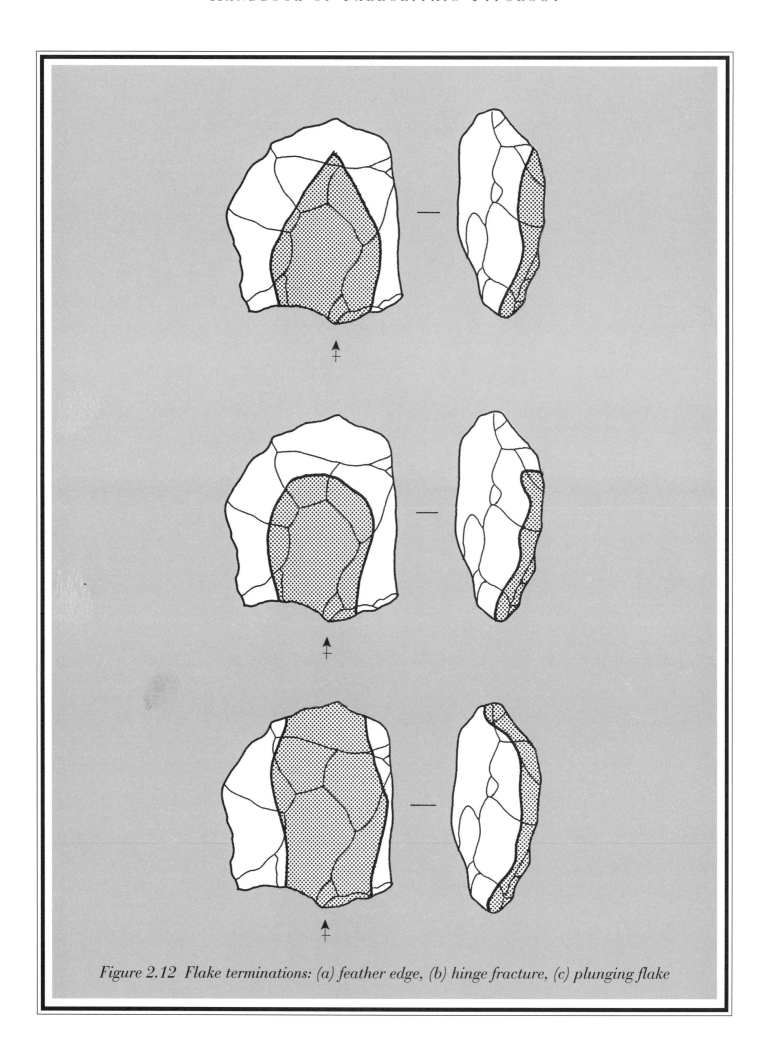

Figure 2.12 Flake terminations: (a) feather edge, (b) hinge fracture, (c) plunging flake

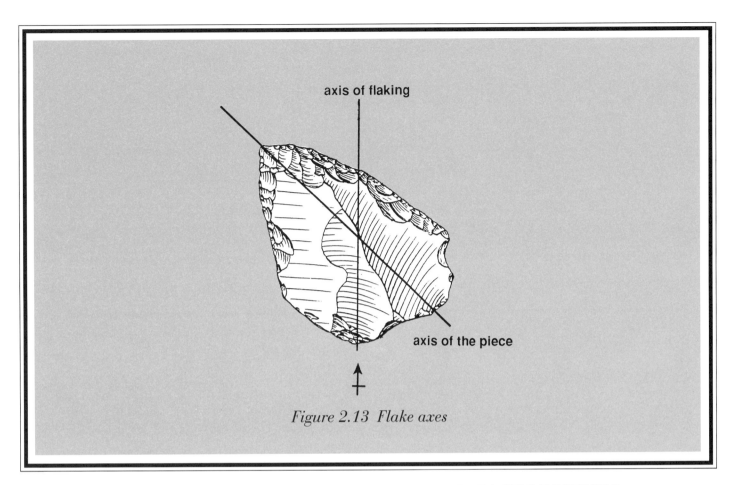

Figure 2.13 Flake axes

feather, termination occurs when the interior surface of the flake gradually intersects the exterior surface, resulting in a sharp edge (Figure 2.12a). If not enough force is given relative to the mass of material being removed, the interior surface can rise abruptly toward the exterior surface, and sometimes even turn back toward the proximal end of the flake. This is called a **hinge** fracture (Figure 2.12b). If too much force is given, the interior surface can proceed through the distal end of the core, sometimes even plunging away from the exterior surface. These are often termed **overshot**, or **plunging** flakes (Figure 2.12c). When a flake snaps distally as it is removed, it results in a **step fracture** that can only be recognized on the core itself, since a step fracture on a flake cannot be distinguished from a snap that occurs after the flake was removed.

Following the terminology of Bordes (1961), which is fundamental for the classification of certain of his types (e.g., transverse and déjeté scrapers [types 21–24—see Chapter 6]), a flake has two axes (Figure 2.13): the **axis of flaking** (technological axis) and the **axis of the piece** (morphological axis). The axis of flaking (sometimes called the "axis of the flake"), is defined as the vector that originates at the point of percussion and proceeds distally and perpendicular to the platform surface, thus bisecting the bulb of percussion. The axis of the piece is the longest axis of symmetry of the piece.

MEASUREMENTS

As is true for all measurements in empirical science, there are problems of definition, interpretation, and reliability of metrical approaches in lithic analysis. Theoretically, there are an infinite number of different metric observations that can be taken on flakes and retouched tools. Of course, the research questions being addressed should dictate the choice of measurements taken, but it is often the case in lithic analysis that choosing variables is still not easy since so few of the factors that affect morphological variability are understood to any great degree. This leads to a significant problem in operationalizing such basic concepts as length and width, but also to very serious problems in interpreting the results. To make matters worse, there are almost as many different ways of taking the "same" measurement as there are researchers taking it! This lack of measurement standards often results in a lack of comparability in the results of various researchers.

Unfortunately, this Handbook cannot review the more theoretical aspects of lithic measurement; there are, indeed, few studies available that do so (see Fish 1979; Leach 1969). What it will do is to present definitions of some of the more basic measurements. Of course, it is imperative that all lithic studies define how the measurements were made, so that others can attempt to replicate the results or

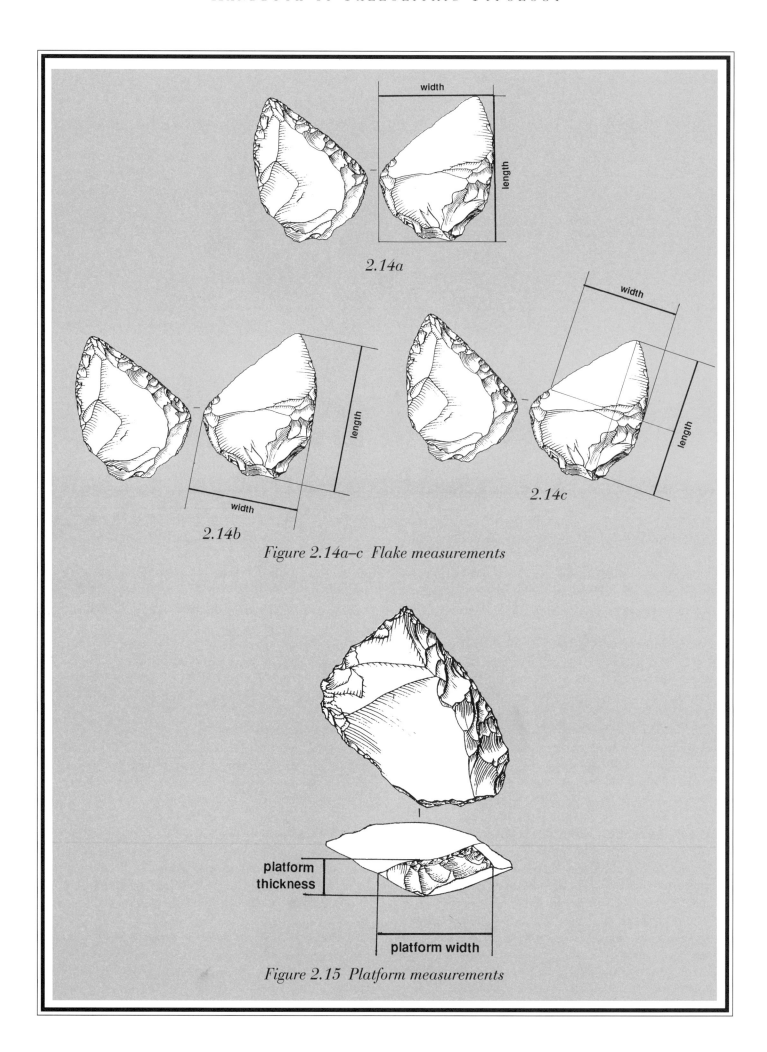

2.14a

2.14b

2.14c

Figure 2.14a–c Flake measurements

platform
thickness

platform width

Figure 2.15 Platform measurements

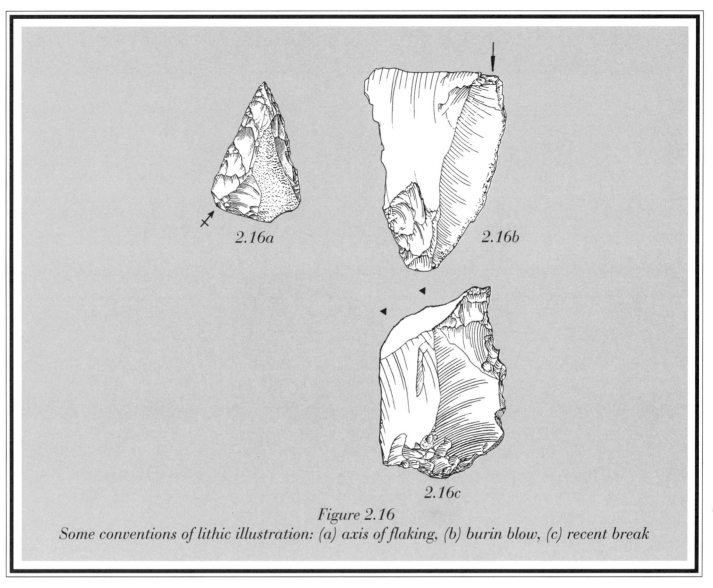

Figure 2.16
Some conventions of lithic illustration: (a) axis of flaking, (b) burin blow, (c) recent break

Chapter
2

make direct comparisons.

There are at least three methods for measuring the length and width of complete flakes. One of these, what is often termed the "box" method, is to record them as the dimensions of the smallest rectangle that can completely contain the flake (Figure 2.14a). A second approach is to measure length as the longest axis from the platform to the most distal point on the flake; and to measure width as the maximum distance between two edges of the flake as measured perpendicularly to the length axis (Figure 2.14b). The third approach is to measure length from the point of percussion to the most distal point on the flake, and width between the flake edges at the midpoint of, and perpendicular to, the length axis (Figure 2.14c). Clearly, these three techniques will yield different results. Thickness is usually taken as either the maximum thickness of the piece or at the intersection of the length and width axes.

Platform width is usually measured from one lateral margin of the platform to the other (Figure 2.15), though this measurement is difficult when the platform surface grades smoothly into a lateral border, as in a naturally-backed piece (see, for example, Figure 2.4). In this case, the surface being measured should be along a chord that is perpendicular to the length axis. Platform thickness is usually measured along the platform surface from the point of percussion to the exterior margin of the flake, and perpendicular to the interior surface of the flake. This last axis also serves as one side for measuring the interior platform angle (preferably to a point below the bulb of percussion) and the exterior platform angle (along the exterior surface of the flake).

Edge angles are difficult to measure and there are many different techniques that vary considerably in terms of reliability (see Dibble and Bernard 1980). A further problem is the fact that edge angle can vary along an edge.

Bordes (1961) utilized several standardized measurements of bifaces as a basis for their classification. These measurements will be presented in Chapter 11.

CONVENTIONS OF LITHIC ILLUSTRATION

In this Handbook, flakes and tools are illustrated at lifesize where space permits, and oriented vertically along the axis of the piece with the proximal end down; if the axis of flaking is significantly different from the axis of the piece, the former is indicated by a small, crossed arrow (Figure 2.16a). One or more small arrows are used to indicate burin blows, tranchet blows, or similar removals (Figure 2.16b). Breaks or retouch that occurred post-depositionally are left blank (Figure 2.16c). For certain objects, several views may be shown to illustrate particular characteristics, as well as an outline of the cross-section. For bifacial objects, if both surfaces are not illustrated then the one that is illustrated will usually be the one that is more convex, always with the long axis oriented vertically and the more pointed extremity of the piece oriented toward the top of the page. Lighting is always shown as coming from the upper left portion of the piece. The orientation of flake scars is usually indicated by shading lines that schematically correspond to ripples (with their concavities pointing toward the direction of blow). For further information and conventions of lithic illustration, see Addington (1986).

CHAPTER THREE

PALEOLITHIC TECHNIQUES AND TECHNOLOGIES

Flaking Techniques
Flaking Technologies
Retouching Techniques and the Fashioning of Tools

IN FRENCH LITERATURE THERE ARE stronger distinctions made between flaking techniques, technologies, and reduction sequences than is generally true in American literature. At the most fundamental level are the **techniques** involved in the application of force to the material. At a higher conceptual level is the flaking **technology**, which involves a consistent pattern of core preparation and the application of specific flaking techniques. The various by-products obtained, not including the finished tool, are referred to as **debitage**. At the highest level is the French concept of the *chaîne opératoire*, which is only roughly translated into English as "reduction sequence." The *chaîne opératoire* refers to the totality of the various processes beginning with the procurement of raw material, its preparation, the production of flake blanks, and their final retouching into finished tools. It includes a very strong notion of intentionality on the part of some of the prehistoric flintknappers, i.e., that every stage is preconceived for the production of certain final and desired endproducts. Examples of reconstructed *chaîne opératoires* have been proposed by Geneste (1985) for Levallois (see Chapter 4) and by Turq (1989) for the production of Quina flake blanks (see also Boëda et al. 1990).

FLAKING TECHNIQUES

As outlined by Bertouille (1989), stone flaking techniques encompass many different factors, including the manner of applying force; the manner in which the piece being flaked is held; the means of application of force; the shape of the object used to apply force; and the relative hardness of the two elements in contact. It was primarily on the basis of the first of these that Bordes (1947) differentiated several distinct flaking techniques for the Paleolithic, namely **direct percussion** (which includes simple direct percussion, anvil, *par contre-coup*, and bipolar techniques), **indirect percussion**, and **pressure flaking**. These techniques are still the basic techniques recognized.

Simple direct percussion. This appears to have been one of the simplest and most common of the techniques used during, and for long after, the Paleolithic. It consists of striking an object or piece of raw material directly with a hand-held hammer. The hammer itself can be of a variety of materials, including "hard" hammers of stone and so-called "soft" hammers made of wood, bone, or antler—even small splinters of bone were used in at least one case (Chase 1990).

Bertouille (1989) distinguishes two extremes in the forms of hammers: those whose shape is roughly spherical and which make contact with the struck object at a single point; and those which are long and, ideally, cylindrical, which make contact as a line or surface. However, exactly what effect different hammer types and materials have on flake morphology is not well understood (see Bonnichsen 1977; Hayden and Hutchings 1989). It is often stated that flakes obtained by simple direct percussion with a hard hammer are usually relatively short and often present well-developed bulbs, ripples, and fissures, while flakes produced with a soft hammer tend to be longer and thinner, with less-developed bulbs and other characteristics of their interior surfaces. In fact, both flake and platform morphology may depend much more on aspects of the platform and surface preparation than on the hammer itself (see Dibble and Whittaker 1981).

Anvil technique. This technique, also referred to as "Clactonian technique" (it was first described for the site of Clacton-on-Sea, England; see below), consists of striking a core against a large, stationary block. It is often stated that this technique results in a large platform, a high interior platform angle, pronounced ripples, and a rather diffuse (and sometimes multiple) bulb, though again these features are probably more the result of characteristics of the platform surface (especially the preparation or use of a very low exterior platform angle) rather than the use of a stationary anvil.

Contre-coup. This is a special case of the anvil technique that has been described by Bordes (1947:16) for producing burins. It consists of placing the part of the blank to be retouched on an anvil of stone or bone, and then striking the exterior surface of the object, thus removing small flakes from the same surface that was struck.

Bipolar technique. Bipolar technique, which was first named by Breuil (1954), consists of placing the object to be worked on a stationary flat surface (or anvil), and then striking the object with a hand-held hammer. Objects worked in this fashion are characterized by a small bulb of percussion and traces of the opposing shock on the distal extremity of the object. This technique was often used for the production of backing, and also for working small pieces of raw material, e.g., in the Pontinian industries of Italy (Taschini and Bietti 1979). The term "bipolar" is often confused with **bidirectional**, which refers to the removal of flakes from two opposite ends of a core.

Indirect percussion. In the case of indirect percussion, or punch technique, an intermediate object (the "punch") of antler, bone, wood, or stone, is placed on the core, and the punch is then struck with a hammer. This technique facilitates very precise blows since the accuracy of the blow is controlled by the stationary punch. There is general consensus that punctiform platforms result from this technique, especially when the punch is of a softer material (antler or bone), though, again, it has not been demonstrated that it is the use of the punch itself rather than aspects of platform preparation that is responsible for the platform characteristics.

Pressure flaking. This technique consists of placing the point of a retoucher (for example, an antler tine or tooth) against the edge of a blank and applying increasing pressure inward and then sharply downward toward one of the surfaces. The resulting flakes, while not dissimilar to those obtained through direct percussion, tend to be much smaller, thinner, more regular, and with less pronounced interior features. This is due in part to the more precise control of the force being applied. Pressure flaking does not appear to have been used during the Lower and Middle Paleolithic, but was first consistently used in Europe during the Solutrean.

While these are some of the principal techniques that are generally recognized for Lower and Middle Paleolithic industries, many others were employed at various times and places in prehistory. The reader is, therefore, advised to consult a number of more specialized works for these. More general overviews of basic flaking techniques, as well as treatments of fracture mechanics, can be found in Crabtree (1972), Hayden (1979), Dibble and Whittaker (1981), Tixier et al. (1980), Brézillon (1968), and Cotterell and Kamminga (1987).

FLAKING TECHNOLOGIES

A number of flaking technologies were used during the Paleolithic to produce blanks or to shape the core into a finished tool. Some technologies were extremely simple—the removal of one to two flakes from a pebble to produce a cutting edge; others were quite elaborate, such as Levallois technology. In French terminology, a major distinction is made between those technologies that involve a distinct stage of core preparation—so-called "predetermination" of the form of the blank to be removed—and those that do not.

PREPARED-CORE TECHNOLOGIES: Traditionally, it has been believed that in a number of technologies of the Lower and Middle Paleolithic the core was intentionally shaped or prepared in such a way as to predeter-

mine the shapes of flakes taken from it. It is true, of course, that in spite of the effects of different hammers and other technical aspects, flake form is primarily a function of core surface morphology. Thus, the forms of virtually all flakes are, in a sense, predetermined by surface morphology. But the term "prepared-core" refers to the production of flakes that have particular desired forms or morphologies that were preconceived in the minds of the flintknapper. Thus, as expressed by Tixier et al. (1980:44), "the guiding notion of these flaking technologies is in the production of similar elements, that is, a standardization of form, where the morphology of each flake pre-existed in the imagination of the artisan."

The principal prepared-core technology of the Lower and Middle Paleolithic is **Levallois**, of which there are many varieties (Bordes 1980). The term *Levalloisien* was introduced in the literature by Breuil (1926), although the technique was first described by Commont in 1909 under the name of "Mousterian" technique. In 1950, Bordes was able to replicate the technique experimentally and later described it as follows (Bordes 1961:14):

Chapter

3

> In order to make a classic Levallois flake, one must take a flint nodule, preferably one that is flattish and oval, and that can be flaked along the margins. After removing a succession of flakes to serve as striking platforms, the upper surface of the core is peeled off with centripetal flakes, resulting in a surface which somewhat resembles the back of a turtle. A striking platform is then prepared at one end, either by small facets or by one large flake removal, which is almost perpendicular to the flaking surface of the core. A blow given with a hard hammer to the striking platform determines a flake that cuts through the centripetal preparation flake scars, resulting in an oval flake having a form close to the form of the core (therefore being of a predetermined form) and presents on its exterior surface the traces of the centripetal preparatory flake scars. If the striking platform of the core was made by a single flake scar, then the flake will have a plain platform, but will still be a Levallois flake.

Thus, for Bordes (1950:21), a Levallois flake is a flake with a form predetermined by a special preparation of the core *before* the removal of the flake.

Geneste (1985), building on the work of Bordes, Tixier, and, more recently, Boëda and

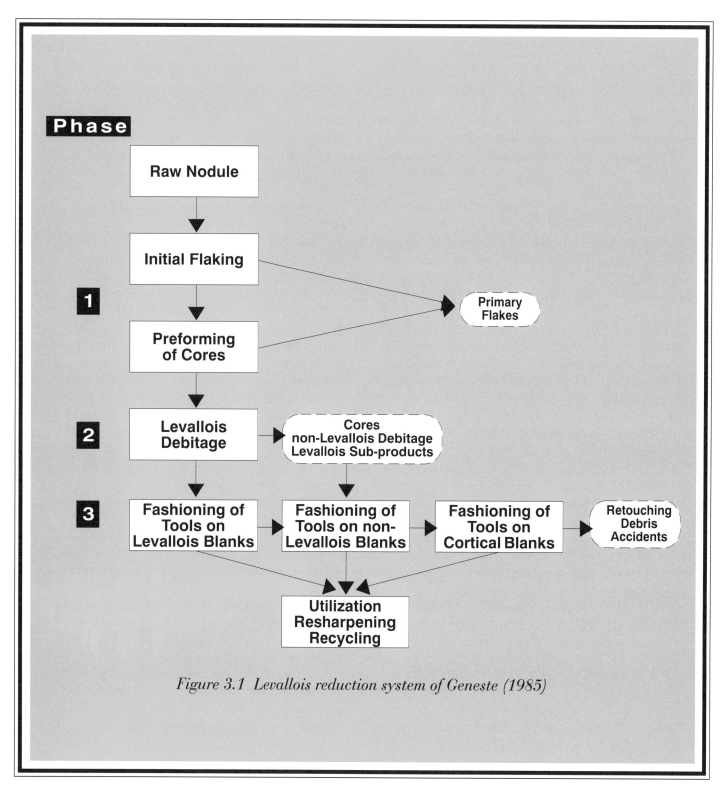

Phase

Raw Nodule

Initial Flaking

1

Preforming of Cores

Primary Flakes

2

Levallois Debitage

Cores
non-Levallois Debitage
Levallois Sub-products

3

Fashioning of Tools on Levallois Blanks

Fashioning of Tools on non-Levallois Blanks

Fashioning of Tools on Cortical Blanks

Retouching Debris Accidents

Utilization Resharpening Recycling

Figure 3.1 Levallois reduction system of Geneste (1985)

Pelegrin (1983), defines what he calls a "Levallois system." This system consists (Figure 3.1) of two reduction sequences, the principal one for the production and utilization of Levallois flake blanks, and a concurrent or parallel reduction sequence concerned with the by-products of Levallois manufacture. He outlines four phases in the principal sequence: Phase 0, concerned with the testing and acquisition of suitable raw material; Phase 1, during which the core surface is prepared; Phase 2, which results in the production of actual Levallois blanks;

and Phase 3, which covers the utilization or retouching of blanks. Phases 2 and 3 are also present for the parallel non-Levallois sequence. Each of these phases is accompanied by the production of various products, including cortical flakes, platform preparation flakes, retouch flakes, atypical Levallois flakes, and debris.

Levallois cores are traditionally classified according to the form of the final flakes obtained from them as either **flake** (Figures 3.2–3.5), **point**, or **blade** cores. Levallois point cores (Figures 3.6

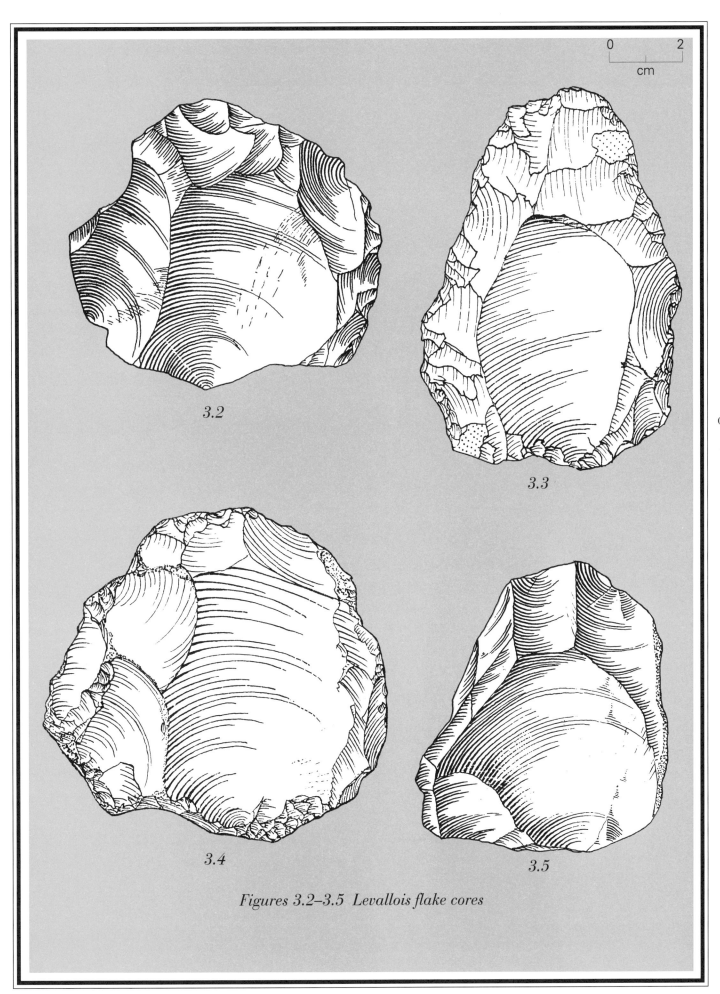

0   2
cm

3.2

3.3

Chapter
3

3.4

3.5

Figures 3.2–3.5 Levallois flake cores

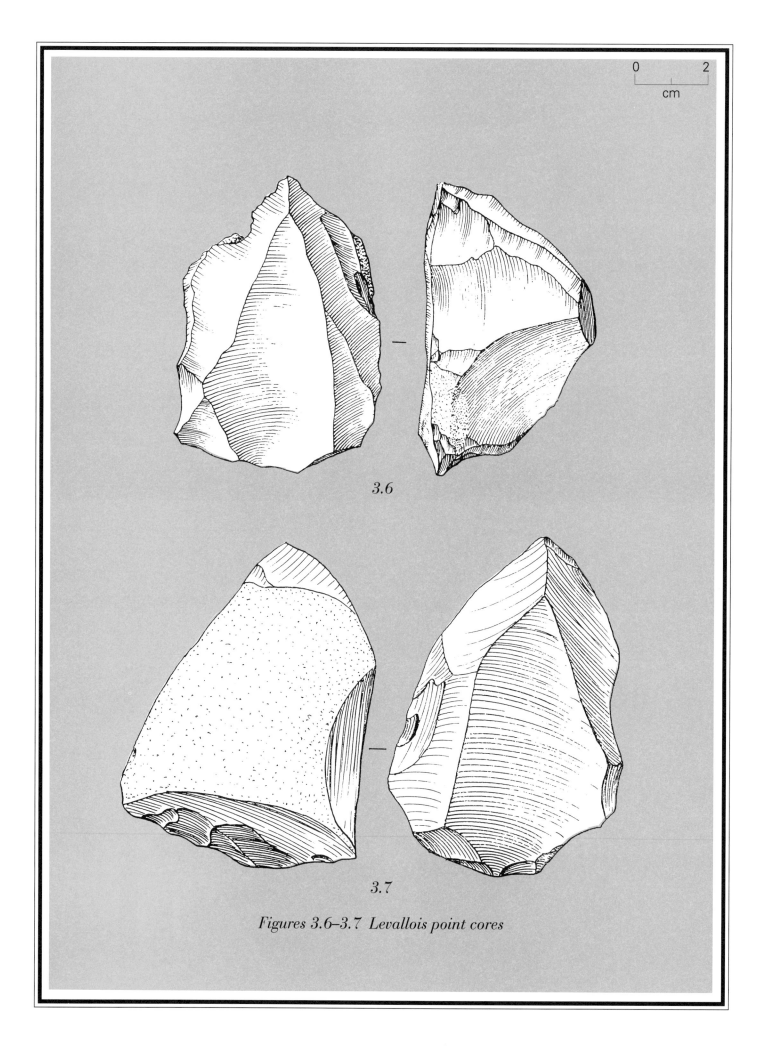

0 2
cm

3.6

3.7

Figures 3.6–3.7 Levallois point cores

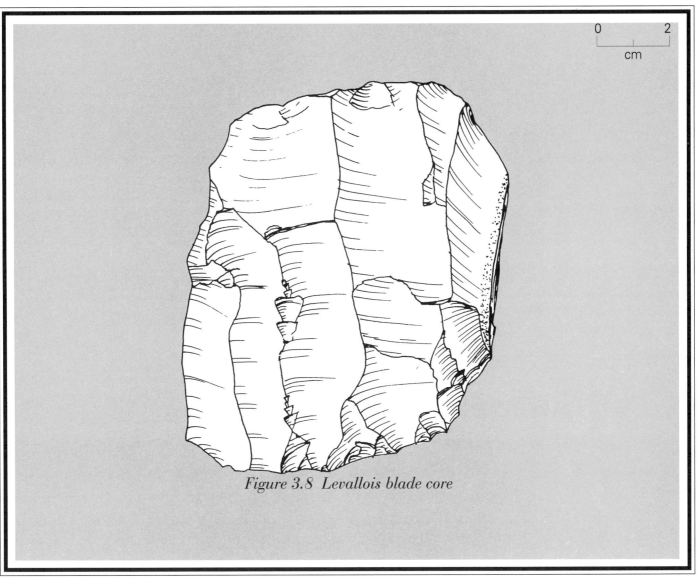

0   2
cm

Figure 3.8 Levallois blade core

and 3.7) are prepared to have (usually) a single central ridge, which results in a pointed flake as the last flake removed. Levallois blade cores (Figure 3.8) are characterized by a series of parallel flake scars, which can be uni- or bidirectional (from one or two opposing platforms, respectively), and these cores can resemble cores of the Upper Paleolithic blade industries. Of course, given the dynamics of flint-knapping a core that was initially prepared for the production of one kind of Levallois product can later be used to produce other kinds. Similarly, the technology may change completely as the core is being reduced. In either case, the morphology of the discarded cores may reflect little, or not at all, the earlier technologies that were applied.

As just described, the Levallois technique can be used for the production of blades as well as flakes and points, and in fact, the distinction between Levallois and other blade technologies is not very clear (see Boëda 1990). Like Levallois, the repeated production of blades often requires considerable preparation of the core to achieve a series of parallel ridges which serve to guide the removal of the blades. One way of initializing this series of ridges is through the production of a **crested blade** (Figure 3.9). This is often achieved through a bifacial flaking along one edge of a nodule, which results in a more or less sharp ridge or crest on the core. After the preparation of the striking platform at one end of the core, the first blade is struck along this crest, which is thus preserved on the exterior of the blade and gives it its name. The lateral margins of this first blade result in two other parallel ridges on the core, both of which can then guide the removal of subsequent blades (see Tixier et al. 1980:55; Bordes and Crabtree 1969). Such a technology certainly involves core preparation and is thus, in this sense, Levallois-like, though most prehistorians would nonetheless differentiate it from Levallois. Given, however, that true blade industries do occur before the Upper Paleolithic in Europe (Tuffreau 1984; Pradel 1952), as well as in the Levant (Jelinek 1990) and Africa (Singer and Wymer 1982), this distinction based on the production of crested blades may be somewhat arbitrary.

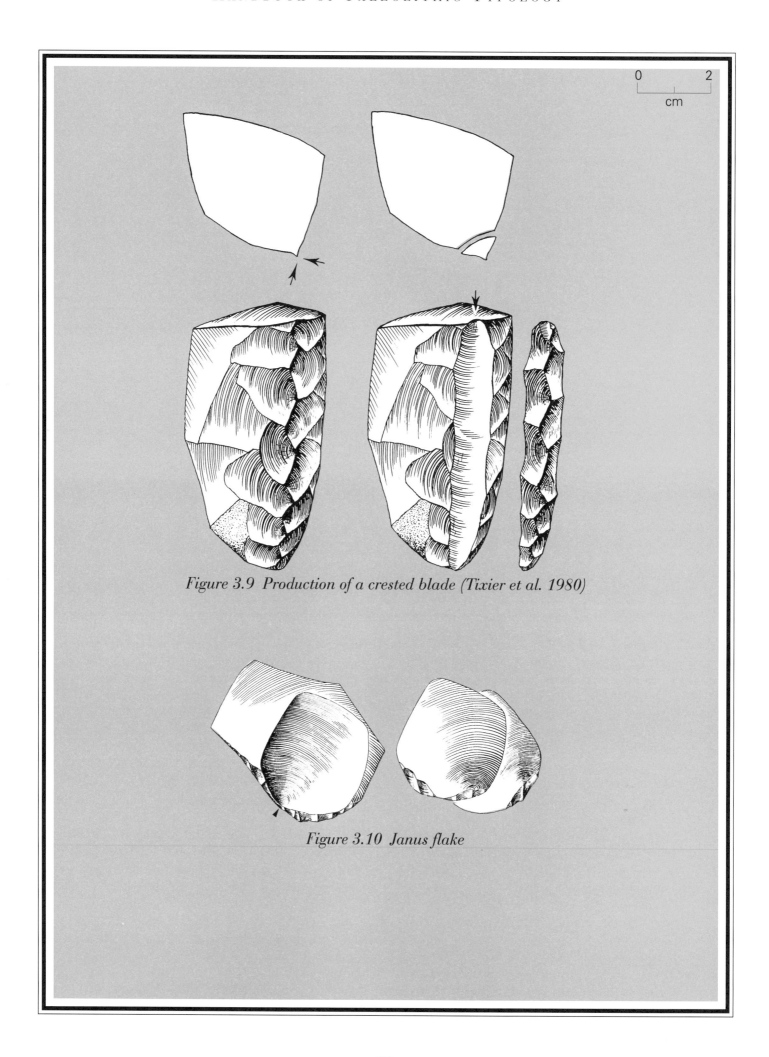

Figure 3.9 Production of a crested blade (Tixier et al. 1980)

Figure 3.10 Janus flake

The distinction between Levallois and other blade technologies is really only the tip of a very large iceberg of problems surrounding the concept of Levallois, its application and interpretation. Virtually any patterned or consistent flaking technique "prepares" a core surface and "predetermines" the resulting flakes, thus resulting in products that are less variable in morphology than would be true for a set of flakes that were struck randomly from a core. As we have just seen, blade techniques involve preparation and produce standardized results, but so does bifacial reduction, and the latter also results in less variable products (Dibble 1989). The problem is to know where to draw the line in calling these various technologies Levallois or not.

There is also a certain degree of variability within Levallois as it is recognized today, with the inclusion of flakes, blades, and points under the single technological system. Bordes (1980) also suggested that several other technologies, some of which occur outside of Europe, should be recognized as being Levallois. However, a consensus has not been reached as to whether these technological variants should be considered as varieties of a general Levallois technology, or whether the term "Levallois" should be reserved for only some of them and new names given to other prepared-core techniques.

Unfortunately, the debate over the definition of Levallois is likely to continue for some time and thus we are unable here to offer any precise and objective criteria for its typological classification. There is also some disagreement as to the level of preconception involved in Levallois technology (cf. Dibble 1989; van Peer 1991).

Bordes (1961:16) also used the term **Proto-Levallois** for "clumsily made" flakes that are somewhat reminiscent of true Levallois flakes. This subjective category is not consistently applied. Another similar term, **Para-Levallois**, refers to Middle Stone Age material from South Africa which is Levallois-like in style, but most often characterized by thick flakes that are often wider than they are long. This technique, which is also called **Victoria West** technique, is rarely seen in Europe.

Another so-called prepared-core technique, also generally associated with some African material though occasionally recognized in Europe, is the **Kombewa** technique. As described by Tixier et al. (1980:55), it consists first of the production of a flake with a large and quite pronounced bulb of percussion. A second flake then removes the bulb from the interior surface of the first, resulting in a very regular circular, semi-circular, or oval flake. The resulting Kombewa flake (seen in the righthand portion of Figure 3.10) often retains a remnant of the platform of the original flake. Such flakes are also sometimes called **Janus** flakes.

OTHER TECHNOLOGIES: One of the simplest technologies, called by Bordes (1961) the **Abbevillian** and **Lower Acheulian** technique (after the earliest European industries), consists of the more or less random detachment of flakes with a hard hammer. Often the flake scar remaining on the core after one flake removal served in turn as the striking platform for a subsequent removal, resulting in a number of plain platforms. Obviously, flakes produced from such an unpatterned technique tend to be highly variable in their morphology. Cores resulting from this technology tend to be completely reduced, and are generally classified as globular cores (Figure 3.11) or sometimes as "shapeless" (Figures 3.12 and 3.13), with flake scars originating from multiple surfaces. Sometimes, however, the cores present adjacent parallel scars that are reminiscent of Levallois blade cores, or pyramidal or prismatic cores (Figures 3.14 and 3.15) that are not dissimilar from those of the Upper Paleolithic.

A related technology is the so-called **Clactonian** technique, which was originally interpreted as involving the use of an anvil (see above). The flakes present platforms that are quite large, with very pronounced interior platform angles (greater than 105 degrees) and diffuse bulbs of percussion (Figure 3.16). Again, the lack of any surface preparation results in flakes that are highly variable both in form and thickness.

The **Mousterian**, or **disc-core** technique, is characterized by a centripetal flaking around the entire core margin, on one or both surfaces (Figures 3.17–3.20). Although it is not dissimilar to Levallois in both the technique and the form of the removed flakes, it nonetheless lacks clear evidence that the surface morphology of the core was specially prepared to achieve a flake of a particular form. It must be admitted, however, that this is a subjective criterion and, in fact, there is evidence that the two techniques may be related (see Baumler 1988). Two characteristic results of this technique are the pseudo-Levallois point (type 5 in Bordes' typology—see Chapter 4) and the disc core itself. The latter is generally circular in form, with centripetal flake scars, and typically has a flaking surface that is quite high, or even pointed, at the midpoint.

A number of other specialized, though still considered unprepared, flaking techniques are seen in certain Mousterian assemblages. One of these results in so-called "**salami slices**" (Bourlon 1907), which

Chapter

3

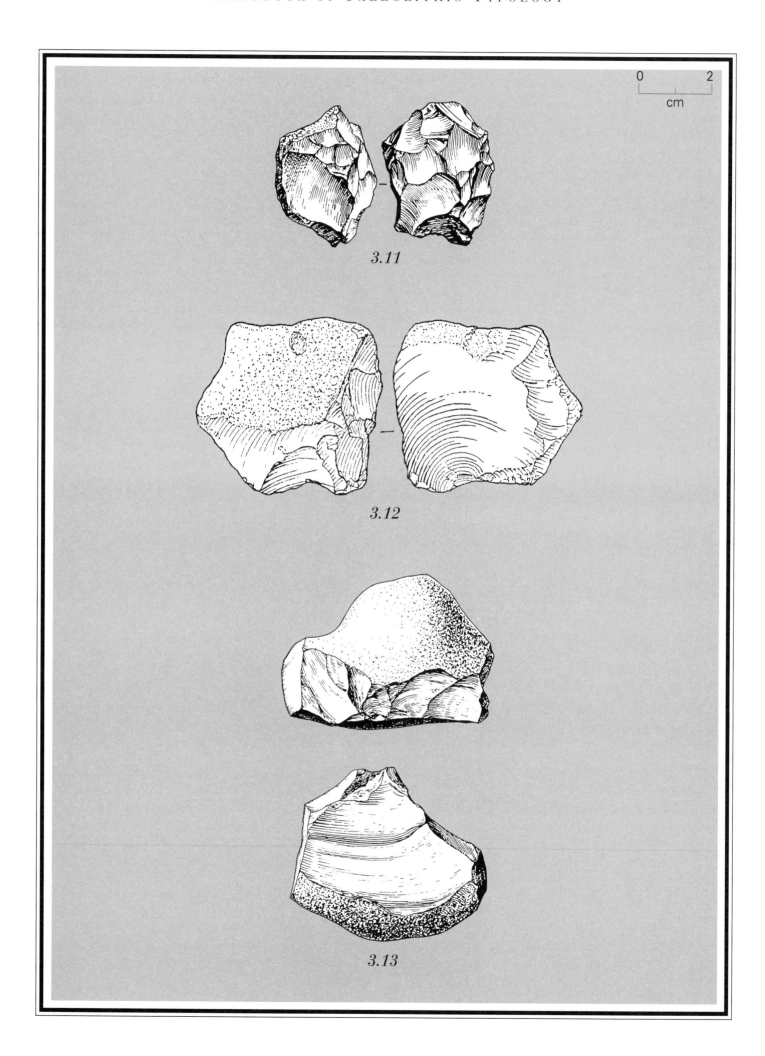

3.11

3.12

3.13

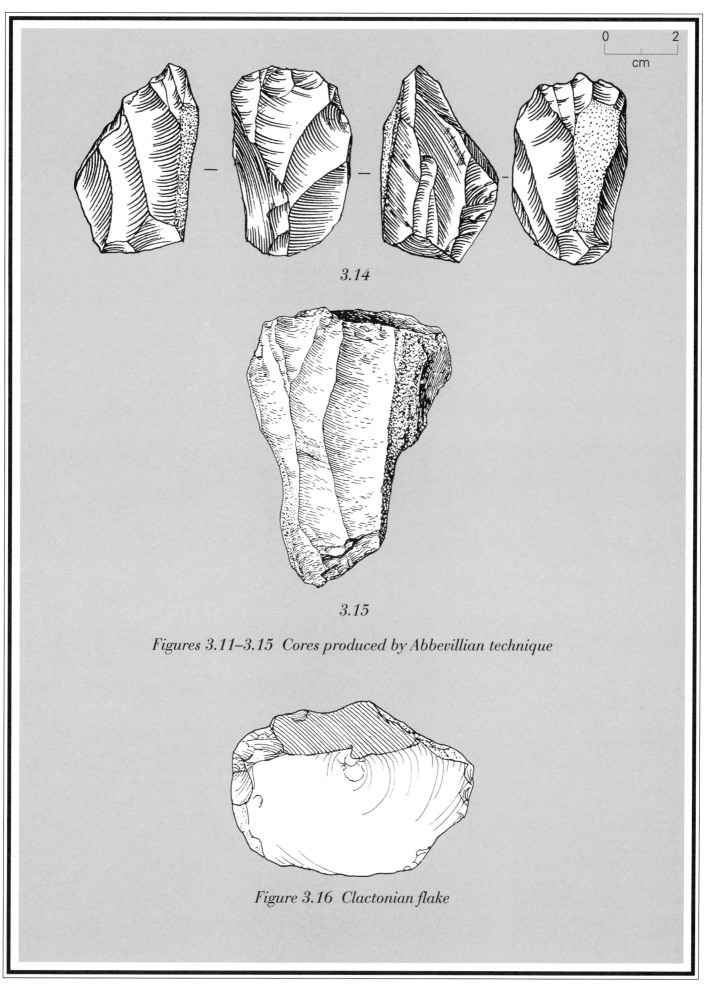

3.14

3.15

Figures 3.11–3.15 Cores produced by Abbevillian technique

Figure 3.16 Clactonian flake

Chapter

3

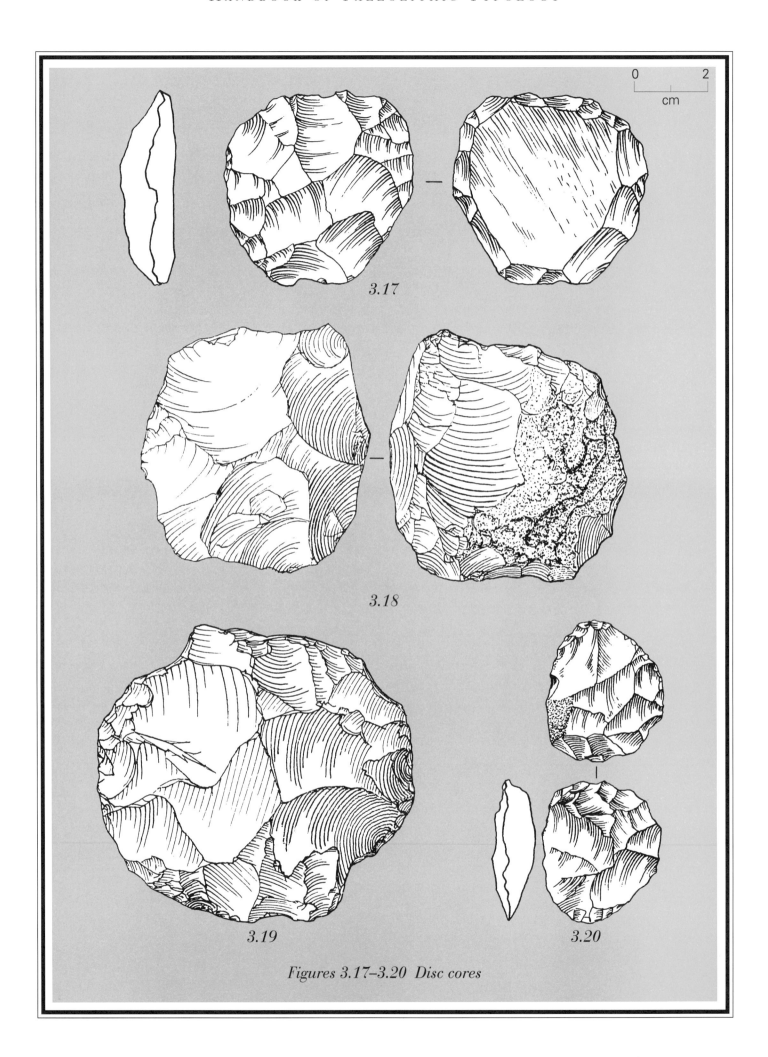

3.17

3.18

3.19

3.20

Figures 3.17–3.20 Disc cores

are thick and often very wide flakes that are sometimes associated with Quina-type transverse scrapers (for a fuller discussion of the total reduction sequence of this technology, see Turq 1989). In instances where raw material exists in the form of smaller pebbles, there is often exhibited a technique for splitting these pebbles into thick halves, and using these "**citrus slices**" as blanks (e.g., in the Erd Mousterian industry or the Pontinian in Italy— Gábori-Csánk 1968; Taschini and Bietti 1979). Smaller nodules of raw material are also associated with the production of higher frequencies of naturally-backed knives (Fish 1981).

RETOUCHING TECHNIQUES AND THE FASHIONING OF TOOLS

With the exception of the types defined solely on the basis of the technology of blank production (Levallois flakes, pseudo-Levallois points, naturally-backed knives, etc.—see Chapter 4), formal tools are fashioned on blanks through **retouching** along the edges. This involves the removal of small retouch flakes, either by percussion or pressure, (1) to shape or otherwise achieve an effective working edge; (2) to prepare the piece for hafting; or (3) as a preparatory stage in subsequent retouching. Of course, the term "tool" is being used in the traditional typological sense, since unretouched flakes can and undoubtedly were used in a variety of tasks. Note also that to be considered as such, the retouch must be applied after the blank was removed from the core. Thus, platform preparation or small flake scars resulting from core preparation are never considered retouch.

Different types of retouch are variously defined by different authors on the basis of a number of characteristics (see Bordes 1961 and Laplace-Jauretche 1964). Tixier et al. (1980) lists seven of the principal aspects:

- The surface(s) that were retouched, i.e., exterior, interior, or both. There are also three options in the latter case: **alternating** (i.e., one flake scar on the exterior surface, then one on the interior surface, and so on along the edge), **alternate** (where one edge is retouched on the interior and an opposing edge is retouched on the exterior), or **bifacial** (where both interior and exterior retouch occurs at the same location along the edge). Retouch on the interior surface is often called **inverse** retouch.

- The location of the retouch on the blank. In other words, the retouch may occur on the proximal, distal, or medial part of the blank, or around the entire perimeter.

- The distribution of the retouch along the edges, i.e., whether it is **continuous** or **discontinuous** along the edge.

- The shape of the retouched edge as viewed from the exterior surface (e.g., convex, straight, concave, notched, or denticulated).

- The extent or amount of development of the retouch, often expressed as being **light** to **heavy** depending on how far the retouch scars extend in from the edge (i.e., how **invasive** the retouch is), or on how much material has been removed through retouching (see Kuhn 1990).

- The angle formed by the two surfaces comprising the edge. When this angle is high (generally greater than 75 degrees), the retouch is considered to be **abrupt**.

- The morphology of the retouch scars.

Some of the major recognized retouch morphologies are listed below.

CONTINUOUS RETOUCH: Scalar retouch (Figure 3.21a and b), in which the retouch flake scars tend to become wider as they proceed in from the edge. This is a type of retouch that typically occurs in Middle Paleolithic assemblages, though it does also appear in earlier industries. It can be produced through direct percussion with either a hard or soft hammer.

Stepped retouch (Figure 3.21c), which can be considered a "multi-tiered" retouch, in which the retouch scars tend to end in either step or hinge fractures. When very pronounced it is referred to as **Quina** retouch, which was well-developed in some of the industries of the site of La Quina (France), where it was often found on thick blanks. Atypical Quina retouch (or **demi-Quina**) is that which is stepped but not very invasive on a thick scraper. In a somewhat less developed form and in an Upper Paleolithic context, Quina retouch is referred to as **Aurignacian** retouch (de Sonneville-Bordes 1960:20). There is some discussion as to whether Quina retouch was intentionally produced (Lenoir 1973, 1986), or whether it is the unintentional result of resharpening a thick blank (Dibble 1984a, 1987).

Parallel (Figure 3.21e) or **subparallel retouch** (Figure 3.21d) which is, as its name implies, retouch where the margins of the retouch scars are more or less parallel. This kind of retouch, which is often achieved through pressure technique, is significantly developed in the Solutrean of the Upper Paleolithic, though it is present in limited frequency in some Mousterian artifacts.

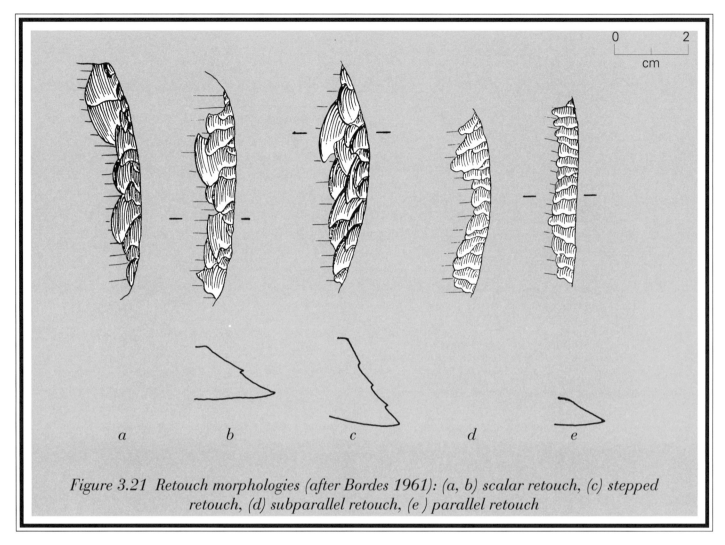

Figure 3.21 Retouch morphologies (after Bordes 1961): (a, b) scalar retouch, (c) stepped retouch, (d) subparallel retouch, (e) parallel retouch

The preceding retouch types are characterized as continuous retouch that extends some minimum distance (about a centimeter) along an edge, minimally invasive in from the edge, and forming a smooth cutting edge with an angle that is usually not too abrupt. These retouch types do grade into other kinds of retouch, however. Extremely light, but continuous and often abrupt retouch is referred to as **nibbling** and is characteristic of certain types, such as raclettes. Abrupt (i.e., steep), continuous retouch is called **backing** if it is opposite a sharp cutting edge, or **truncating** if it occurs at either or both ends of a flake or blade. If the retouch is abrupt, discontinuous, and alternating, it is usually not considered as retouch at all, but rather as macroscopic use wear or, usually more correctly, post-depositional edge damage (see Chapter 9).

Biface retouch consists of the removal of flakes from both the interior and exterior surface of a flake or core, usually with a soft hammer. The flakes thus removed, which are called **biface retouch flakes**, often have special characteristics (cf. Hayden and Hutchings 1989; Ahler 1989), including a small platform (often with evidence of grinding on the exterior margin), a distinct lip on the interior margin of the platform, and a rather diffuse bulb of percussion. They are often quite thin (Figure 2.10).

NON-CONTINUOUS RETOUCH: **Notching** refers to the production of a single, relatively deep concavity on the flake margin. It can be produced in two ways, either by a single blow (what is referred to as a **Clactonian notch**; see Figure 3.22a) or by several small, contiguous retouch scars that together shape the concavity (called either an ordinary or complex notch; see Figure 3.22b and c).

Denticulation is retouch that is formed by a series of contiguous notches or serration along the edge (Figure 3.23a and b). Sometimes an uneven scraper retouch can grade into a denticulated retouch, at which point some prehistorians like to speak of a denticulated scraper. Sometimes denticulation can be so continuous and regular that the retouched edge is difficult to distinguish from a rough scraper edge.

Burins are pieces where a lateral (or, occasionally, a transverse) edge is removed with one or more blows that follow the ridge formed by the sharp margin of the flake, resulting in a surface that is more or less perpendicular to the original flat surfaces of the

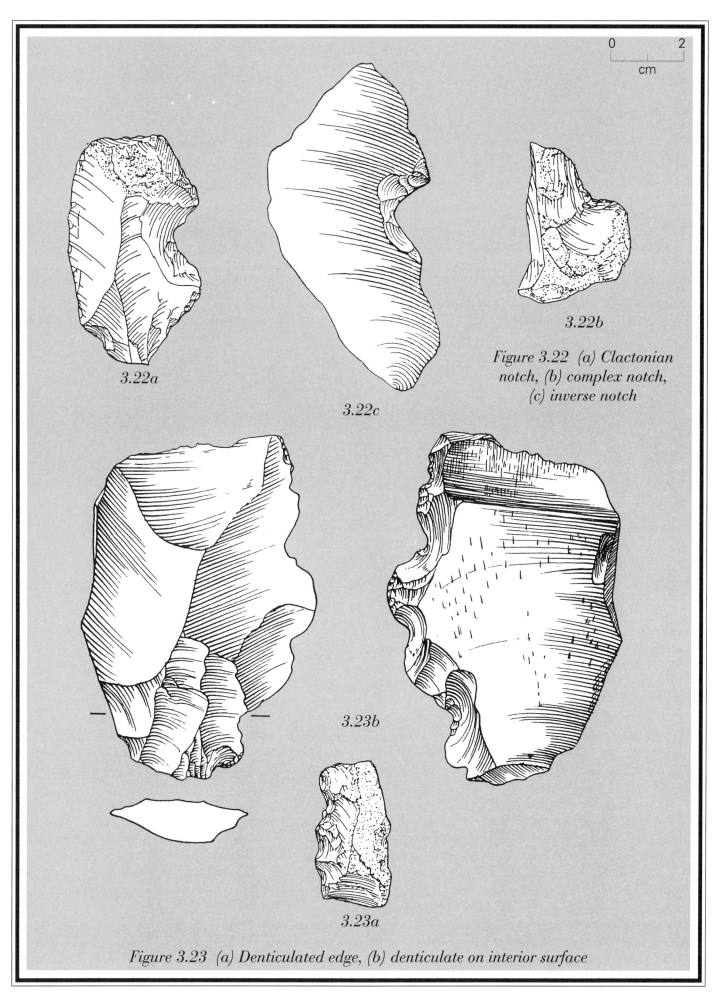

0   2
cm

3.22a

3.22c

3.22b

*Figure 3.22 (a) Clactonian
notch, (b) complex notch,
(c) inverse notch*

Chapter

3

3.23b

3.23a

Figure 3.23 (a) Denticulated edge, (b) denticulate on interior surface

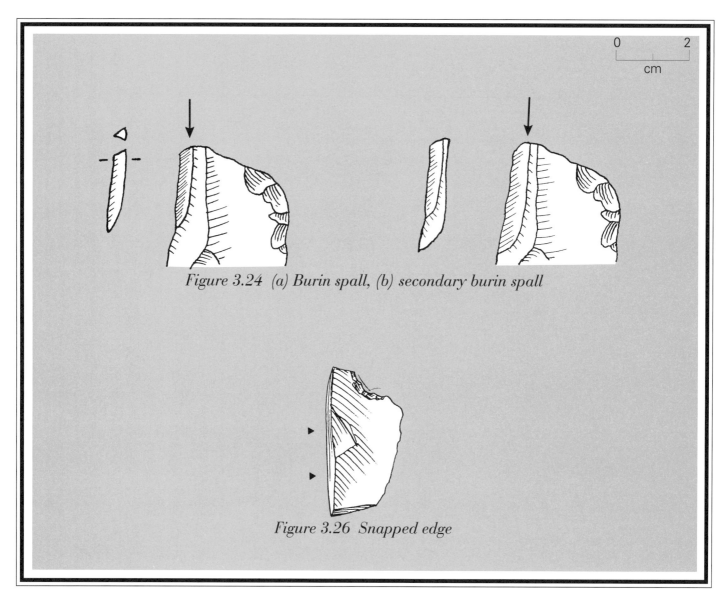

0   2
cm

Figure 3.24 (a) Burin spall, (b) secondary burin spall

Figure 3.26 Snapped edge

flake. The small flake that is removed, usually markedly triangular in cross-section, is called the **burin spall** (Figure 3.24a). Burins often exhibit evidence of resharpening, in which case the subsequent removals are called **secondary burin spalls** (Figure 3.24b).

The most common mistake when learning to recognize burins is to classify simple breaks as burins since, superficially, the flat edge produced by a snap can resemble the flat edge of a burin. Burins can be identified by the presence of the striking platform, often with a small negative bulb of percussion, and/or by faint ripples running along the burin edge (see, for example, Figure 3.25, which shows burin scars on a core-like piece). Moreover, the margins of the burin edge, that is, the intersection of the burin edge and the interior and exterior surfaces of the flake, are quite sharp. Conversely, a snapped edge will usually exhibit lipping or rounding on one or both edges (Figure 3.26), what Cotterell and Kamminga (1987) refer to as "finials." One must also take care not to confuse a real burin with what

is often called a "pseudo-burin," which is a flake that splits longitudinally when it is struck (Figure 3.27). At one time these were called "Mousterian burins" or *burins de Siret* (Siret 1933:121); however, such splits are purely accidental and are recognizable because they exactly intersect the point of percussion and the bulb.

A **tranchet blow** (Figure 3.28) is somewhat related to the burin technique, consisting of the production of a flat chisel-like sharp edge on the distal end of a piece by a single transverse (or sometimes lateral) blow. **Thinning** is a term often used for flat retouch on either the interior or exterior of a piece, usually near the proximal end, where it appears it was applied to thin the piece for hafting. It is usually not considered to be typologically significant; that is, it can be present without changing the classification of the piece.

One of the things to keep in mind regarding these various retouch types is that often it is the kind of retouch that defines the tool. In other words, a "burin" is a flake that has been modified with a

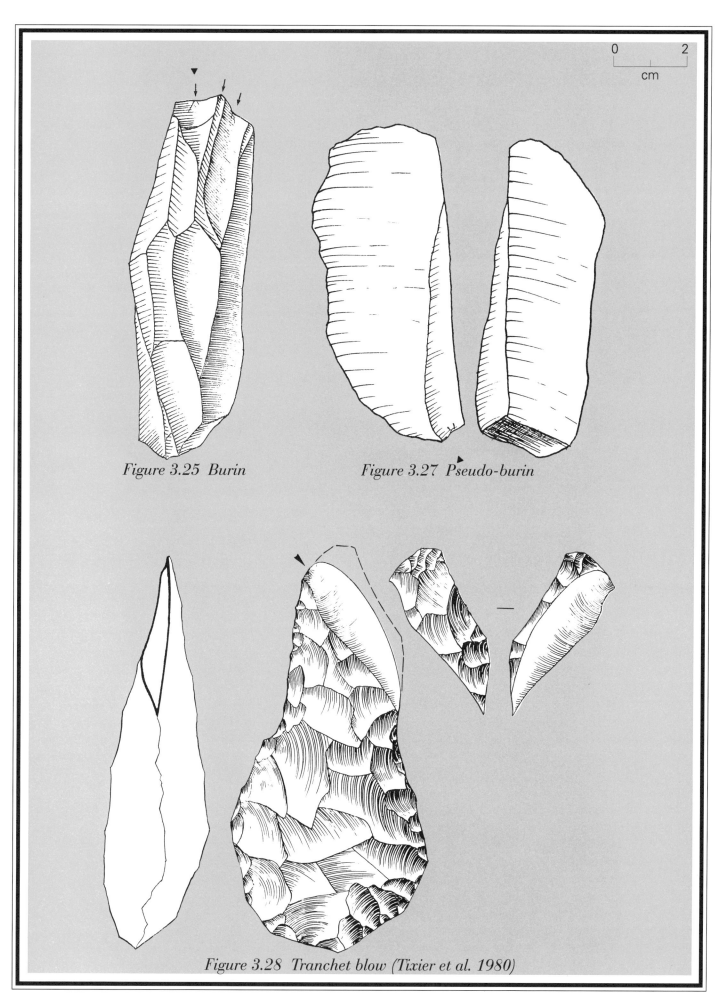

0   2
cm

Figure 3.25 Burin

Figure 3.27 Pseudo-burin

Figure 3.28 Tranchet blow (Tixier et al. 1980)

burin blow, and a "notch" is an object with a notch removed from one or more edges. But "burin" and "notch" also refer to the retouched area itself. So, for example, we can speak of a core with a notch on it, referring to the application of that particular retouch type on a part of the core; or we can say that a burin has a notch, meaning that the same flake exhibits both a portion that was notched and another portion that was burinated. In other words, several tool "types" may be represented on the same physical object. Following strict Bordian methodology, however, a single object will only be counted once, meaning that a decision must be made as to which of the different retouch types present will characterize the piece (see Appendix I and discussion of miscellaneous pieces [type 62—see Chapter 9]).

PART II

MODIFICATION

Non-retouched

LEVALLOIS
Typical Levallois flake (1)
Atypical Levallois flake (2)
Levallois point (3)

NON-LEVALLOIS
Pseudo-Levallois point (5)
Naturally-backed knife (38)

DEBITAGE
Cores
Normal flakes
Shatter and debris

Retouched

RETOUCH TYPE

Notching
Notch (42)
End-notched flake (54)
Notched triangle (52)
Alternate retouched bec (44)
Denticulate (43)
Tayac point (51)

Burin
Typical burin (32)
Atypical burin (33)

Perçoir
Typical perçoir (34)
Atypical perçoir (35)

Core-like
Chopper (59)
Inverse chopper (60)
Chopping-tool (61)
Rabot (56)

Other
Mousterian tranchet (41)
Pseudo-microburin (53)
Irreg. ret. on interior (45)
Pieces with abrupt and alternating retouch (46–49)
Stemmed point (57)
Stemmed tool (58)
Miscellaneous (62)

Continuous

RETOUCHED SURFACE

Interior
Scraper on interior surface (25)

Alternate
Scraper with thinned back (27)
Alternate scraper (29)

Exterior

Bifacial Retouch
Scraper with bifacial retouch (28)
Bifacial foliate (63)
Bifacially retouched piece (50)
Hachior (55)
Truncated-faceted piece

LOCATION OF RETOUCHED EDGE

Parallel Edges
Double straight scraper (12)
Double straight-convex scraper (13)
Double straight-concave scraper (14)
Double convex scraper (15)
Double concave scraper (16)
Double convex-concave scraper (17)

Single Lateral Edge

Convergent Edges
Retouched Levallois point (4)
Mousterian point (6)
Elongated Mousterian point (7)
Limace (8)
Straight convergent scraper (18)
Convex convergent scraper (19)
Concave convergent scraper (20)
Déjeté scraper (21)

Distal/Proximal
Straight transverse scraper (22)
Convex transverse scraper (23)
Concave transverse scraper (24)
Typical end scraper (30)
Atypical end scraper (31)
Truncation (40)

EDGE ANGLE

Non-abrupt
Single straight scraper (9)
Single convex scraper (10)
Single concave scraper (11)

Abrupt
Abrupt scraper (26)
Typical backed knife (36)
Atypical backed knife (37)
Raclette (39)

AN OVERVIEW OF BORDES' TYPOLOGY

In this part of the Handbook we will define and discuss various named types recognized in European Lower and Middle Paleolithic industries, building on the typology of Bordes.

Since the typology is simply a list of categories, there are many potential ways to organize it. Bordes himself eventually assigned numbers to each of his types, which standardized their order for producing cumulative graphs (see Appendix I). This order was in part dictated by similarities in morphology or retouch types, but in large part it was designed to maximize the separation among Middle Paleolithic industries using this graphical technique. In this Handbook we have not followed this numerical order, but instead have organized the presentation according to the major typological groupings that have been historically recognized, either because of common overall morphology (e.g., Chapter 5: Points), retouch type (e.g., Chapter 6: Scrapers), or other considerations (such as the Upper Paleolithic types presented in Chapter 7). Where appropriate, Bordes' type numbers are included in the definition of each type, and a complete typelist with type numbers can be found in Appendix I. Types without numbers are those that were not included in Bordes' original typology.

While this may be a logical organization for purposes of presentation, it still does not necessarily reflect the actual decision-making process that one goes through in deciding the proper type to which a particular object should be assigned. As was discussed in the Introduction, learning to apply Paleolithic typology is not a matter of comparing prehistoric artifacts with ideal forms representing each type. While "typical" pieces do occur with some frequency, a very large percentage of retouched material from any assemblage will not quite fit, for one reason or another, any idealized type. For these cases, it is more a matter of matching certain aspects of the objects with the defining characteristics of the types.

Figure II.1 on the facing page presents one possible way of organizing the main typology according to selected criteria. By stepping through each of these in turn (i.e., retouched or not, type of retouch, which surface is retouched, etc.) one can usually arrive at a satisfactory typological assignment for virtually any object.

CHAPTER FOUR

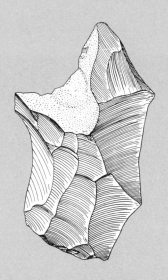

TECHNOLOGICALLY
DEFINED TOOLS

THIS CHAPTER PRESENTS A NUMBER OF types which are defined on the basis of certain specialized technologies of blank production rather than on specific morphologies brought about through retouching. Except for the retouched Levallois points, all of the technologically defined types presented in this chapter are unretouched. To quite a degree, then, these types are in marked contrast to the other types in Bordes' typelist, which mostly categorize objects that were deliberately retouched and for which the shape, location, and other characteristics of the retouched edge represent the primary criteria for classification. Thus, the distinction between "tools" and "debitage" becomes blurred, and the inclusion of the latter in the typology makes it a rather uneven mix of technological and formal attributes.

The types based on Levallois technology are typical and atypical Levallois flakes (types 1 and 2, respectively), Levallois points (type 3), and retouched Levallois points (type 4). In the discussion of technology presented in Chapter 3, it was pointed out that there is a great deal of confusion regarding the definition and classification of Levallois technology. Since these first four of Bordes' types are defined as Levallois products, it follows that these are among the least reliably recognized types in Lower and Middle Paleolithic industries (see, for example, Perpère 1986).

Once it is decided that a blank is Levallois, then the main criteria for classification become the presence (or absence) and character of retouch and the form of the blank.

To be classified as one of types 1–3, the blank must not be retouched. If it is, then it is typed according to the standard criteria for the other retouched types. In other words, a Levallois flake that has been retouched into a scraper will be classified as a scraper, not as a Levallois flake. Types 1–3 can, however, exhibit macroscopic traces of "utilization" or other forms of edge damage, and therefore Levallois flakes, blades, or points should never be placed in the categories of abrupt and alternating retouched pieces (types 46–49—see Chapter 9).

The only distinction based on form is whether or not the piece is a Levallois point. If so, then it may be classified as a type 3 or 4, depending on the presence of light, marginal retouch (see below). All other Levallois forms (flakes or blades) are regarded as types 1 or 2, depending on the "quality" of flaking. Likewise, all other possible distinctions based on core preparation are ignored. Thus unidirectional, bidirectional, and centripetal preparations are all considered the same as far as this classification is concerned.

Chapter

4

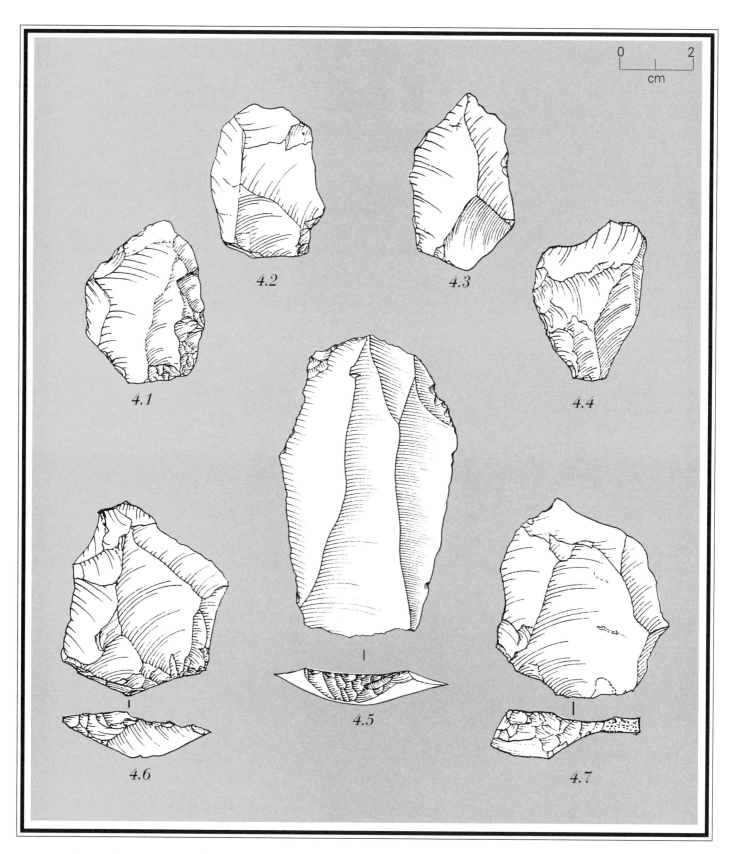

Typical and atypical Levallois flakes (Types 1 and 2; Figures 4.1–4.21). These two types represent all of the unretouched, Levallois products without points, including both flakes and blades. The difference between typical and atypical Levallois flakes is highly subjective. Typical Levallois flakes and blades (Figures 4.1–4.14) are generally symmetrical about the axis of flaking, are thin relative to their length and width, and have fairly flat exterior surfaces. Size is not considered a defining characteristic, and some typical Levallois flakes can be quite small (2–3 cm in length). Typical Levallois flakes can exhibit platform preparation of any kind, including faceted or dihedral, or no preparation (either cortical or plain).

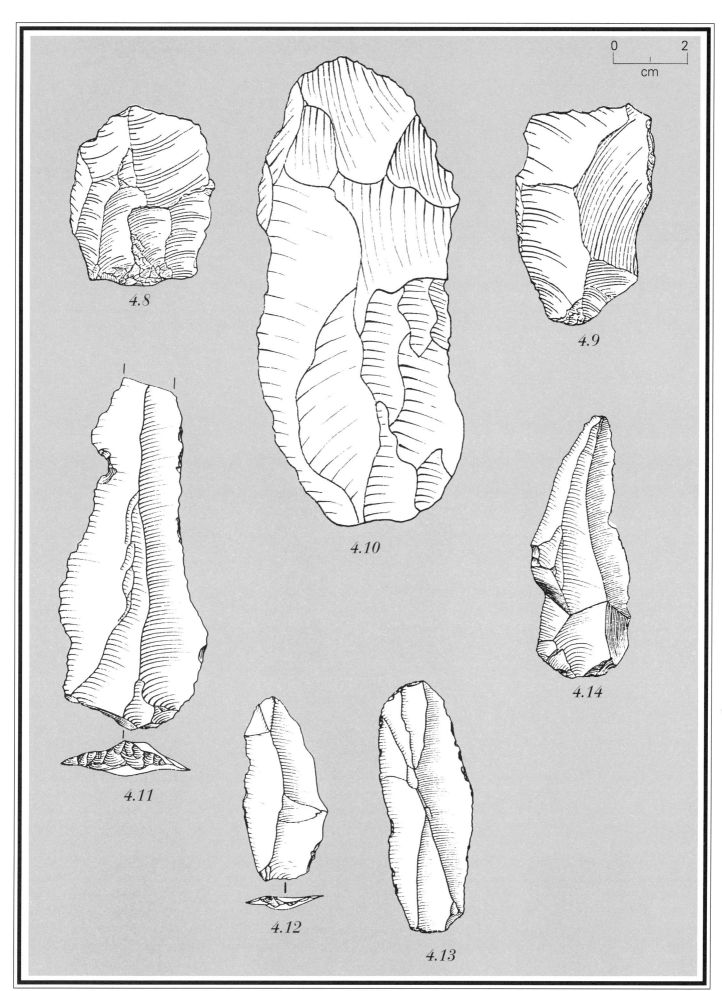

0   2
cm

4.8

4.9

4.10

4.11

4.12

4.13

4.14

Chapter

4

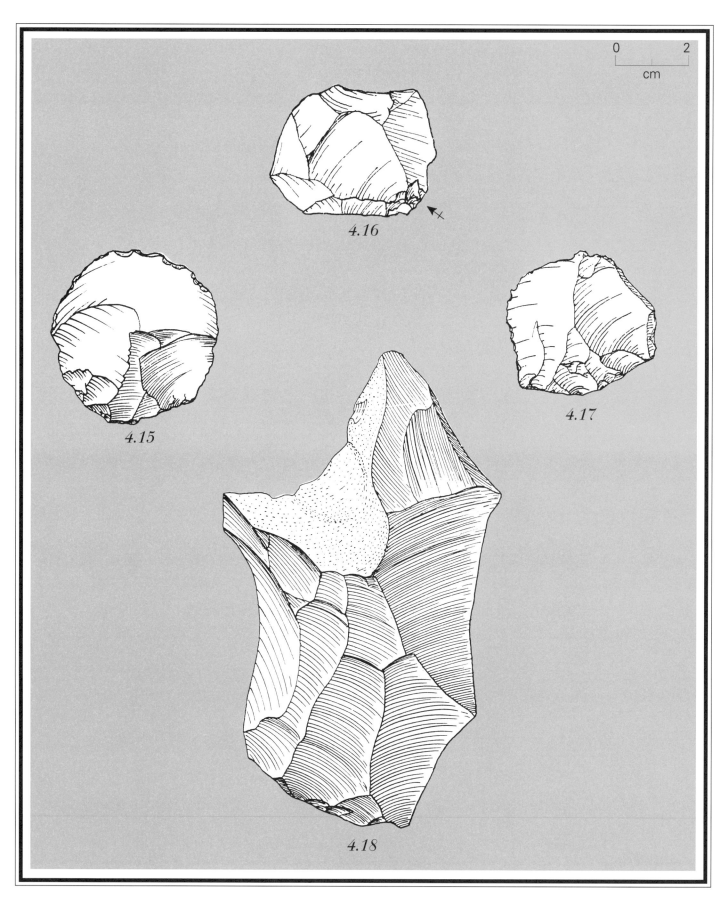

0 2
cm

4.16

4.15

4.17

4.18

There are many different criteria for classifying a piece as an atypical Levallois flake or blade (see Figures 4.15–4.21). Thickness is one criterion (Figure 4.21), as are faults such as overshooting the end of the core or pronounced hinge fractures. A Levallois flake is also considered atypical if it exhibits significant amounts of cortex (Figure 4.18). Note in this case that a Levallois flake that has lateral cortex should not be classified as a naturally-backed knife (type 38; see below), regardless of the

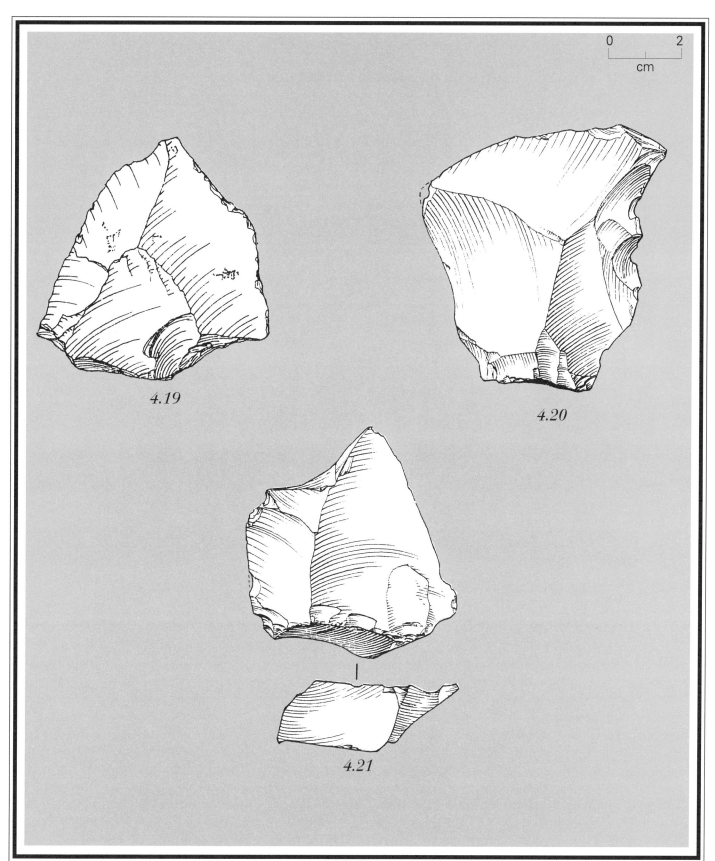

4.19

4.20

4.21

Chapter

4

abruptness of the cortical back. Geneste (1985:220) proposes placing in this category also those Levallois flakes whose long axis is divergent from their axis of flaking (Figure 4.16). In practice, many Levallois flakes exhibiting uncomplicated or incomplete exterior flake scars are often called atypical (e.g., Figures 4.15, 4.17, and 4.20). In any case, it must be kept in mind that atypical Levallois flakes are definitely products of Levallois technology, that is, they are not "Proto-Levallois" or flakes that are "almost" Levallois.

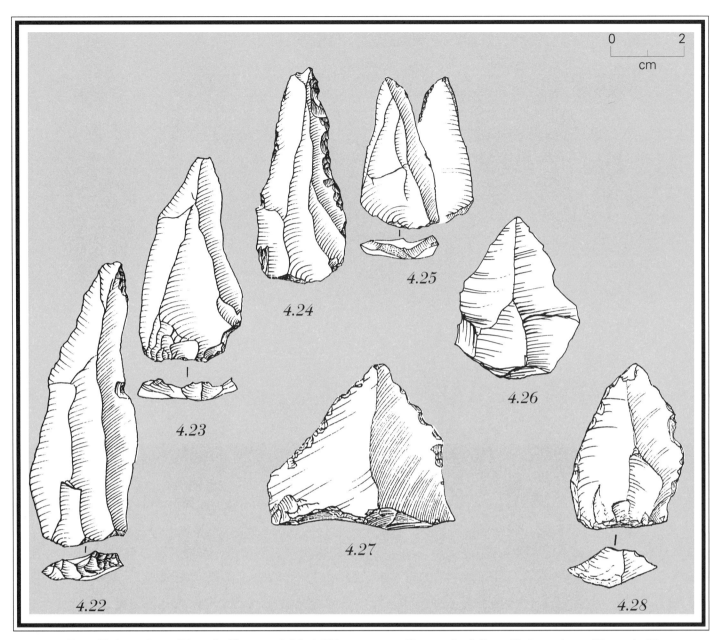

0   2
cm

Levallois points (Type 3; Figures 4.22–4.28). Although the term "Levallois point" was coined by Bordes (1953a), the definition given by Tixier (1960:182) is perhaps clearer: "a triangular flake with a central or medial ridge, sometimes possessing a triangle at the base due to the prior removal of a small flake. It is this medial ridge which guides the removal and predetermines the triangular form."

Although he did not give them different type numbers, Bordes did make a distinction between first-order Levallois points, which exhibit only the central ridge (e.g., Figure 4.27, which is also a very thick example), and second-order Levallois points, which exhibit also the triangular negative scar near the base left by the removal of an earlier first-order point (most clearly seen in Figure 4.23). Bordes also distinguished between triangular, ogival (i.e., shaped like a pointed arch), and elongated Levallois points, although none of these distinctions are retained in the typology, either.

Retouched Levallois points (Type 4; Figure 4.29). By definition, a Levallois point (that is, a type 3 tool) is not retouched. If a Levallois point blank is retouched, then it is classified as type 4, a retouched Levallois point (Figure 4.29). However, the retouch should be generally light and, as Bordes (1961:24) put it, represent an "accommodation retouch made to regularize the lateral margins of the point." If, on the other hand, the retouch is relatively heavy and on both edges, then the piece should be typed as a Mousterian point (types 6 and 7—see Chapter 5). Note that if a Levallois point is made into a different type of tool (notch or denticulate, for example), the classification of the piece will be according to the type of retouch. Note also that a Levallois flake or blade (not a point) that is made to be pointed through the application of bilateral retouch is correctly typed as either a Mousterian point (type 6 or 7—see Chapter 5) or a convergent scraper (types 18–21—see Chapter 5). Abrupt and possibly alter-

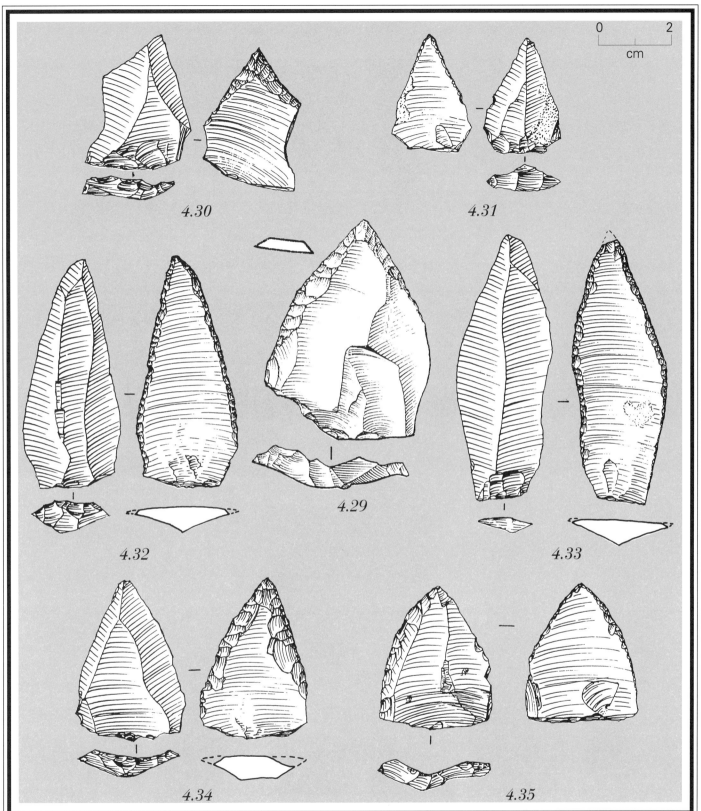

0   2
cm

4.30

4.31

4.29

4.32

4.33

4.34

4.35

nating retouch, as in the case of Figures 4.24 and 4.27, does not warrant classification as a retouched Levallois point (nor, again, as types 46–49), nor does the extremely light interior retouch seen in Figure 4.25.

The **Soyons point** (Figures 4.30–4.35) was defined by Combier (1955:433–434) as a Levallois point with continuous, light retouch on the interior surface of both margins.

It is not generally thought that Levallois points, retouched or not, represent real projectile points, though such a case has been made by Shea (1989a, b) on the basis of microwear analyses of Levantine Mousterian material.

The following types are not products of Levallois technology.

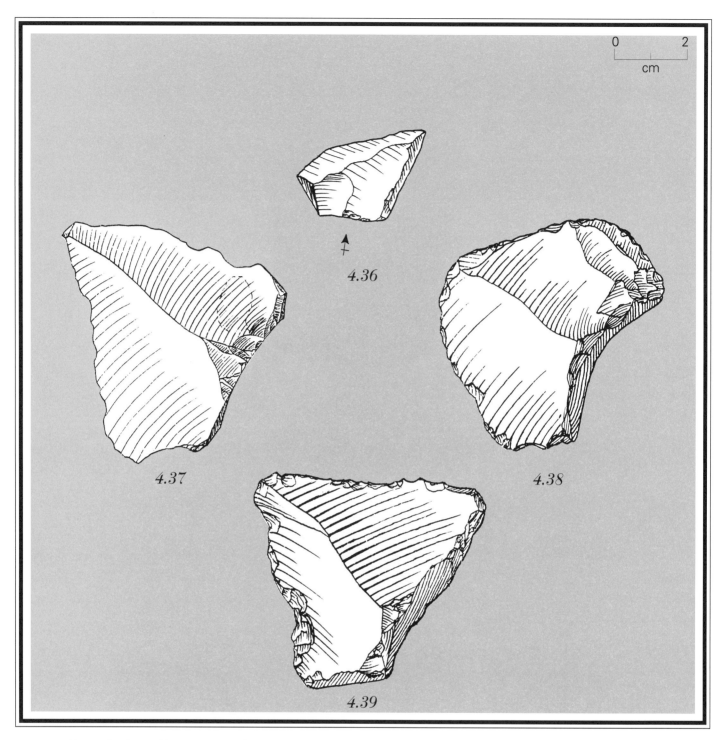

0 _____ 2
cm

4.36

4.37

4.38

4.39

Pseudo-Levallois points (Type 5; Figures 4.36–4.39). These can resemble Levallois points in that they are sometimes triangular and can exhibit a similar scar morphology. However, in general they are produced by a disc-core technology and their long axes, i.e., the axis defined by the distal point, are oblique relative to their axes of flaking (generally the divergence between these two axes is greater than 45 degrees). Also, pieces which exhibit a converging or even a near unidirectional scar orientation oriented obliquely from the proximal to distal end, and which retain a significant portion of core edge as a lateral extension of the platform are often classified as pseudo-Levallois points. In fact, these "points"

are often not pointed at all and can exhibit a marked polygonal form when the flaking surface intersects several previous flake scars of the core, as in Figure 4.38. Such pieces are also called *éclats débordants*, or core trimming elements, and are characteristic of particular techniques of preparing the surface of a Levallois flake core (Boëda et al. 1990), though they, themselves, are not Levallois flakes.

Pseudo-Levallois points may also show evidence of non-deliberate edge damage without being otherwise classified as types 46–49 (Figure 4.39). If, however, deliberate retouch is present, then the piece should be typed according to the character of that retouch.

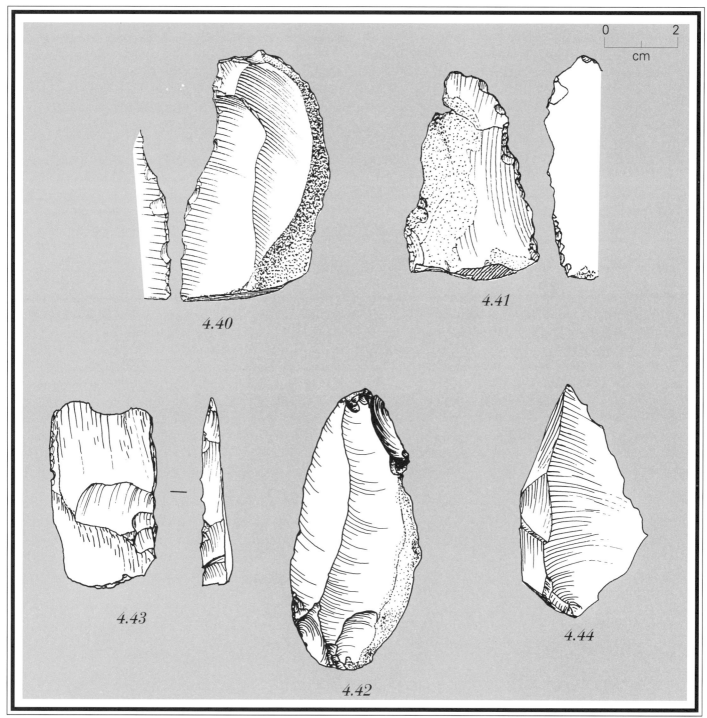

0   2
cm

4.40

4.41

4.43

4.42

4.44

Naturally-backed knives (Type 38; Figures 4.40–4.44). Although knives have been recognized by prehistorians for a long time, the distinction between knives with a prepared (i.e., retouched) back (types 36 and 37—see Chapter 7), and the naturally-backed knives described here, is relatively recent (Peyrony 1934; Tixier 1960; Bordes 1961; de Heinzelin 1962). Bordes (1961:33) defined naturally-backed knives as unretouched flakes or blades that have a sharp cutting edge on one margin and a natural cortical surface (the "back") on the opposing edge which is perpendicular, or nearly so, to the interior surface. For him, such a piece may or may not show traces of "utilization," or edge damage, on the

cutting edge. However, if the back is not cortex but some other natural flat surface perpendicular to the flaking surface of the blank (for example, a remnant of the lateral edge of a core as in Figures 4.43 and 4.44), then Bordes felt that such an object could be counted as a naturally-backed knife *only* if it presents traces of "utilization" on the sharp edge.

A major source of ambiguity in this definition is that if the backing is cortex, then that is enough to classify it as a recognized type. If the backing is the result of some other natural flat surface, then Bordes required evidence of utilization on the opposite sharp edge. In order to be consistent, the definition of this type should either always require the presence of

Chapter

4

such utilization or ignore it entirely.

There are arguments on both sides concerning whether or not such traces of utilization should be considered. If this type is to be used to monitor specific activities, i.e., cutting or slicing, then independent evidence of such use would be important. If so, then a more consistent definition for naturally-backed knives would be as follows: flakes or blades exhibiting a natural cutting edge *with* macroscopic traces of utilization opposite a margin that is nearly perpendicular to the interior surface. If the back is of cortex, then it could be considered a **typical** naturally-backed knife (Figures 4.40–4.42); if the back is non-cortical (i.e., plain, broken, or formed by flake scars produced before the blank was removed), then it should be considered an **atypical** naturally-backed knife. In this case, all naturally-backed pieces without traces of utilization should not be typed. Pieces without cortical or natural backs which exhibit macroscopic traces of utilization should be regarded only as utilized flakes.

On the other hand, such evidence of utilization is, of course, rather subjectively determined and in any case its presence depends on the use of the piece intensely enough or on materials sufficiently hard as to leave recognizable traces. It is also true that such traces do not always reflect use, but may be damage resulting from post-depositional factors (Bordes 1961:46; Kantman 1970a; Keeley 1980:25–28) or "spontaneous retouch" (Newcomer 1976) obtained when the flake was removed. While such factors should not be exaggerated, it does mean that the macroscopic damage is not an unequivocal indication of use and thus the presence or absence of such traces may not be particularly relevant to the definition of this type. In this case, the assignment of type should rest only on the morphology of the flake, that is, that there is a naturally blunt edge opposite a sharp *potential* cutting edge. In this case, the type would not monitor use or activity, but rather technology. If the flat surface is a previous core-edge, then the object should be classified as an *éclat débordant* or pseudo-Levallois point (type 5—see above).

In any case, the presence of abrupt, discontinuous retouch, or edge-damage, does not mean that they should be classified as types 46–49 (abrupt and alternating retouched pieces—see Chapter 9).

The backing of the naturally-backed knives, whether due to cortex or any other flat surface produced prior to the removal of the flake in question, must be perpendicular or nearly so, to the flaking surface (between 75 and 105 degrees relative to the interior surface). A piece whose lateral edge is blunted by deliberate retouching would be typed as a backed knife (types 36 and 37—see Chapter 7) or as an abrupt scraper (type 26—see Chapter 6). Note, however, that a flat lateral edge resulting from breakage after the flake blank was removed from the core *never* constitutes backing, natural or otherwise. Also note that as in the case of all of these technologically defined tools, the presence of deliberate retouch overrides the technological considerations and so would result in the piece being typed according to the retouch characteristics.

De Lumley (1971) defined another naturally-backed knife, called the **couteau de Bize** (Figures 4.45–4.49), which presents a series of flat retouch scars (which were present before the removal of the blank) on the margin opposite a sharp edge. These flakes are often obtained through Levallois technology, and may also be considered as *éclats débordants* (Meignen and Bar-Yosef 1991:56).

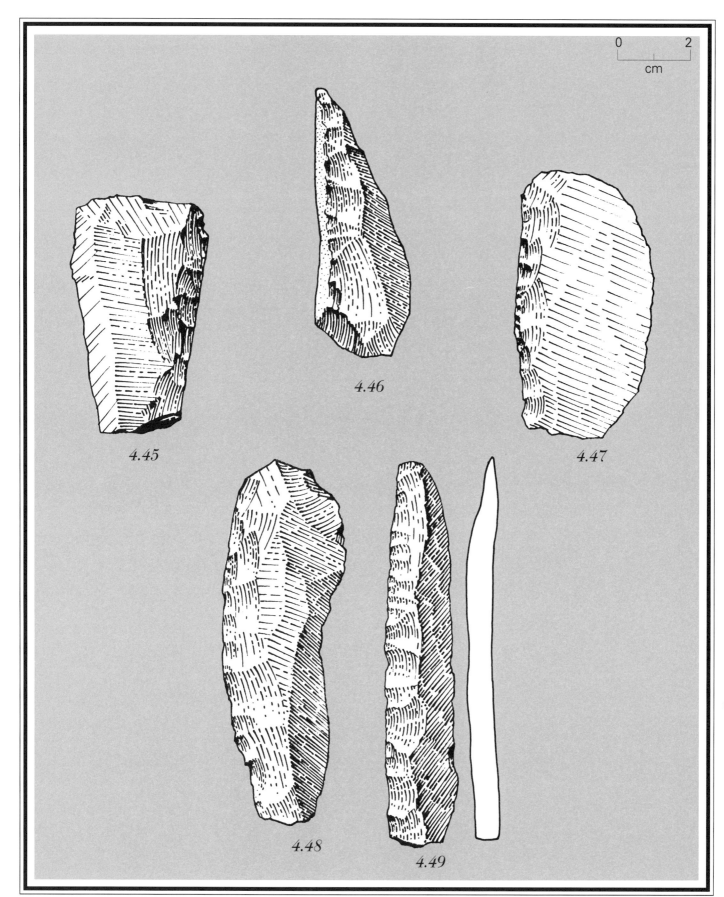

4.45

4.46

4.47

4.48

4.49

CHAPTER FIVE

POINTS

THIS CHAPTER COVERS THE retouched Mousterian points and the double points of Bordes' typology, as well as some other point types that occur in varying frequencies in certain Lower and Middle Paleolithic assemblages. Levallois and pseudo-Levallois points are discussed above in Chapter 4, and Tayac points (which are essentially convergent denticulates) are discussed below in Chapter 8.

As is true of the various kinds of knives, points have long been recognized in Paleolithic contexts and the term "point" has been in the literature since the eighteenth century. However, they have also been poorly defined, with nothing approaching a clear definition until that of Vayson de Pradenne in 1920. Even since then, point typologies have varied considerably among prehistorians. For Cheynier (1954:339), a point was any blade or flake for which an extremity was made pointed by bilateral retouching. Others have proposed more complex point typologies, for example, Pradel (1963), who distinguished—though poorly defined—twelve separate types of Mousterian points. Some authors have classified as points many different sorts of objects that were either pointed or rounded at their extremities, and either retouched or not.

Mousterian points (Type 6; Figures 5.1–5.16) and **elongated Mousterian points** (Type 7; Figures 5.17–5.22). For a long time confused with Levallois points, Mousterian points have been described by a number of authors, including Peyrony (1932), who distinguished two separate types of points based on the presence or absence of a faceting platform. Bordes (1961:22), however, excluded any considera-

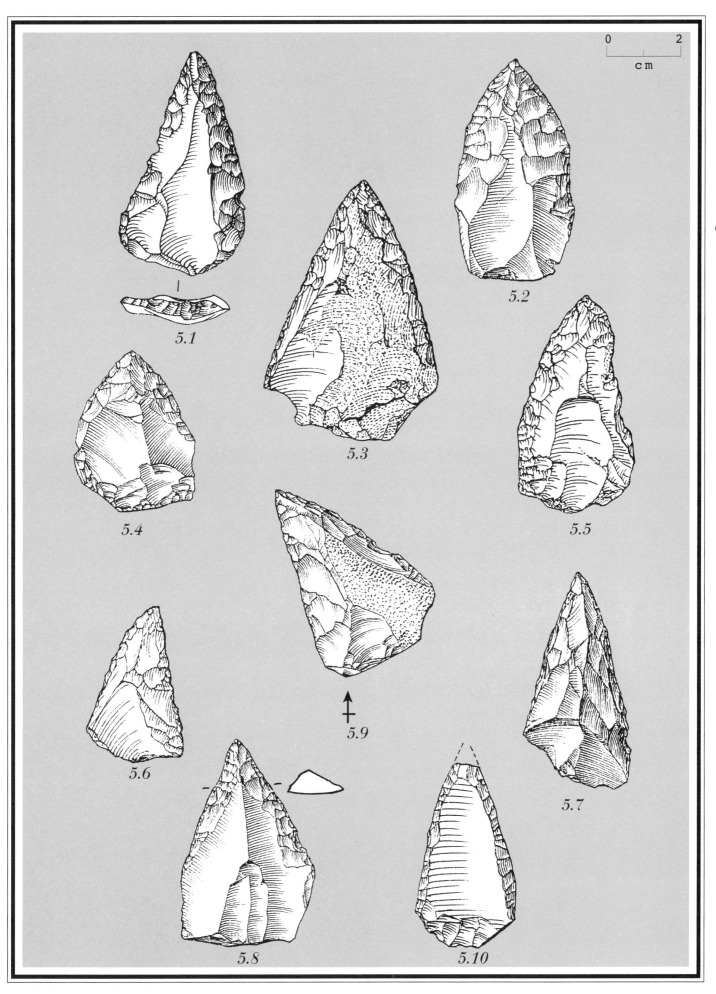

0
2
c m

5.1

5.2

5.3

5.4

5.5

Chapter
5

5.6

5.9

5.7

5.8

5.10

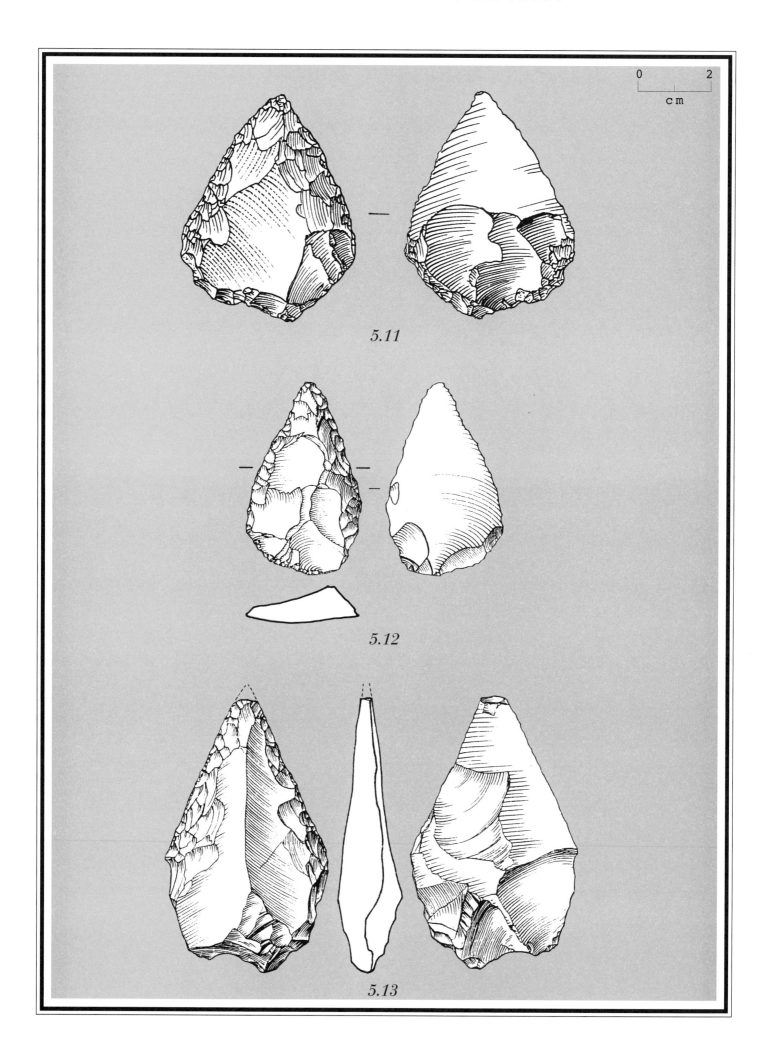

5.11

5.12

5.13

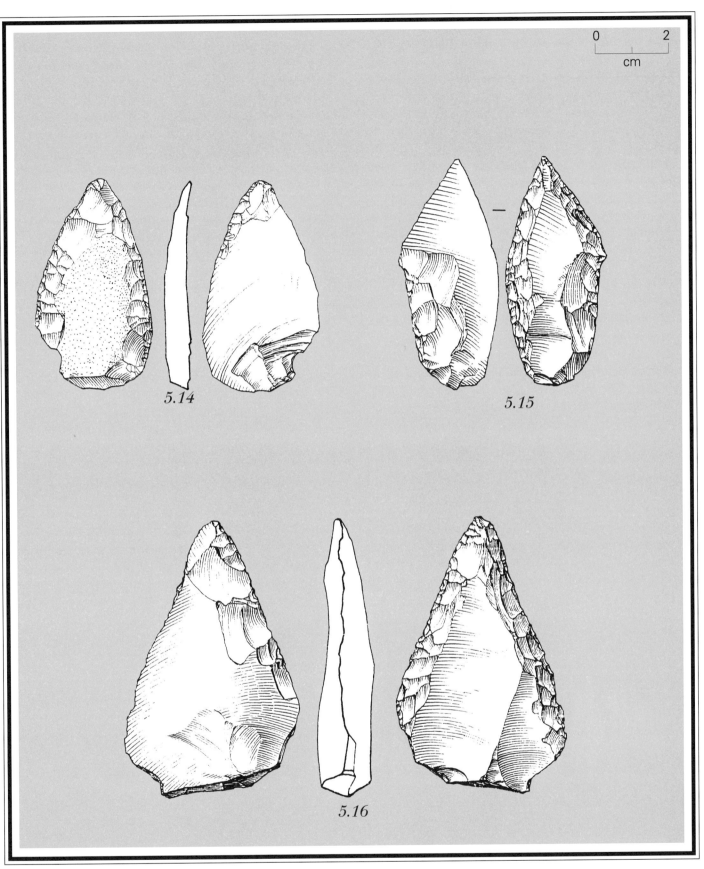

5.14

5.15

5.16

tion of the flaking technique or technology, defining Mousterian points morphologically as "triangular, subtriangular, sometimes lozenge-shaped, more or less elongated, with a pointed end produced by significant retouching, and made on a flake which is either Levallois or not." Further, Mousterian points must be more or less flat in their longitudinal aspect, though they can be skewed, or *déjetées* (Figure 5.9). They may also exhibit thinning, either of the proximal (Figures 5.11–5.15) or distal end (Figure 5.16).

The distinction between Mousterian points and elongated Mousterian points is based only on a length/width ratio: the latter have lengths that are at least two times their widths.

For Bordes (1961:21), the most important characteristic of Mousterian points is that they are pointed. This means that to be typed as a point, the distal extremity of the object must form a sharp angle in the plane of the flaking surface (i.e., as one looks down on the exterior surface of the piece) and also that this end be equally pointed in the plan perpendicular to the interior surface (i.e., when viewed from the side). Thus, the distal end of the piece should neither terminate abruptly nor present a steep edge. However, when the angle viewed from the exterior is extremely sharp one can, at the limit of the definition, still classify the object as a point, even if the end is thick.

Mousterian points can be made on virtually any kind of flake or blade, including Levallois points. As brought out in Chapter 4, the presence of "significant retouch" is what distinguishes Mousterian point types made on Levallois points from type 4—retouched Levallois points. Note also that on a Mousterian point, the "point" itself must be deliberately formed by retouch. Thus, a naturally pointed flake or blade is never considered a Mousterian point, and it is on this basis that one should not confuse Mousterian points with unretouched Levallois points (type 3—see Chapter 4). Mousterian points may also exhibit a flat, invasive retouch (Figure 5.22), which may lead to confusion with a bifacial foliate (type 63—see Chapter 9).

In fact, the major problem in classifying Mousterian points is distinguishing them not from other point types but from convergent scrapers, which also have two retouched edges that converge and meet at one extremity (types 18–20—see

Chapter 6). Bordes (1961) himself offered a light-hearted "functional" criterion, writing that the best way to decide is to haft the piece and try to kill a bear with it. If the result is successful, then it is a point; if not, then it should be considered a convergent scraper. One of the problems with this approach is that it can quickly exhaust the available supply of bears or typologists, depending on the nature of the assemblage. Although various metrical distinctions have been investigated (see, for example, de Heinzelin 1962), the distinction between the two classes remains as a major problem in applying the typology. Figure 5.21 is at the limit between these two types.

In fact, it is not certain that such a distinction is valid, as there are several lines of evidence that suggest that Middle Paleolithic retouched points were probably not true projectile points and instead represent one end of variation in convergent scrapers. First, it is undeniable that they resemble convergent scrapers technologically. Second, they are highly correlated with convergent scrapers, i.e., assemblages that are rich in convergent scrapers are also rich in retouched points, and those that lack one tend to lack the other (Dibble 1988). If these two categories were functionally distinct, such a relationship would not necessarily be the case. Third, an analysis of breakage of points does not show patterns consistent with true points (Holdaway 1989; cf. Shea 1989a, b; Solecki 1992). And fourth, microwear analyses also do not support their consistent use as projectile points (Beyries 1984, 1988; Anderson-Gerfaud 1990). On the other hand, some analysts have observed damage on points that is suggestive of impact fracture (Callow 1986), and there is some microwear evidence of hafting (Anderson-Gerfaud 1990).

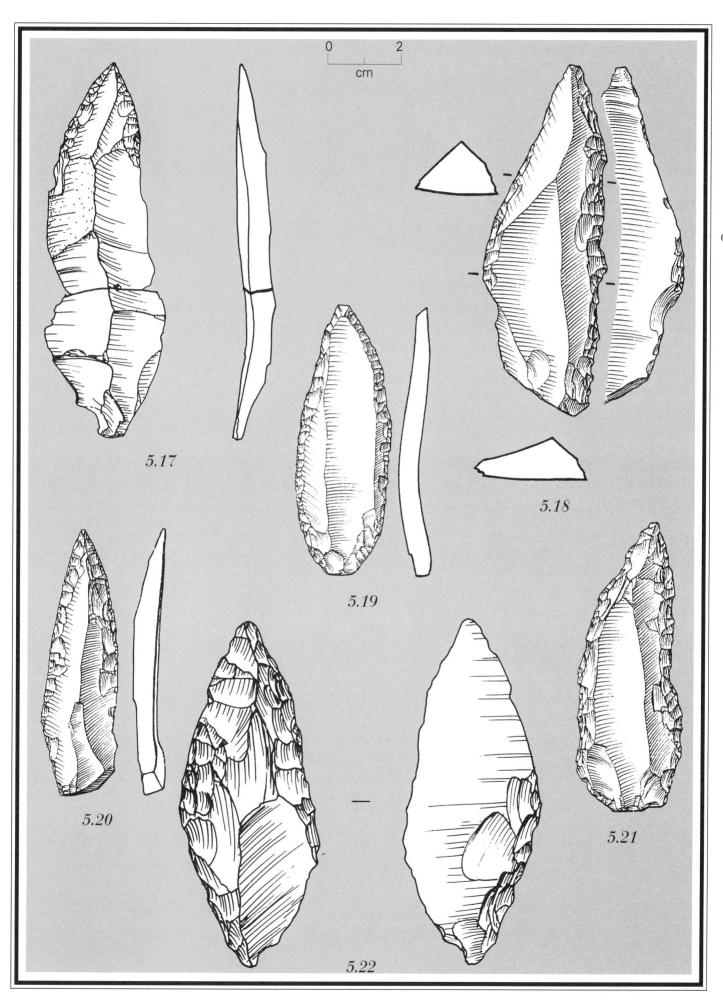

0   2
cm

5.17

5.18

5.19

5.20

5.22

5.21

Chapter
5

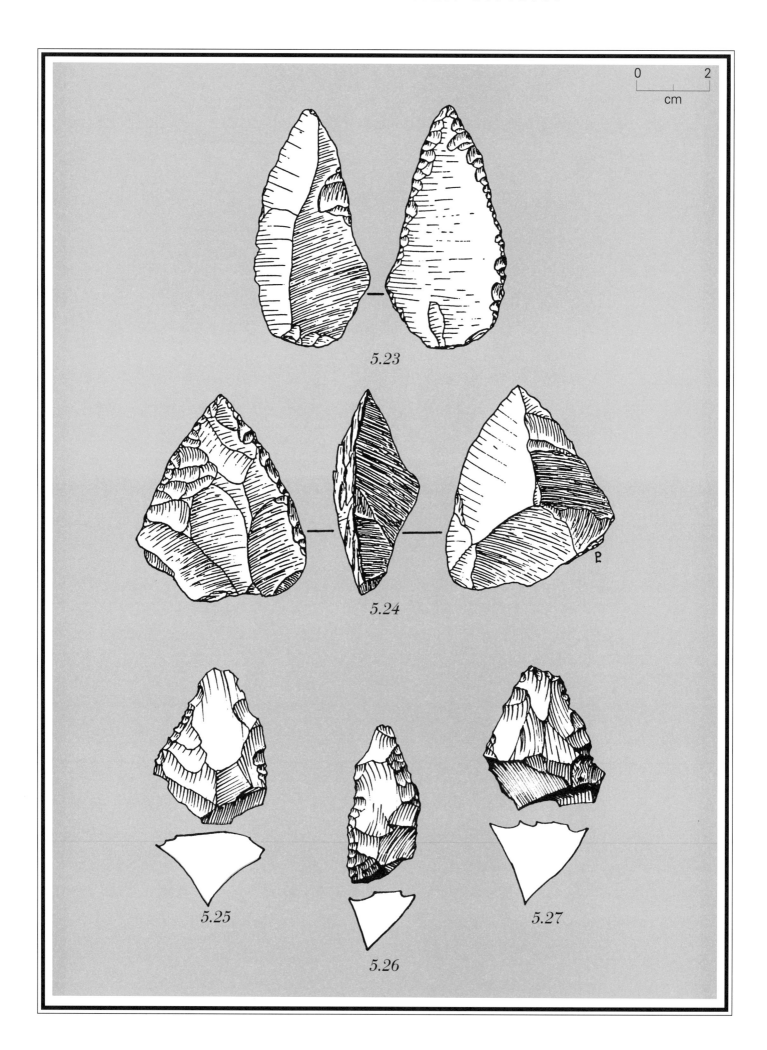

5.23

5.24

5.25

5.26

5.27

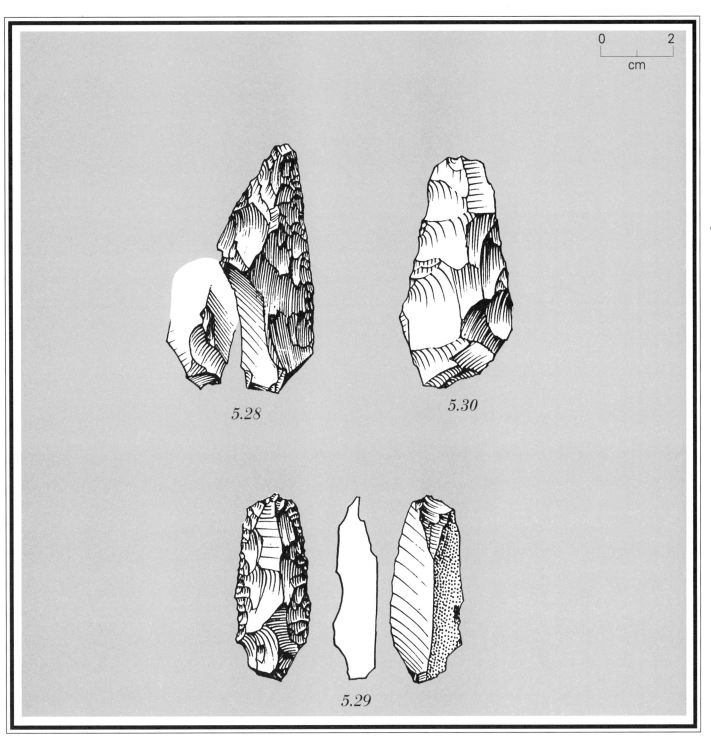

0   2
cm

5.28

5.30

5.29

Chapter
5

Many other point types have been described in the literature which are easily subsumed under types 6 and 7. Examples of allowable secondary characteristics include basal thinning of the bulb and platform, some bifacial retouch, alternate retouch on opposing edges, concave bases, or non-triangular (e.g., ogival, oblong, obtuse, etc.) outlines. Any of these features can be present on Mousterian points without affecting their classification. Two special types deserve mention, however. One, described by Pradel (1963), is the **Fontmaure point** (Figure 5.23), which has continuous, light retouch on the interior surface of both margins, like the Soyons

point described in the previous chapter. However, unlike the Soyons point, the Fontmaure point is on a non-Levallois blank. Another special type is the **pointe de Quinson** (Figures 5.24–5.30), as described by de Lumley and Bottet (1960) from the site of Baume-Bonne in southeast France. It is defined as a pointed "piece with a triangular section, with one of the three surfaces covered by retouch, and the other two faces left plain" (Bordes 1961:43). These may have a retouch that is either abrupt or stepped (Figure 5.30) or so flat and invasive that it is almost core-like (Figure 5.29). Neither of these types are recognized in Bordes' typology.

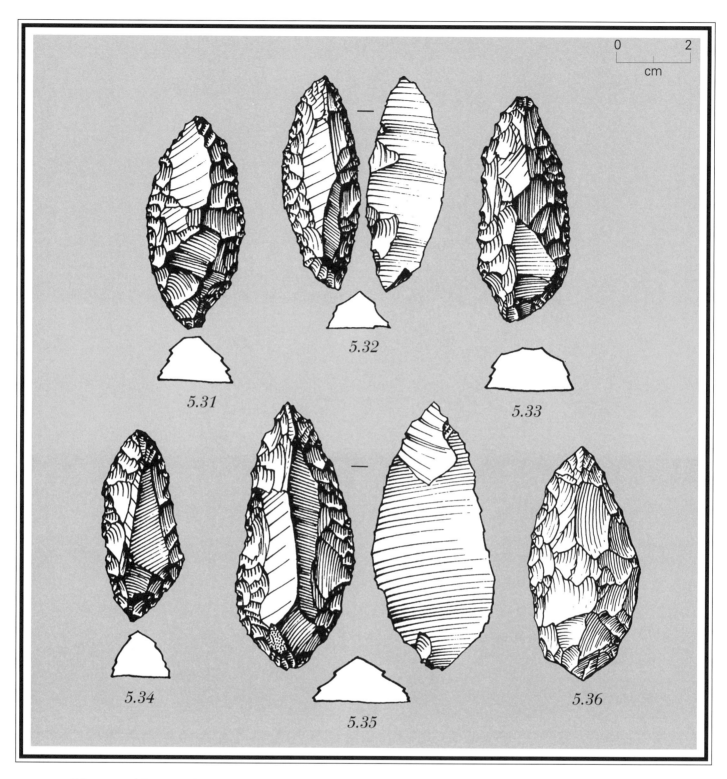

Limaces (Type 8; Figures 5.31–5.42). The term *limace* was first used in a typological sense by Martin (1923:112) to describe double pointed objects from the site of La Quina. According to most authors, limaces are considered either as points or convergent scrapers, though Bordes grouped them with the former in terms of his numerical order of the types (see Appendix I).

Typical limaces (Figures 5.31–5.36) are retouched so as to be pointed at both ends (with the platform removed through lateral retouching) and symmetrical. However, pieces can still be considered limaces even when the platform is not completely removed or when the pieces retain an appreciable amount of cortex, as long as the proximal edges converge significantly. In contrast to the more tightly defined Mousterian points, the retouched ends of limaces may be somewhat rounded (Figures 5.37–5.42). However, the extremity cannot be so rounded as to require its classification as an end-scraper (Figure 5.42 is at the limit). Usually limaces are quite thick and generally exhibit scaled and stepped (i.e., Quina) retouch, though this is not essential for an assignment to this category.

Chapter

5

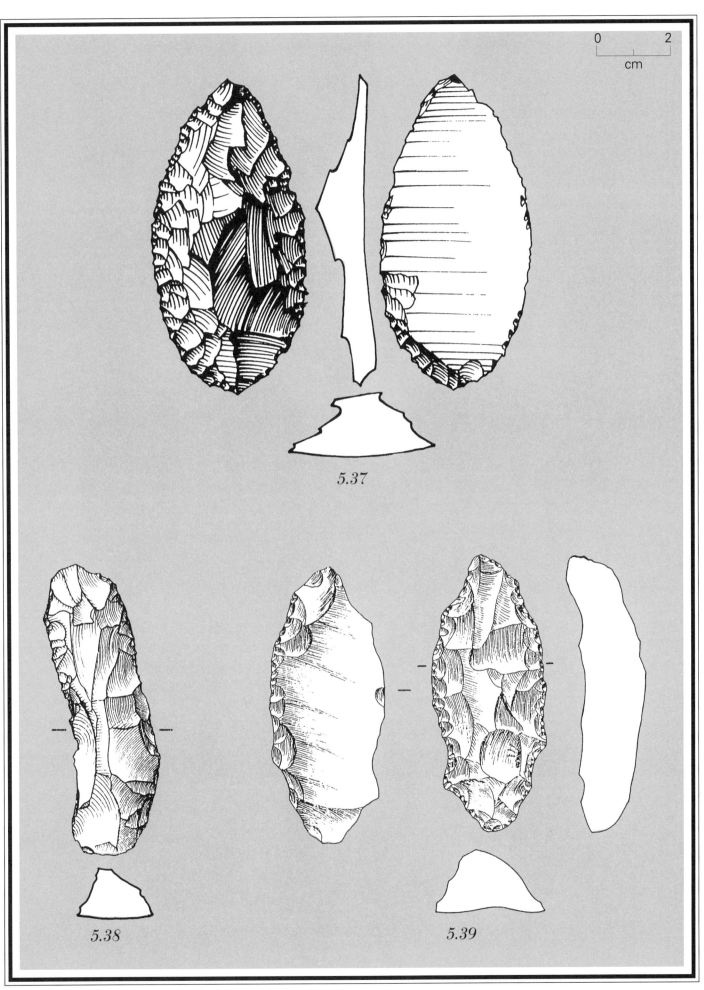

5.37

5.38

5.39

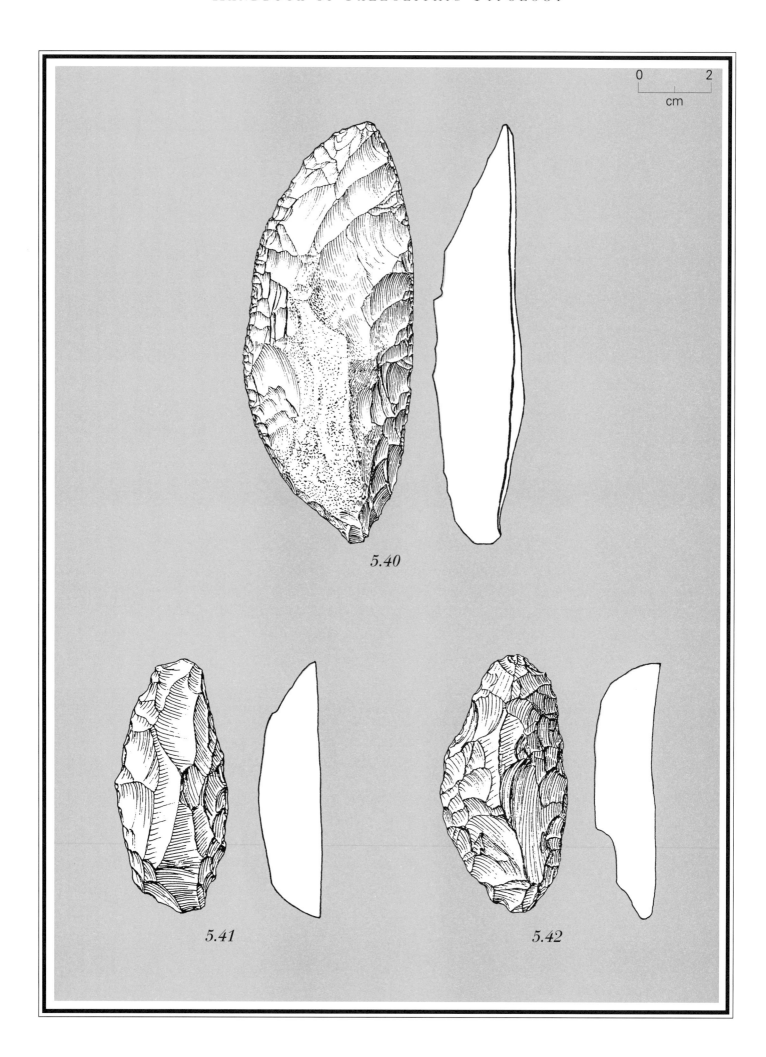

5.40

5.41

5.42

CHAPTER SIX

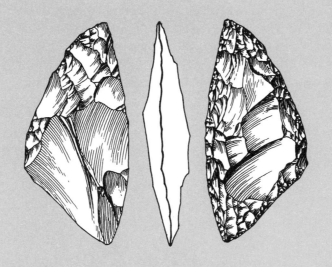

SCRAPERS

SCRAPERS, OR *RACLOIRS*, ARE AMONG THE oldest recognizable tool forms, extending back into the Oldowan industries of more than two million years ago. By the time of the Acheulian of Europe, which begins at least 750,000 years ago, scrapers are classifiable into many different types and, in a sense, reach their apogee, both in terms of diversity and frequency, in the Charentian Mousterian (Quina and Ferrassie groups) of France and similar industries elsewhere in Europe, the Near East, and Africa. In fact, scrapers of various types are the most frequently occurring tool in the European Middle Paleolithic and, along with denticulates and notches, represent one of the most important aspects of variability among those assemblages (Dibble 1988). There are also more subdivisions among the scrapers than exist for any other typological group in Bordes' typology.

The term *racloir* was used for the first time by Boucher de Perthes (1847), and since then many definitions and typologies have been suggested. In fact, Brézillon (1968) has counted about sixty different types of scrapers defined by various authors. Most of these classifications take into account several criteria: for some the form of the blank is most significant (Pittard and Montandon 1914; Martin 1923; Laplace-Jauretche 1964); others emphasize primarily the type and location of the retouch (Gruet 1959; Bordes 1961). Some, especially the earliest prehistorians, insist that the interior surface of scrapers cannot be retouched, though for others this is not important. There are typological lumpers as well, such as Leroi-Gourhan (1964) and Dibble (1987), who emphasize the morphological or technological unity of these kinds of tools.

The general definition of scrapers presented by Bordes (1961:25) is as follows: "an object made on a flake or a blade, Levallois or not, with continuous retouch that is flat or abrupt, scaled or not, on one or more margins, in order to produce a more or less cutting edge which is straight, convex, or concave, with no deliberate notching or denticulation." With such a broad definition it is not surprising that the morphology and other characteristics of these types can be quite variable. But it does have the advantage of separating the type definition from the technology that produced the blank. The only feature in common is that the retouch is continuous, regular, and smooth (i.e., not denticulated) along at least one edge.

Bordes' definition also emphasizes the functional aspect of these tools. He felt that scraper retouch was not meant to sharpen the edge of the tool, but rather to regularize it and even partially to blunt it in order to give it more resistance for scraping (which he believed was performed perpendicularly to the flat plane of the tool). These notions are supported by some microwear research (Beyries 1988; Anderson-Gerfaud 1990) for at least some scraper types. However, it is by no means certain that all scrapers were actually used for that function, i.e., scraping, as they could easily have been used for cutting or for other tasks as well. Probably, like most stone tools in the Lower and Middle Paleolithic, they were used for a variety of tasks. For this reason, the use of the term "scraper" is probably not fully justified.

In Bordes' typology, the major classes of scrapers are defined on the basis of the number of, location of, and relation between, the retouched edges. Within most of the major classes, minor subdivisions are made at the level of the individual types for differences in edge shape, i.e., straight, convex, or concave, as seen in plan view. There are no metric criteria for determination of edge shape, however. Bordes simply placed a straight edge (such as a pencil) against the center of the retouched edge: if one point of the tool's edge touches the pencil, then the edge is convex; if two points touch the pencil, the edge is concave; and if the edge touches along a line, it is considered a straight retouched edge. If the edge is sinuous or presents any other combination of edge shapes, such as straight and convex, then it is classified according to the longest and/or most pronounced portion.

It is not known whether these shape distinctions are informative in behavioral or other terms. It appears that variability in edge shape is continuously distributed, with the average edge shape being moderately convex, a few pieces either strongly convex or straight, and even fewer pieces being concave (Barton 1990). This distribution suggests that the partitions of convex, straight, and concave may be arbitrary. It should also be noted that concave scrapers grade into notches (see Chapter 8).

In fact, even beyond the distinctions based on edge shape, it has been suggested that most of the major scraper types defined by Bordes are more or less arbitrary partitions along a continuum of reduction of blanks through resharpening (Dibble 1984a, 1987), with two, and probably more, reduction sequences related to blank form (Dibble 1991; Kuhn 1992). While this hypothesis does not affect the typology of these forms, it does have implications for the interpretation of these various types.

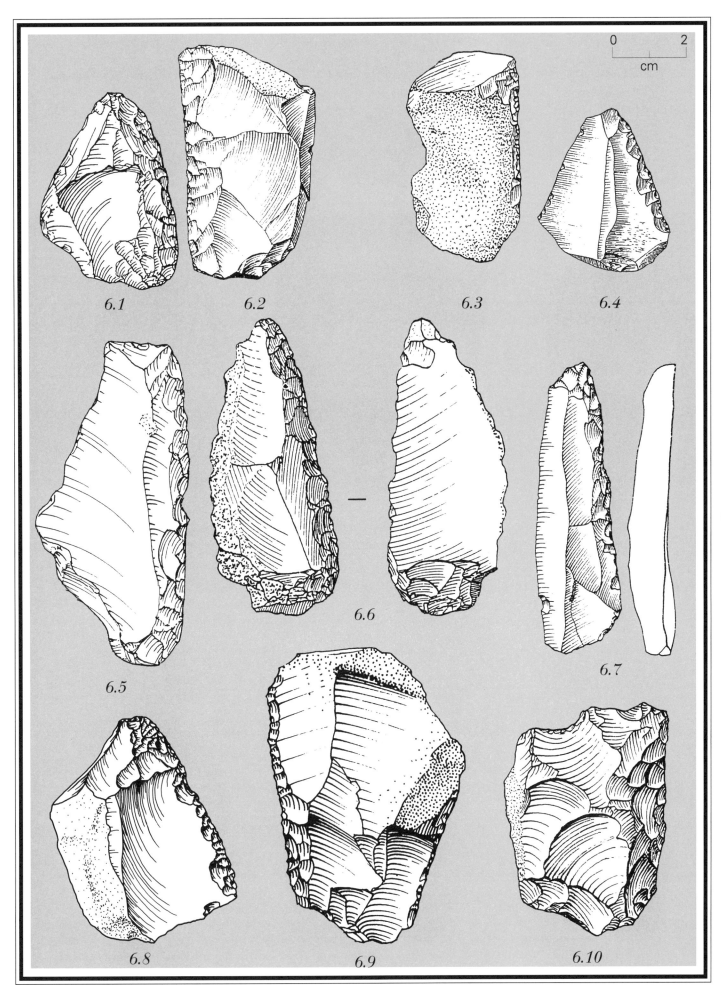

0 ‹——› 2
cm

6.1   6.2   6.3   6.4

6.5   6.6   6.7

6.8   6.9   6.10

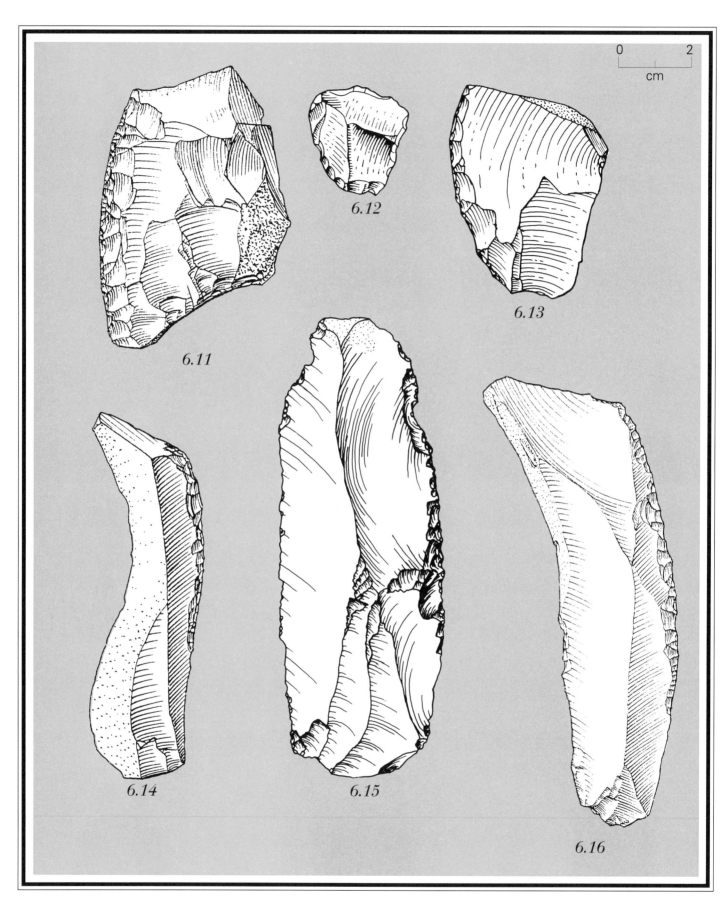

0   2
cm

6.11

6.12

6.13

6.14

6.15

6.16

Single scrapers (Types 9–11) and **single transverse scrapers** (Types 22–24). Single scrapers have only one retouched edge, with a retouch that is on the exterior and not too abrupt. If it is a lateral edge that is retouched, then the tool is considered a sidescraper. Three separate types of single sidescrapers are distinguished on the basis of the shape of the edge: **straight** (type 9; Figures 6.1–6.10), **convex** (type 10; Figures 6.11–6.28), and **concave** (type 11; Figures 6.29 and 6.30). If the distal edge is

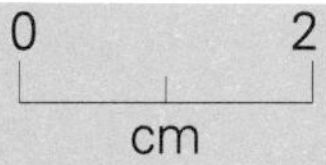

0   2
cm

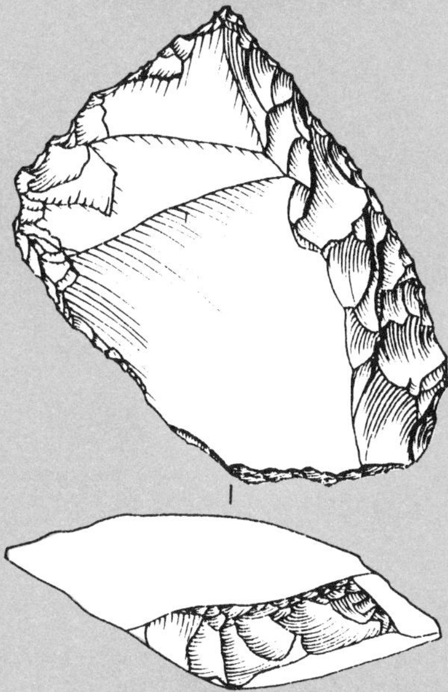

6.17

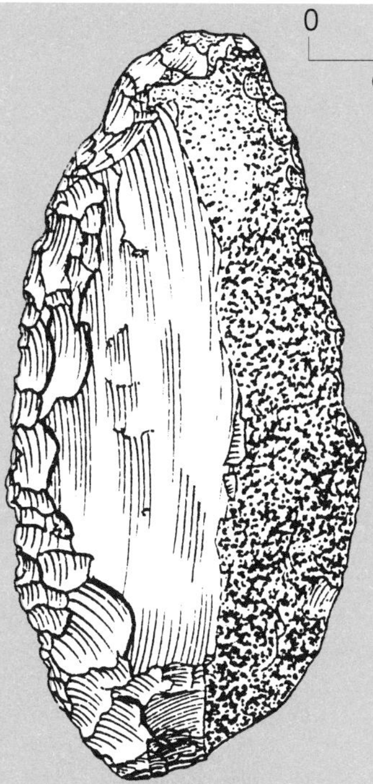

6.19

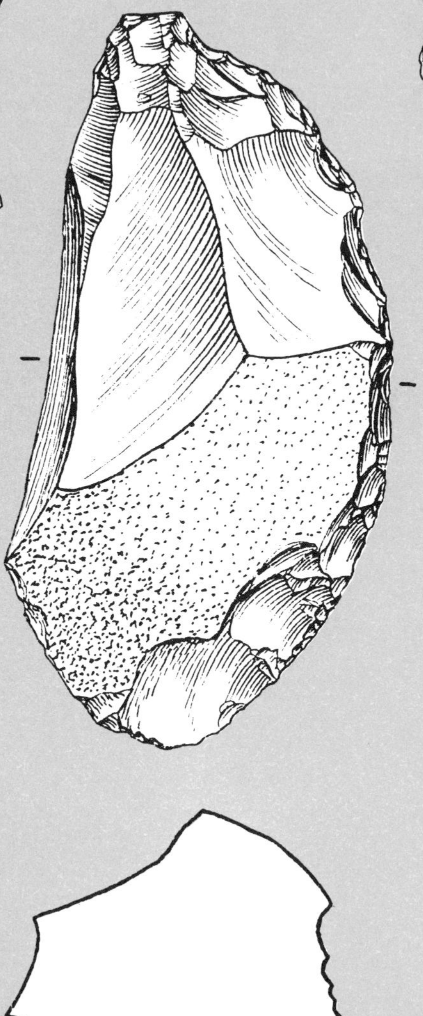

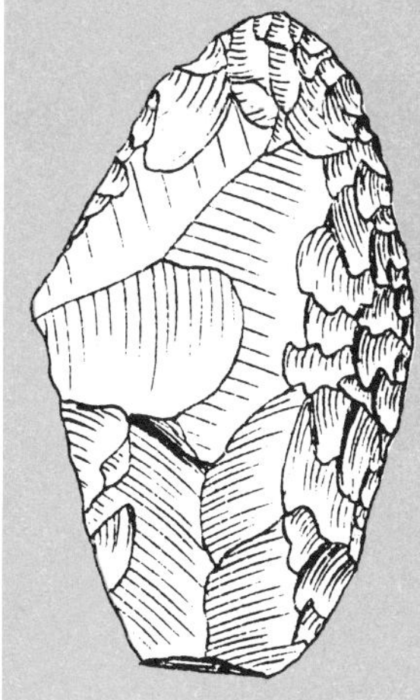

6.20

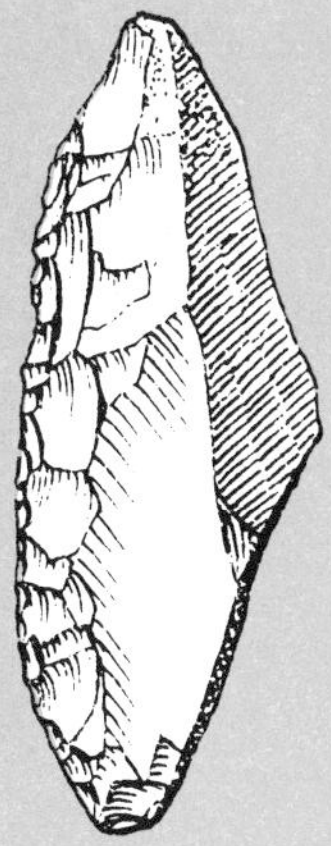

6.21

6.18

6.22

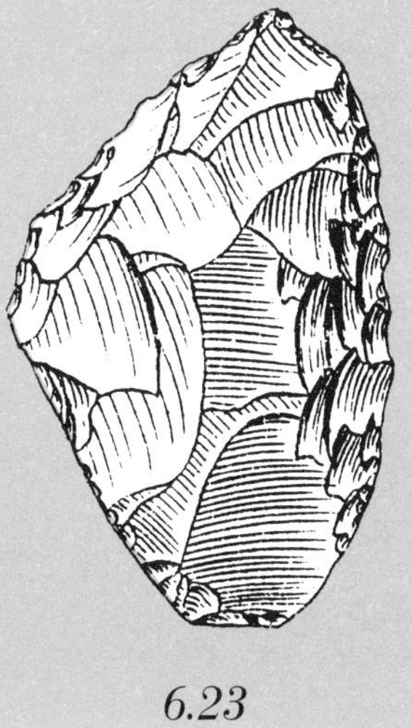

6.23

Chapter

6

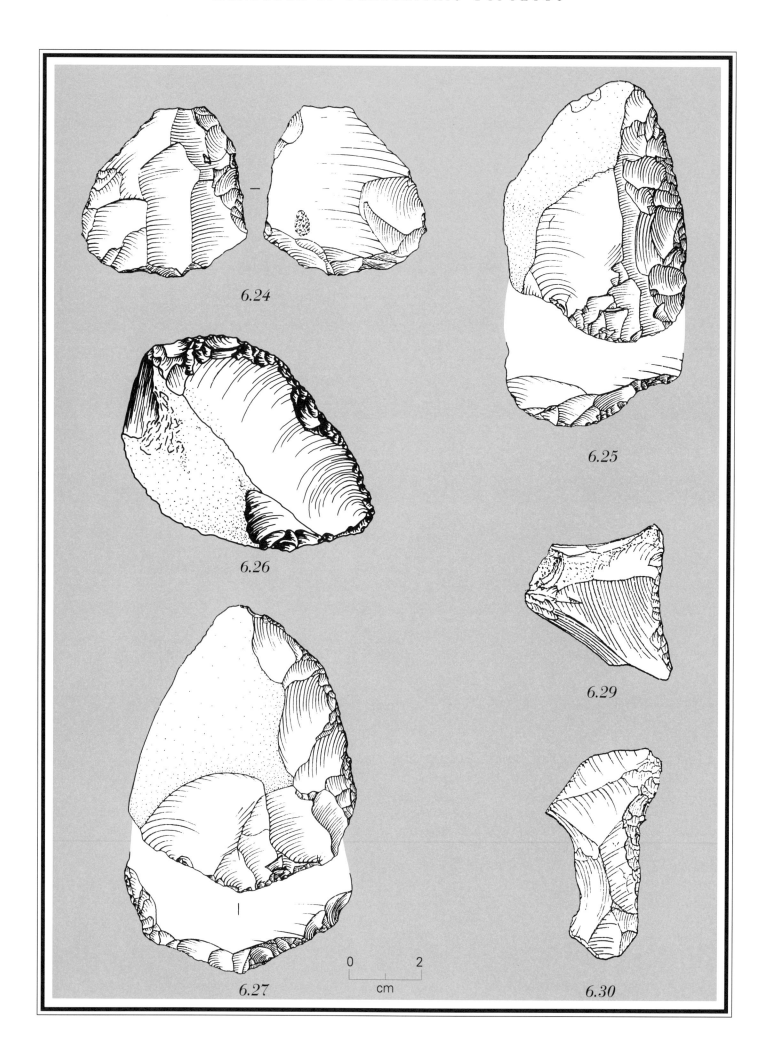

6.24

6.25

6.26

6.29

6.27

6.30

0   2
cm

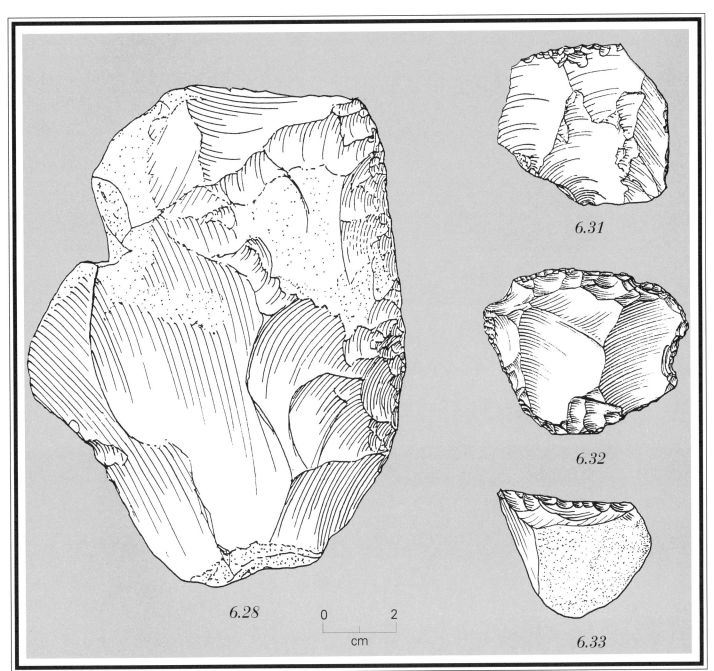

6.31

6.32

6.28

0   2

cm

6.33

retouched, i.e., the edge opposite the platform, then it is a transverse scraper, again with three types defined on the basis of edge shape: **straight** (type 22; Figure 6.31); **convex** (type 23; Figures 6.32, 6.34–6.42); **concave** (type 24; Figure 6.33). Metrically, the distinction between sidescrapers and transverse scrapers is defined in terms of the angle formed by the axis of the retouched edge relative to the axis of the flake. For sidescrapers, these two axes are more or less parallel (where parallel would represent an angle of 0 degrees), while for transverse scrapers this angle can be nearly 90 degrees. The cutoff between the two classes in Bordes' typology is 45 degrees. Although some typologists speak of "oblique scrapers" regarding pieces for which this angle is about 45 degrees (Figure 6.26), there is, in fact, no explicitly defined category for them in

Bordes' typology. Again, there appears to be a continuous distribution of this angle with no evidence of any particular modes that would indicate discrete preferences. Thus, the cutoff between sidescrapers and transverse scrapers may also be arbitrary.

Transverse scrapers can exhibit some interior thinning of the platform which removes part of the bulb of percussion without the modification affecting the classification (Figures 6.34 and 6.35), although sidescrapers with such thinning are classified as a scraper with thinned back (type 27; see below). Thus, the location of the exterior retouch on the distal end overrides the interior retouch. However, if such interior retouch continues all the way to the distal edge, then the piece would be considered a bifacial scraper (type 28; see below).

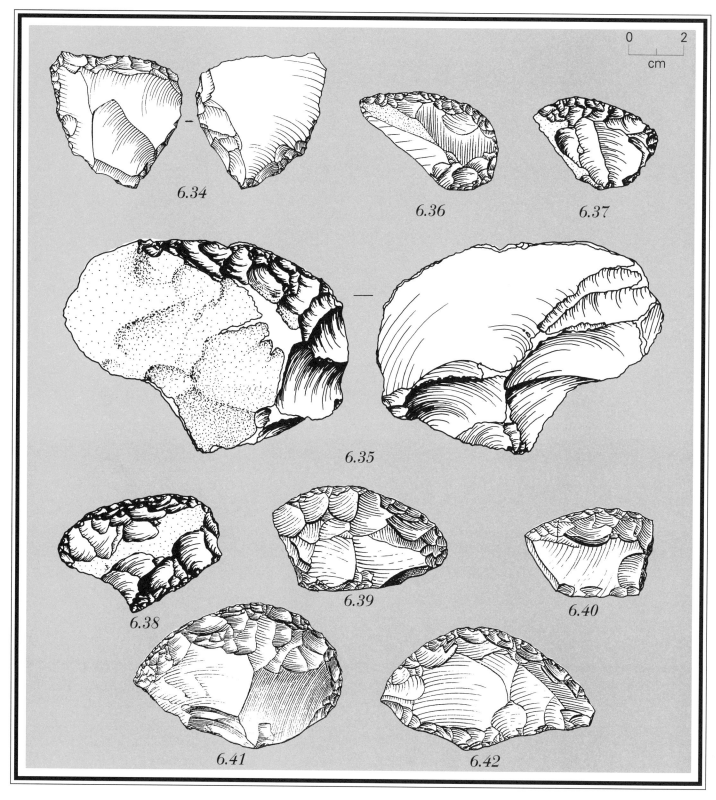

0 2
cm

6.34

6.36

6.37

6.35

6.38

6.39

6.40

6.41

6.42

There is the possibility for some confusion between transverse scrapers and endscrapers (types 30 and 31—see Chapter 7), though the principal distinction between the two classes was made well before the turn of the century by de Ferry (1870; cf. Martin 1923). In general, scrapers are retouched on one or more of the longer edges of a flake or blade. Most often this would be the lateral edge, but for transverse scrapers it is often the case that the distal retouched edge is one of the longest edges on the piece. Endscrapers, on the other hand, have a narrow retouched edge *always* on the distal end of a narrow blank, usually a blade. Thus, the distinction here is made primarily on the overall form of the blank. Moreover, while transverse scraper edges are usually slightly convex, they can also be straight or concave; on the other hand, the retouched ends of endscrapers are almost always strongly convex or roughly semi-circular.

6.43

6.44

6.45

6.46

6.47

6.49

6.48

6.50

0   2

cm

Double scrapers (Types 12–17; Figures 6.43–6.61). Double scrapers were first defined by Rutot (1909) as scrapers having two non-adjacent retouched edges. Bordes differentiated six types on the basis of the shapes of the two edges (Table 6.1).

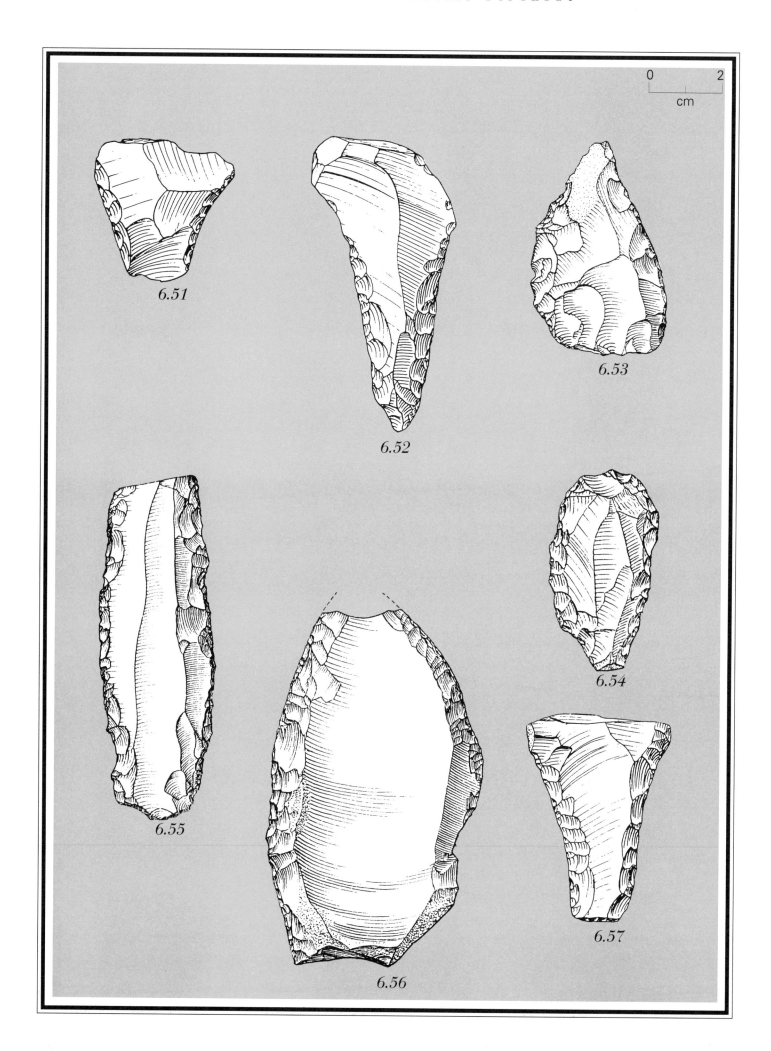

0   2
cm

6.51

6.52

6.53

6.54

6.55

6.56

6.57

First edge	Second edge	Type #	Figure # in present text
Straight	Straight	12	6.43, 6.44
Straight	Convex	13	6.45–6.50
Straight	Concave	14	6.51, 6.52
Convex	Convex	15	6.53–6.56
Concave	Concave	16	6.57
Convex	Concave	17	6.58–6.61

Table 6.1. The six double scraper types of Bordes (1961), differentiated on the basis of their edge morphology.

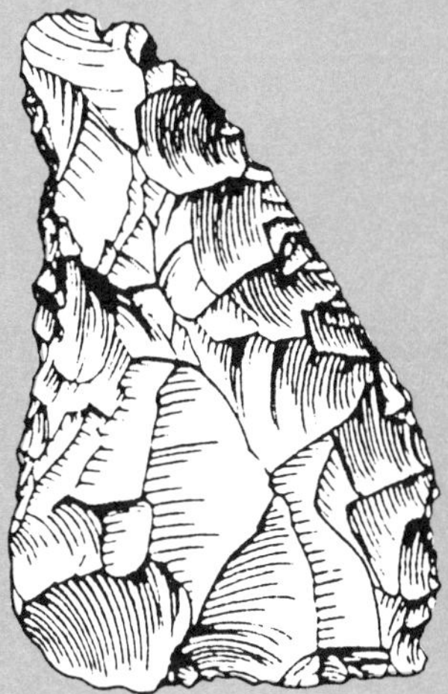

6.59

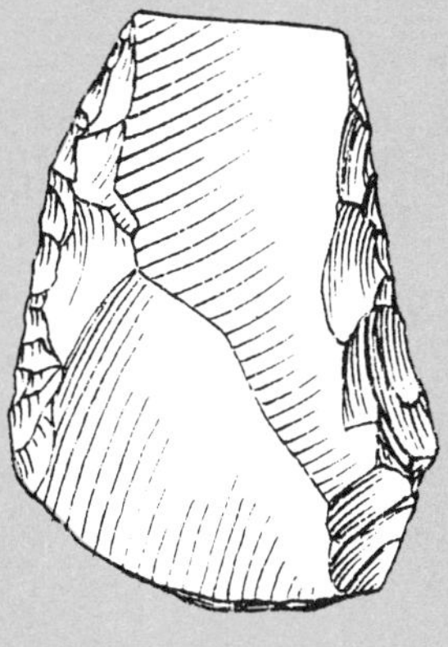

6.58

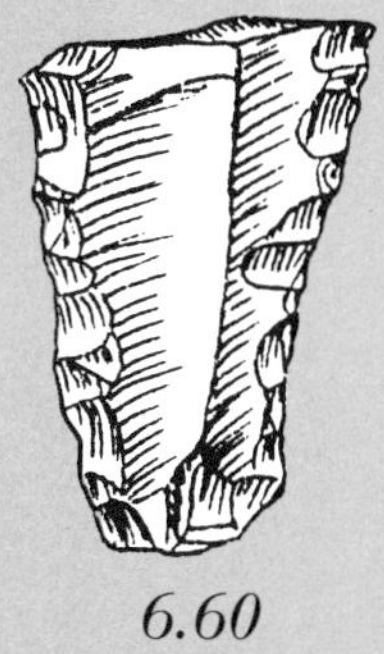

6.60

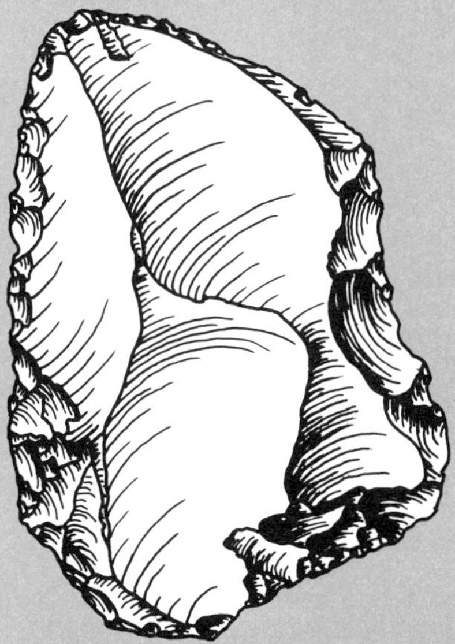

6.61

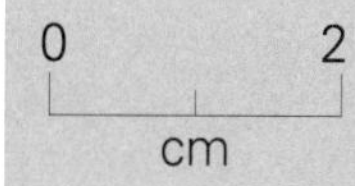

0   2
cm

Chapter

6

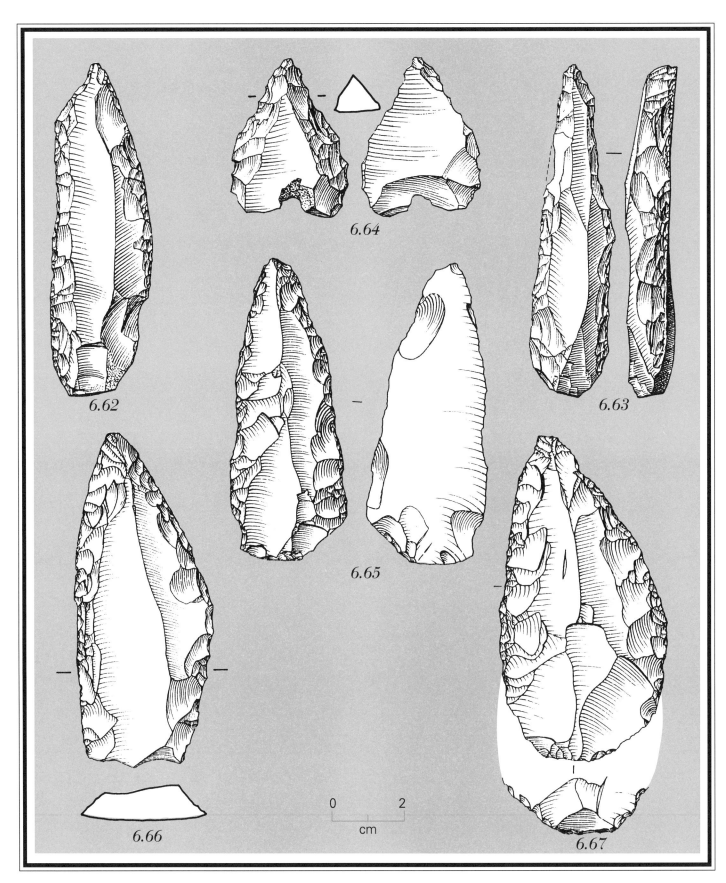

6.64

6.62

6.63

6.65

6.66

6.67

0   2
cm

Convergent scrapers (Types 18–20). Convergent scrapers are defined by Bordes (1961:27) as being double scrapers of which the two retouched edges converge and eventually meet at one end, usually the distal extremity of the piece. The intersection of the two edges should not be too point-ed (see discussion of Mousterian points versus convergent scrapers in Chapter 5), nor should it be too rounded. In the latter case it would be classified as an endscraper, regardless of the presence of retouch along the lateral edges (see Chapter 7).

In theory, the same six edge-shape combina-

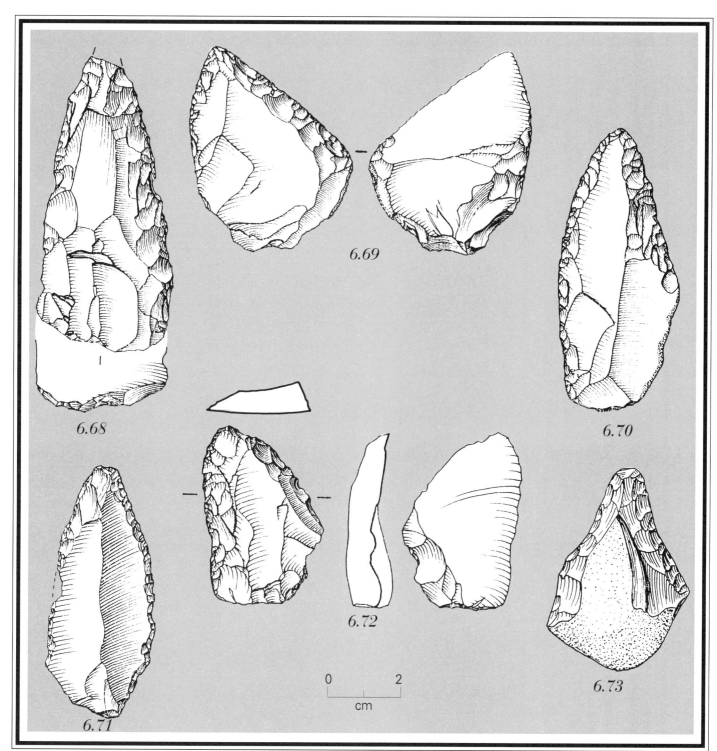

6.69

6.68

6.70

6.72

6.71

6.73

tions distinguished for the double scrapers are also possible for convergent scrapers, though Bordes, following a number of his predecessors, retained only the three distinctions of **straight** (type 18; Figure 6.64), **convex** (type 19; Figures 6.65–6.72), and **concave** (type 20; Figure 6.73). Convex convergent scrapers are the most commonly found. Unfortunately, there is virtually no agreement on the classification of a convergent scraper that has two differently shaped edges, i.e., one convex and the other concave (Figures 6.62 and 6.63). However, if the concavity is sufficiently pronounced then the

piece may be classifiable as a déjeté scraper (see below).

It can be difficult to classify double-edged tools whose distal extremities have been broken off postdepositionally, since often one cannot be certain whether the two edges actually met or not. The general rule of thumb is to follow the general convergence of the two edges, calling the piece a convergent scraper if it seems probable that the two edges would have met (Figure 6.68); otherwise, it should be classified as a double scraper.

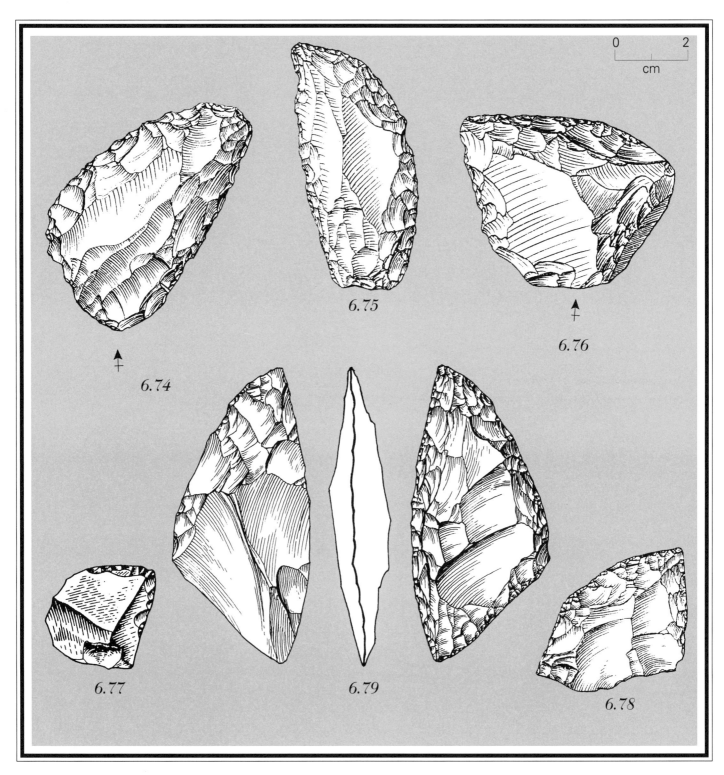

0   2
cm

6.75

6.76

6.74

6.77   6.79   6.78

Déjeté scrapers (Type 21; Figures 6.74–6.79). *Déjeté* (or "skewed") scrapers are convergent scrapers which have an axis of the piece (defined as the bisection of the angle formed by the two retouched edges) that forms an angle greater than 45 degrees relative to the axis of flaking (Figures 6.74–6.78). As pointed out by Dibble (1988), there are two distinct products that are both classified as déjeté scrapers: one where a transverse scraper edge intersects a lateral retouched edge (for example, Figure 6.76); and the other where only the distal end of a convergent scraper is skewed, as with one convex

and one concave edge, or where the long axis of the original flake blank is skewed relative to the axis of flaking (see Figure 6.75). For all déjeté scrapers, the intersection of the two edges can be quite rounded without affecting the classification (Figure 6.74).

Déjeté scrapers can be single (with two edges that meet asymmetrically), double (with three retouched edges), or even triple (Figure 6.79). All of these various forms are classified as type 21. Moreover, there are no distinctions made on the basis of edge shape.

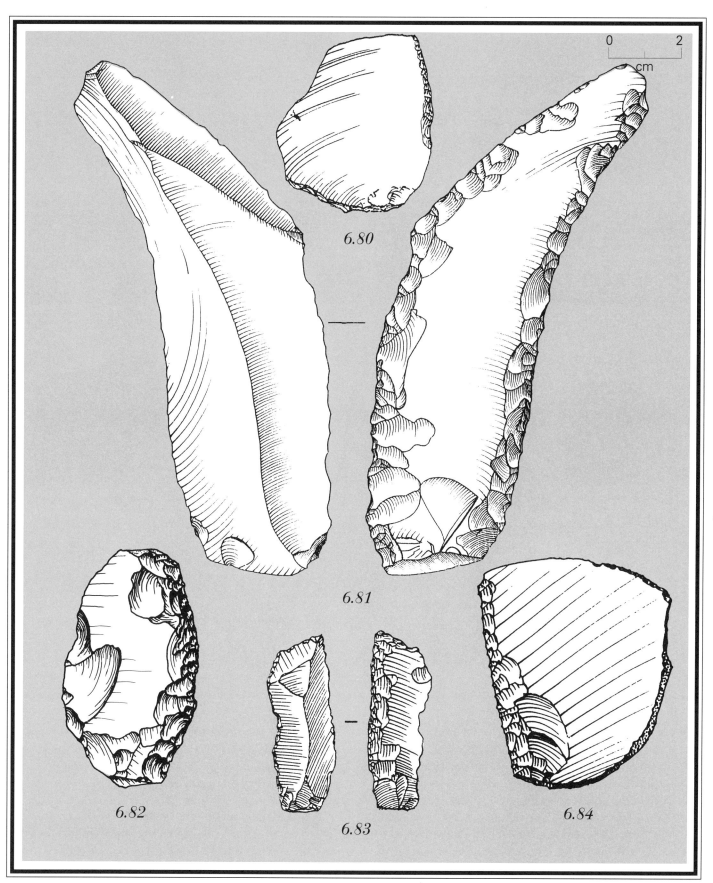

6.80

6.81

6.82

6.83

6.84

Scrapers on interior surface (Type 25; Figures 6.80–6.84). These are rare forms that exhibit a scraper retouch on the interior surface of a flake margin. There are no distinctions made on the basis of edge shape, and they can be single, double, or convergent forms. Note, however, that if one edge is retouched on the interior surface and another edge is retouched on the exterior, then the tool is classified as an alternate scraper (type 29; see below).

Chapter

6

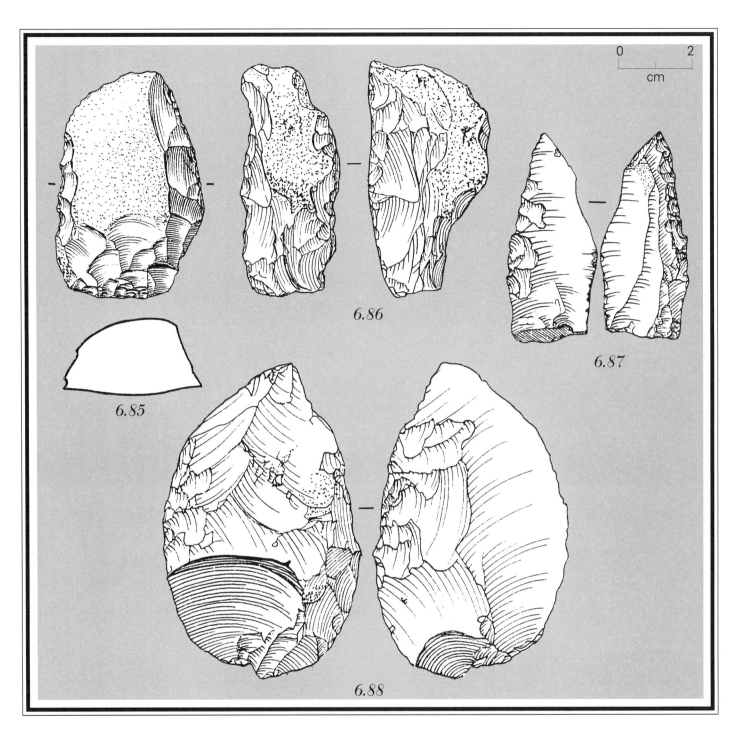

0 2
cm

6.86

6.87

6.85

6.88

Abrupt scrapers (Type 26; Figures 6.85 and 6.86). According to Bordes (1961:29), these are pieces with scraper retouch that is abrupt or semi-abrupt. It is important to distinguish a backed knife (types 36 and 37—see Chapter 7), also with abrupt retouch, from an abrupt scraper. The difference is that a backed knife must have a sharp and unretouched cutting edge opposite the abrupt edge. If the edge opposite the abruptly retouched edge is cortical, retouched, or otherwise not suitable for cutting, the piece should be classified as a scraper. Thus, the distinction between a backed knife and an abrupt scraper is not based on different kinds of retouch (they are the same), but rather on the morphology or character of the opposite, often unretouched edge.

Also, an abrupt scraper should not be confused with a truncation (type 40—see Chapter 7), which has a restricted portion of abrupt retouch on the distal (or sometimes proximal) extremity. In this case, it is the location of the retouch that takes precedence.

Scrapers with thinned back (Type 27; Figures 6.87–6.94). These scrapers present a thinning of the edge opposite the scraper edge, often through the removal of relatively large, flat retouch flakes. Usually the thinning is on the interior surface only, though it can be bifacial; it is generally very irregular. Recall, however, that transverse scrapers with thinning on the opposite (platform) end are nonetheless classified as transverse scrapers (e.g., Figure 6.35).

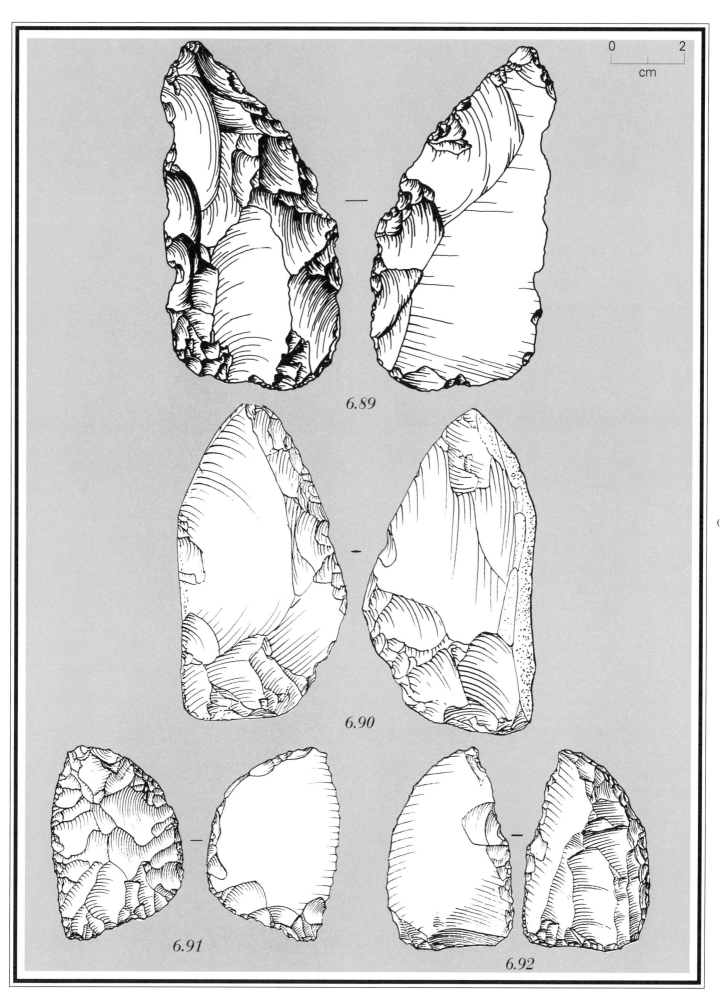

0   2
cm

6.89

6.90

6.91

6.92

Chapter
6

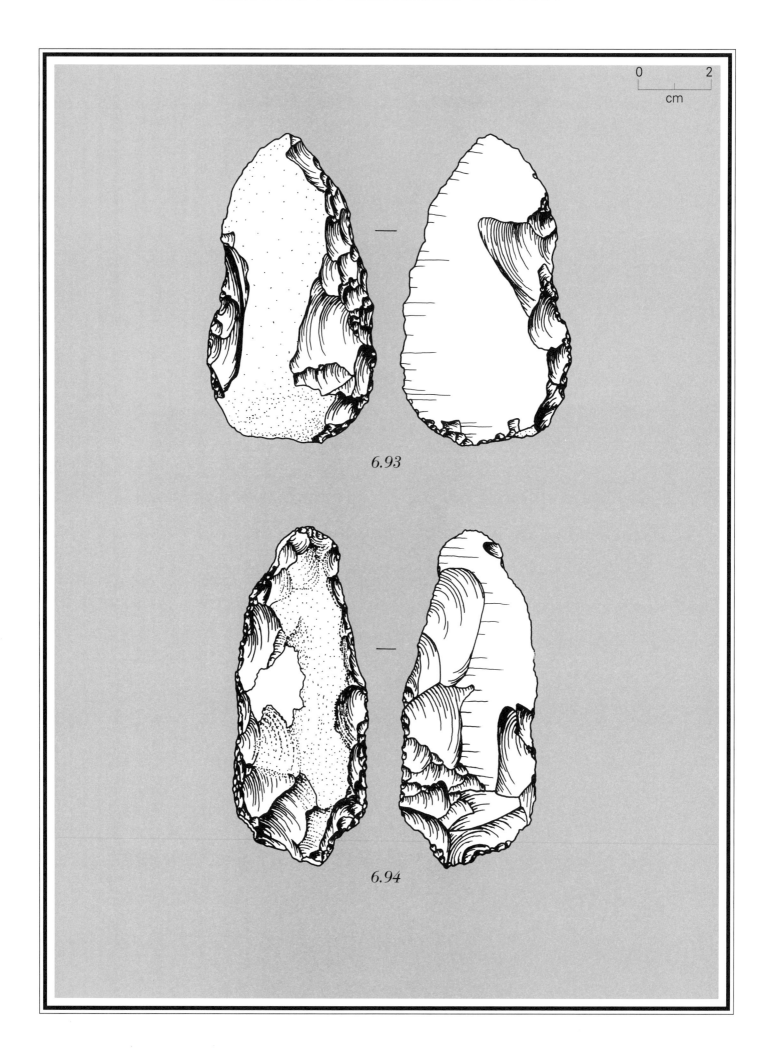

0   2
cm

6.93

6.94

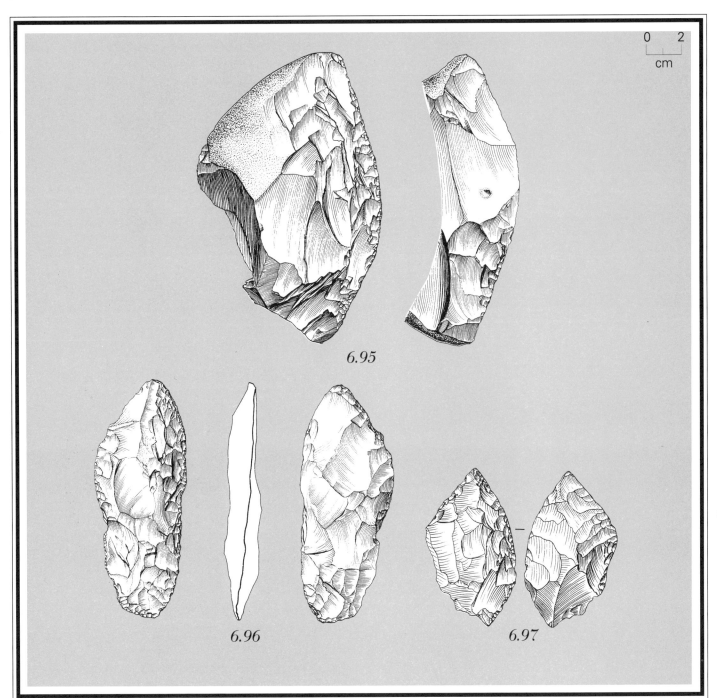

6.95

6.96

6.97

Scrapers with bifacial retouch (Type 28; Figures 6.95–6.97). These are scrapers characterized by a more or less continuous bifacial retouch along one edge. The shape and location of the retouched edge is unimportant. Such objects may be completely bifacially worked, as in Figures 6.96 and 6.97, and in these cases it is the character of the scraper retouch along the edge that results in its classification as a scraper with bifacial retouch and not as a biface or bifacial foliate: bifacial scrapers will have one or more edges that are worked with a continuous, less invasive retouch on one surface than would be typical of bifaces, and this edge must be quite flat (i.e., not sinuous) when viewed from the side. Another factor to consider is the overall shape, which can be quite irregular for bifacial scrapers (e.g., Figure 6.95). Nonetheless, scrapers with bifacial retouch, especially when they are found in a broken condition, can easily be confused with certain handaxes, particularly cordiform types (see Chapter 11).

A variety of this type, often quite large and with a generally asymmetrical cross-section, has been associated with some Quina assemblages. They are called **tranchoirs** (Figure 6.95), though it is important to note that this term has also been applied to many different kinds of objects (de Heinzelin 1962:44; Vaufrey 1955). *Tranchoirs* are not given a separate type in Bordes' typology, however, and so should be classified as type 28.

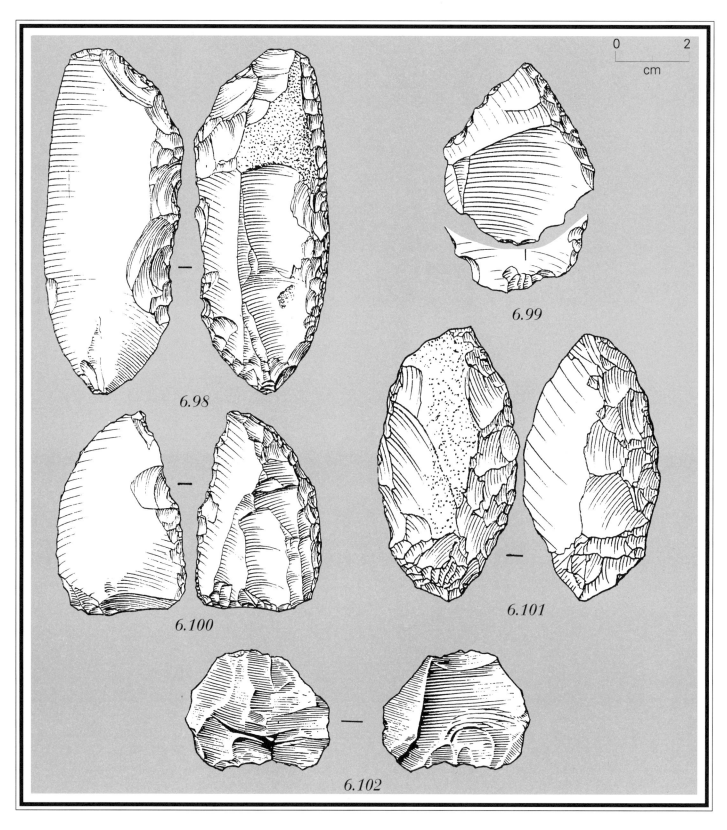

0   2
cm

6.99

6.98

6.100

6.101

6.102

Alternate scrapers (Type 29: Figures 6.98–6.101). As defined by Bordes, these are double scrapers that have one edge retouched on the exterior surface and the other, *opposite edge*, retouched on the interior surface. There is some possibility of confusion between these types and scrapers with thinned backs (type 27; see above), though the interior "thinning" retouch on the latter is much more irregular and usually more invasive.

Alternate retouch, which occurs on two opposite edges, should not be confused with alternating retouch, which alternates between the interior and exterior surfaces *along the same edge*. Pieces with alternating retouch should be classified as one of types 46–49 (see Chapter 9). Note that the retouch on the left margin of Figure 6.99 is only barely passable as being deliberate, in that it is somewhat alternating and irregular.

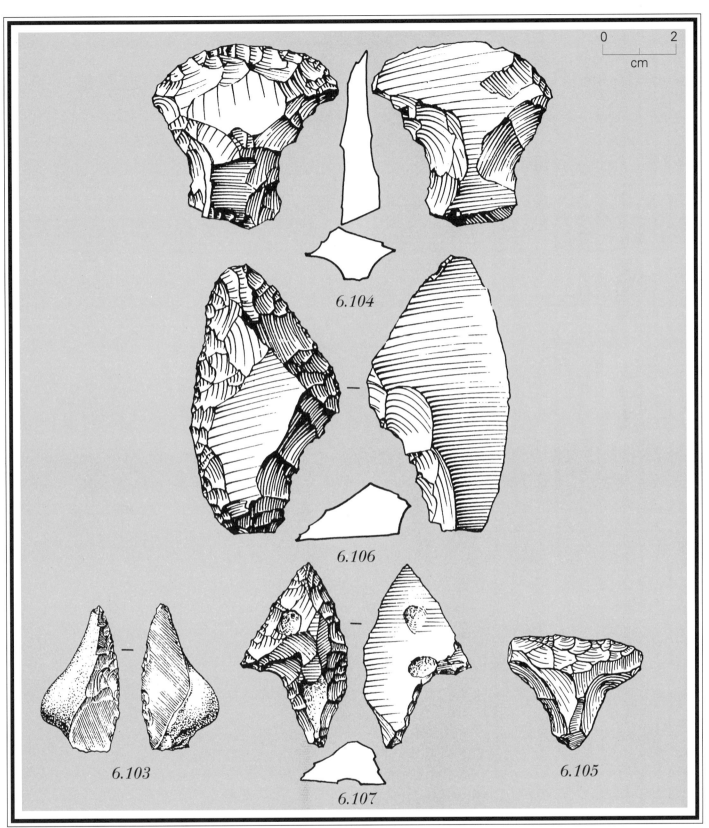

6.104

6.106

6.103

6.107

6.105

Two other scraper types deserve mention, although neither is distinguished in Bordes' typology. The first is the **Tata scraper** (Figure 6.102), named by de Heinzelin (1962:26) after a Middle Paleolithic site in Hungary. He defines it as a "bifacial scraper with flat retouch." Vertés (1964) coined the term **racloirs couteaux** for pieces that exhibit a natural, cortical back opposite a scraper edge (Figure 6.103).

This seems to be a fairly common occurrence for single-edged scrapers and such pieces are usually classified as normal single scrapers. De Lumley (1971) also distinguishes **stemmed scrapers** (Figures 6.104–6.107), although Bordes originally grouped all non-pointed stemmed pieces together in a single type (type 58—see Chapter 9).

Chapter

6

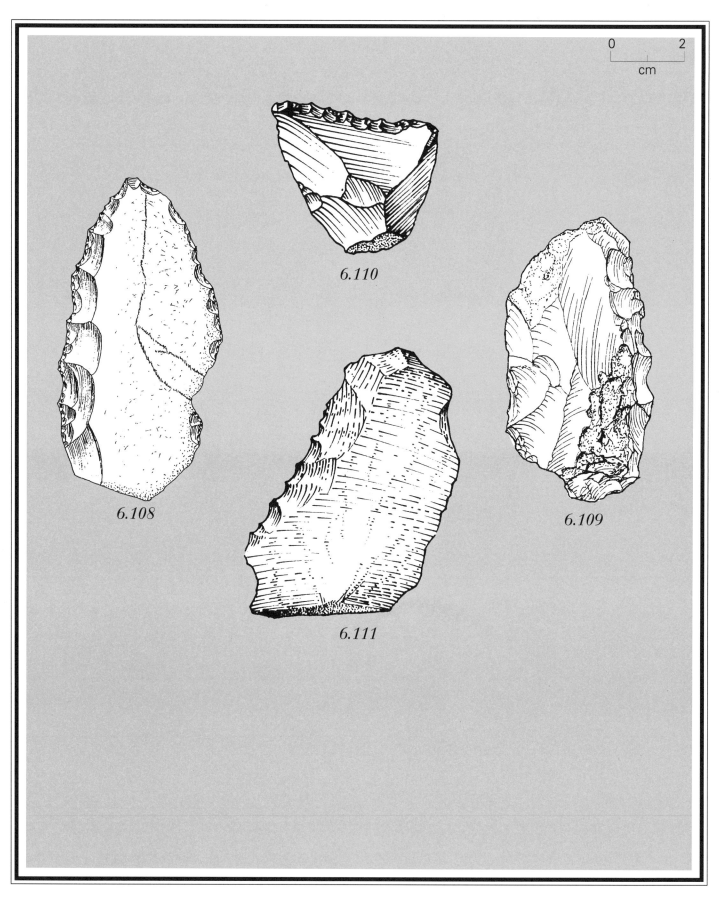

0   2
cm

6.110

6.108

6.109

6.111

A major problem with some scrapers is that they grade into, or are associated with, other types. For example, scraper retouch can be fairly irregular, thus producing a denticulate-like edge. Some examples of such **racloirs-denticulés** (denticulated scrapers) are illustrated in Figures 6.108–6.111. In these cases it is the length and continuous nature of the retouched edges that suggest that they should be typed as scrapers rather than denticulates, but admittedly this can be a subjective call.

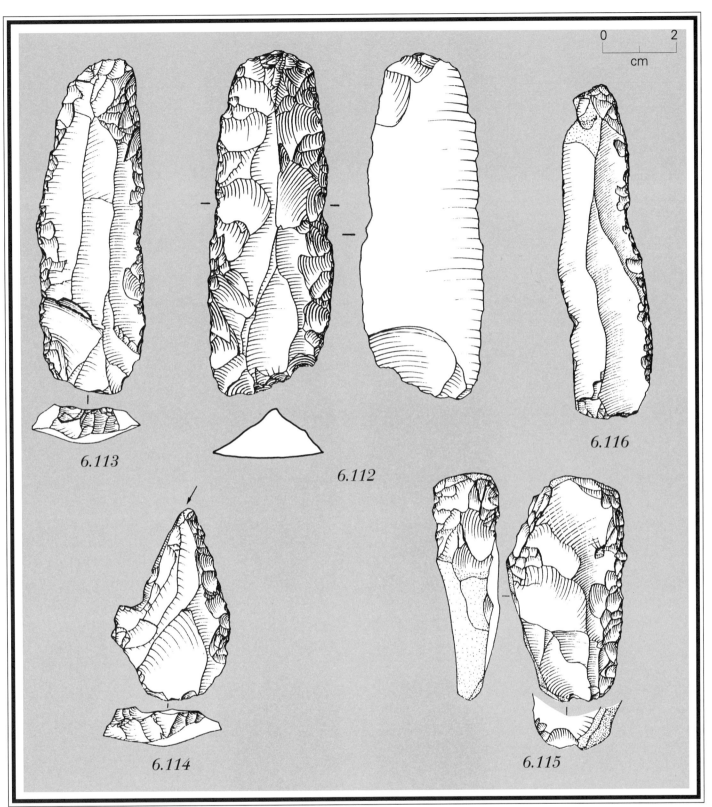

6.113

6.112

6.116

6.114

6.115

Also illustrated here are some combination tools, such as sidescrapers associated with endscrapers (Figures 6.112 and 6.113) and a scraper/burin combination (Figure 6.114). Following Bordes (see Appendix I), such pieces should be typed according to the edge that is most characteristic or well-made, or as the least frequently occurring type in the assemblage. In these cases, they should probably be typed as endscrapers and a burin, respectively. A

scraper with a "backed" edge (Figure 6.115) should be considered an abrupt scraper.

Figure 6.116 illustrates an example of a single scraper with a sinuous edge, which for obvious reasons is difficult to classify as either a convex or concave scraper. Again, the best course is to place it in the least frequently occurring category, probably as a concave scraper.

Chapter

6

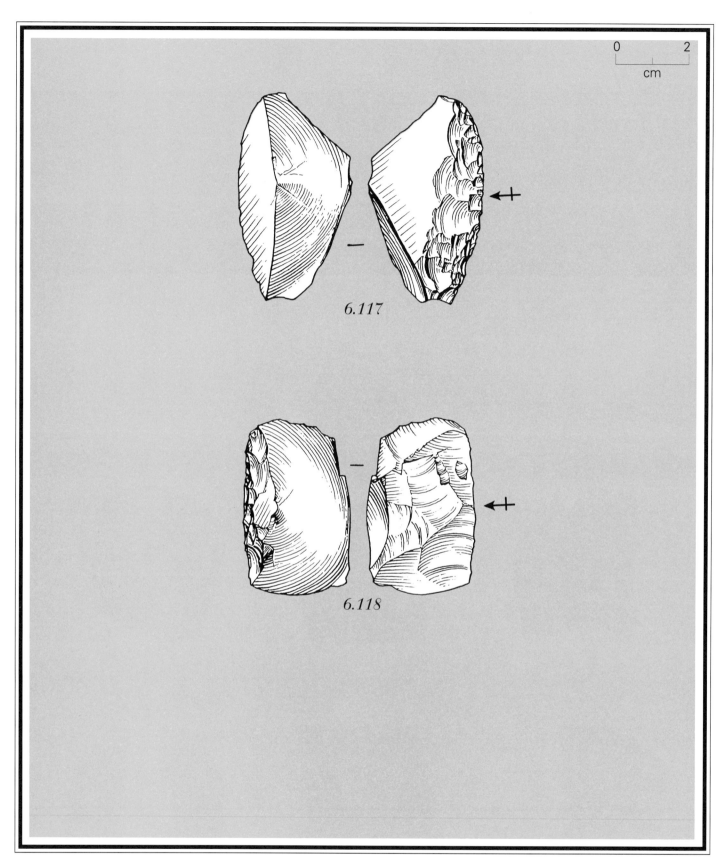

0
2
cm

6.117

6.118

Pieces also exist that exhibit scraper retouch on the exterior surface of the platform (Figure 6.117), or on the platform surface itself (Figure 6.118). Such pieces generally go by the name of **racloirs sur talon,** or "scrapers on the platform," though they have never been explicitly defined. These can be confusing because it is usually the case that any retouch that could have been applied *before* the blank was removed from the core is not used as a criterion for typing the piece, in other words, platform preparation is not typologically relevant. Thus, the problem with possible *racloirs sur talon* is that it must be demonstrated that the platform retouch is not platform preparation.

CHAPTER SEVEN

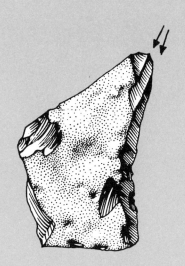

UPPER PALEOLITHIC TYPES

CERTAIN TOOL FORMS THAT ARE CHARacteristic of later Upper Paleolithic industries actually begin to appear within the Acheulian and Mousterian and so are included in Bordes' typology. These types are the endscrapers, burins, perçoirs, backed knives, raclettes, and truncations.

Except for the raclettes and truncations, all of these forms are divided into typical and atypical types, which is probably the biggest source of confusion in learning Bordes' typology. The confusion is not surprising since these distinctions are based on very subjective evaluations: if the piece is "well-made" and closely resembles its Upper Paleolithic counterpart, then it is "typical"; if not, then it should be classified as "atypical." Obviously there is a great deal of variation among typologists in terms of how strictly these comparisons should be made. There is even some feeling that many of the burins, perçoirs, and raclettes of the Lower and Middle Paleolithic are more accidental than deliberate, which renders considerations of their quality somewhat moot.

Endscrapers (Types 30 [Typical] and 31 [Atypical]; Figures 7.1–7.7). According to Bordes (1961:31), an endscraper is a "blade or flake presenting on one of its ends (or both, in the case of a double tool), a continuous, non-abrupt retouch resulting in an edge that is more or less rounded, and rarely straight." In addition, the overall form of the piece should be relatively long and narrow, or at least the retouched end itself should be narrow. Thus, in this case the morphology of the blank itself is also considered, and perhaps is of primary concern in differentiating endscrapers from transverse scrapers. The other significant defining characteristic is the shape and character of the retouched end. If a piece has a distal retouched end that is rounded, then that rounding takes precedent in classifying it as an endscraper regardless of the presence of other scraper retouch on other edges (e.g., as in Figures 7.1 and 7.3). If the retouched end is straight and abrupt, then the tool is classified as a truncation. Notice that this is almost the case for Figure 7.5, but here the retouch is not quite abrupt enough.

Atypical endscrapers (type 31; Figures 7.5 and 7.7) are distinguished primarily on the basis of the "quality" of retouch, which is judged in terms of how continuous and regular it is.

Endscrapers are relatively more abundant in Quina Mousterian assemblages, with some examples that are similar to Upper Paleolithic carinated forms (Figure 7.2).

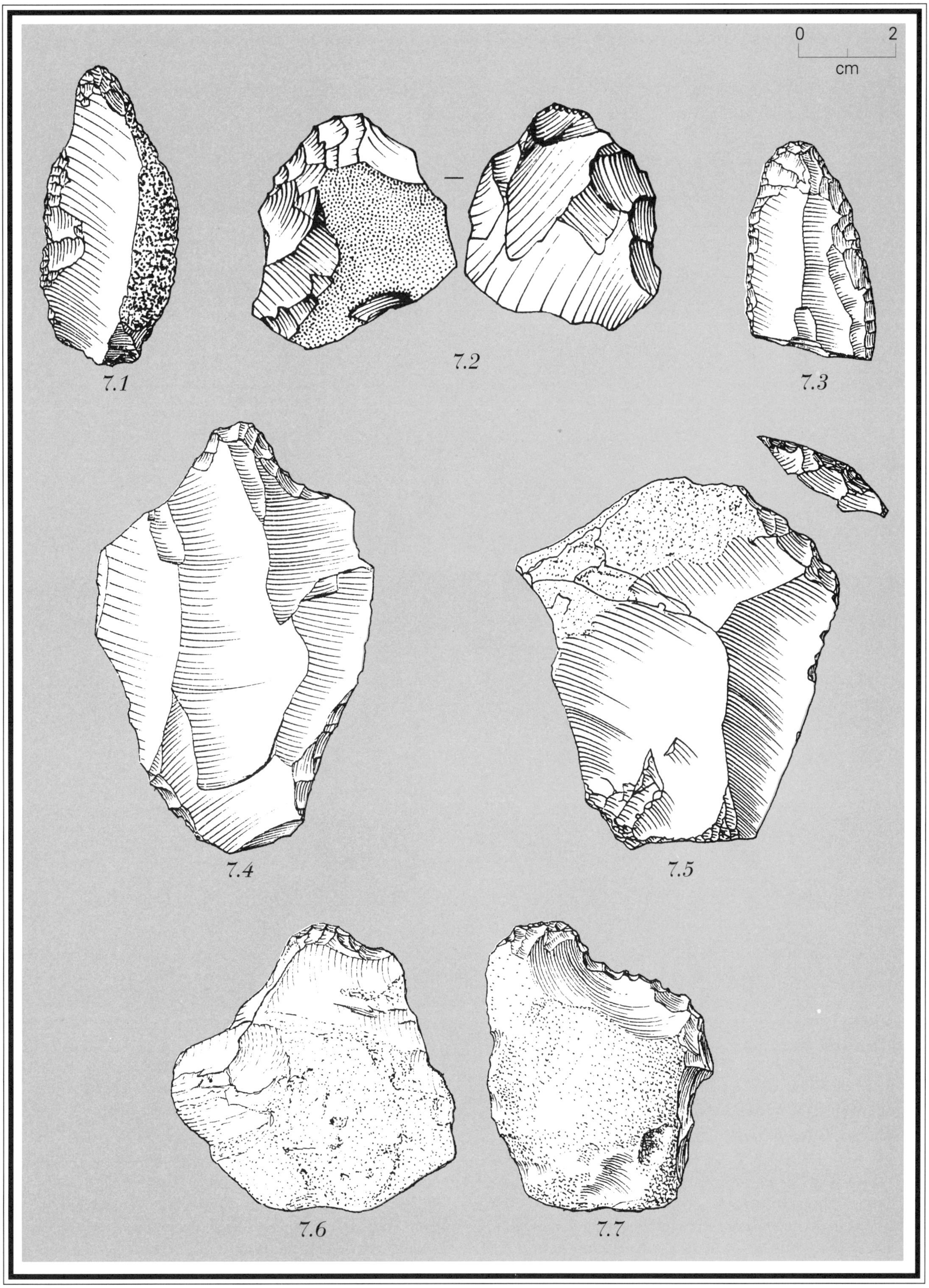

7.1

7.2

7.3

7.4

7.5

7.6

7.7

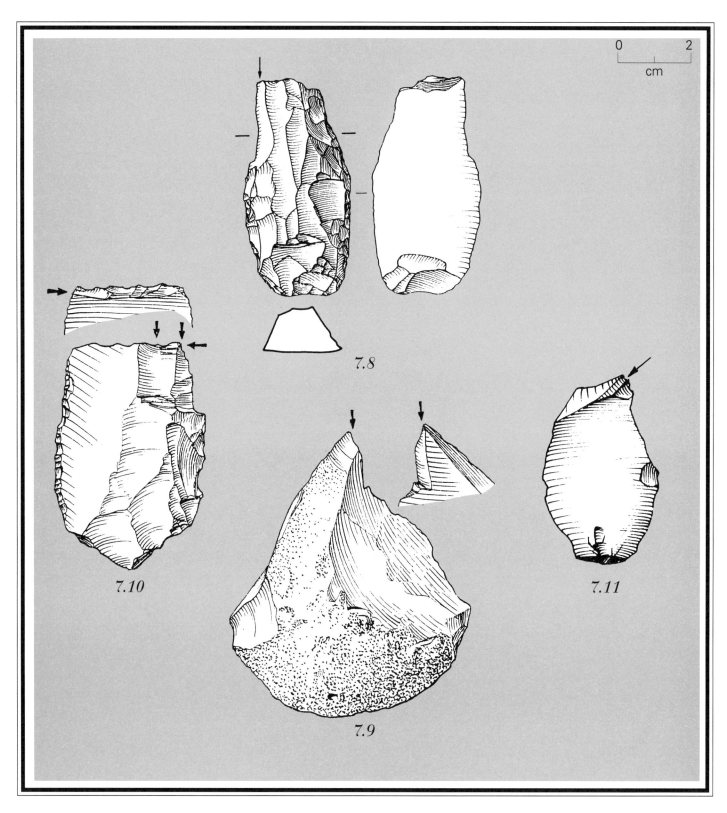

7.8

7.10

7.9

7.11

Burins (Types 32 [Typical] and 33 [Atypical]; Figures 7.8–7.21). Burins ("chisels") have been recognized in Middle Paleolithic assemblages since the time of Commont (1909) and many definitions have been offered by various authors (see Terrade 1912; Peyrony et al. 1930; Pradel 1953; Kelley 1954, 1955). The definition given by Bordes and Fitte (1953:36) is as follows: "the intersection of two flake scars, or one flake scar and a break, forming a dihedral angle, on any kind of flake." Later, Bordes (1961:32) added that the burin scar can also originate from a truncation (that is, that the truncation served as a platform for the removal of the burin spall—see Figures 7.10 and 7.14), and that the burin scar should be relatively perpendicular to the plane of the flake. This second criterion should not be applied too rigorously, however, as Figures 7.8, 7.10, and 7.13 would certainly be considered burins. Burins are thus defined on the basis of a technologically distinct kind of retouch—not primarily on their

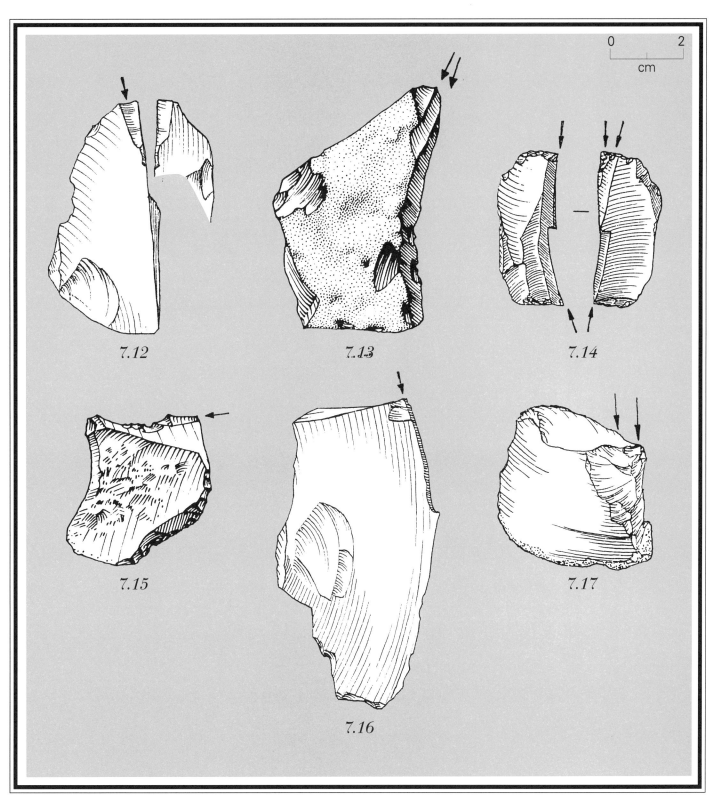

7.12   7.13   7.14

7.15   7.16   7.17

overall morphology—and the burin blow can come from any edge. In illustrations, burins are noted by a small arrow indicating the direction of the blow.

While many Lower and Middle Paleolithic burins appear to be accidental, some appear to be very well made and technologically resemble Upper Paleolithic forms. However, in the earlier industries they are usually made on flake blanks and so often have an overall morphology that is quite different from their Upper Paleolithic counterparts (which are

usually made on blades). Most Lower and Middle Paleolithic burins are simple (i.e., with one burin blow), though occasionally can be multiple (Figure 7.14). The distinction between the typical and atypical forms (the latter are represented by Figures 7.17 and 7.21) is based more on the "quality" of fabrication than a resemblance to Upper Paleolithic forms.

There are a couple of forms that are technologically similar to burins but which are not included in Bordes' typology. Callow (1986) describes a peculiar

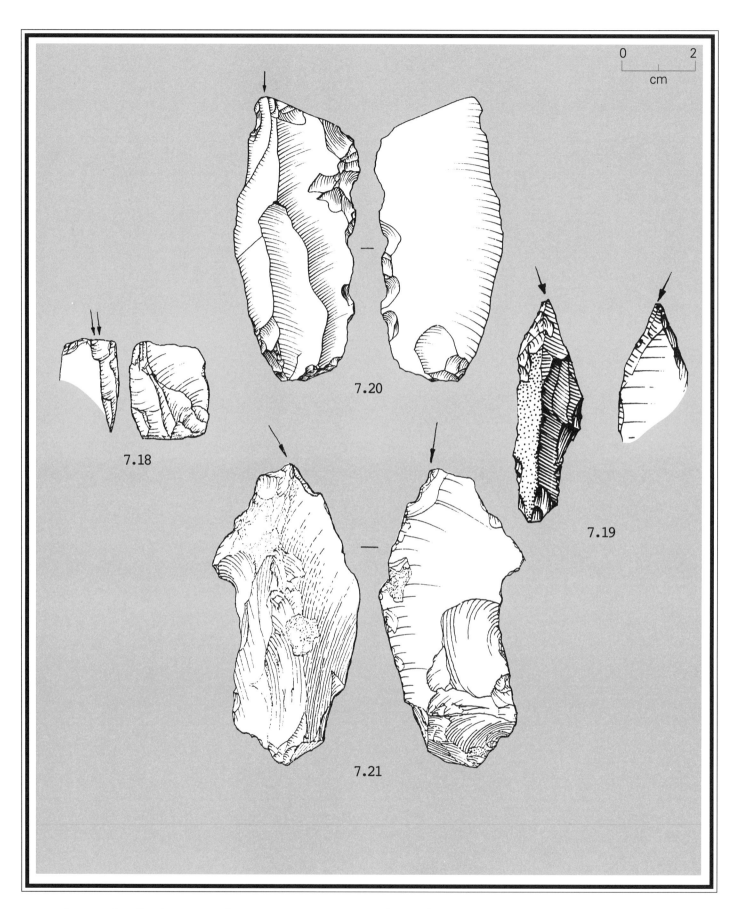

0   2
cm

7.18

7.20

7.19

7.21

technique for "resharpening" or rejuvenating an edge which is accomplished through the removal of a burin spall (see Figure 9.33) that entirely removes the former retouched edge. Because of this interpretation, these pieces were classified by him as type 62

(miscellaneous—see Chapter 9). Truncated-faceted pieces (see Chapter 9) also resemble burins technologically, except that the burin spall, if that would be the correct term in this case, is usually removed from the exterior surface rather than along an edge.

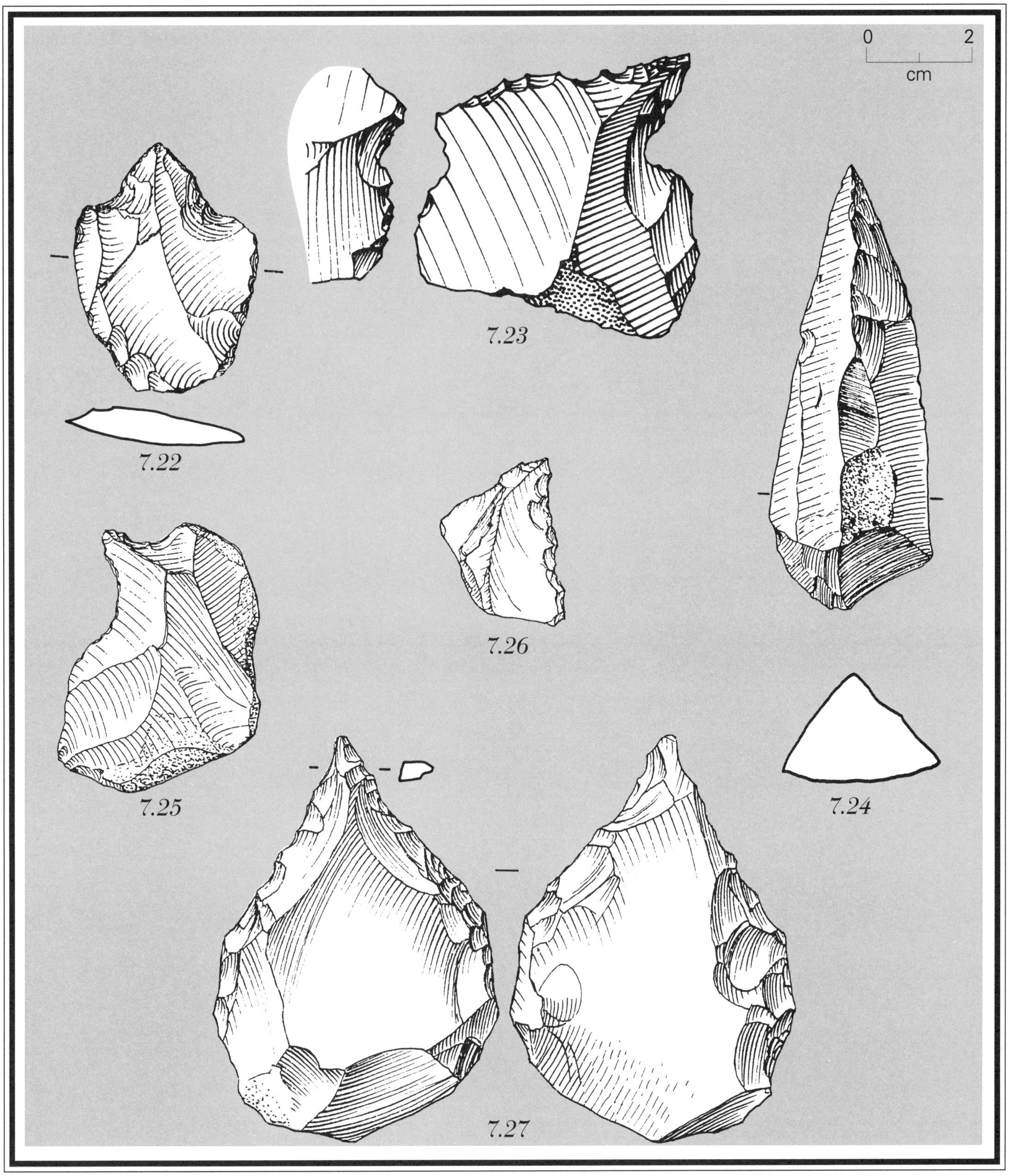

7.23

7.22

7.26

7.25

7.24

7.27

Perçoirs (Types 34 [Typical] and 35 [Atypical]; Figures 7.22–7.27). *Perçoirs*, or "borers," are tools that exhibit one or more small, pointed tips. In the Lower and Middle Paleolithic, such tips can be quite small, usually less than 1–2 mm long and 1 mm wide, and are found on both flakes and blades. When part of the point is a result of a break, or if the point is thick and not well isolated, then the perçoir is considered atypical (Figure 7.27). These should not be confused with alternate retouched becs (type 44—see Chapter 8), which are formed by two contiguous notches, one on the interior *and* one on the exterior surface. A special type of perçoir, formed by a distal truncation with an adjacent notch, is called a **billhook** (Figure 7.23).

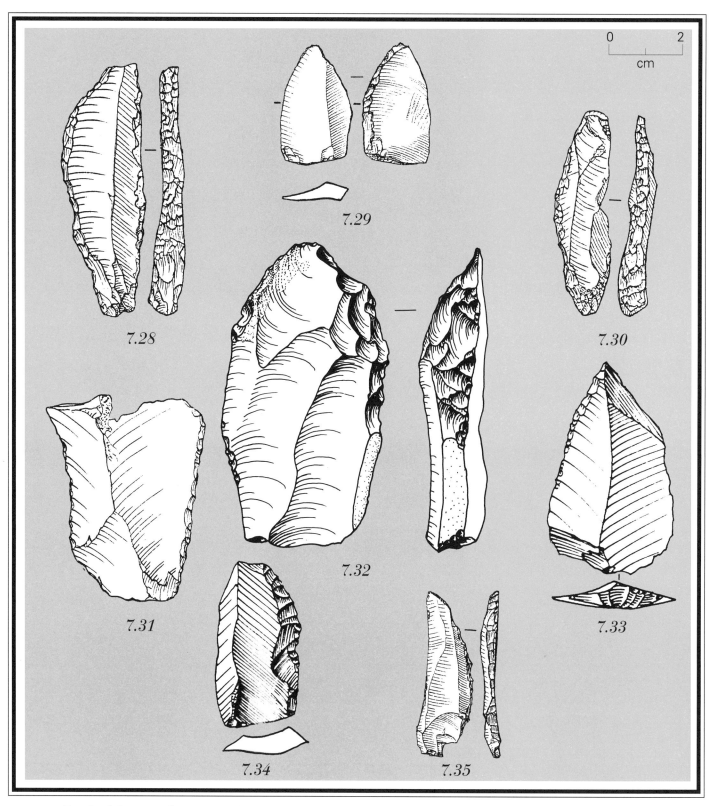

7.29

7.28

7.30

7.32

7.31

7.33

7.34

7.35

Backed knives (Types 36 [Typical] and 37 [Atypical]; Figures 7.28–7.35). Backed knives are present during all of the Lower and Middle Paleolithic. They are defined as blades or flakes that have an abrupt retouched edge opposite a natural, sharp cutting edge. When the backed edge is partly cortical or the retouch is only semi-abrupt, then the piece is classified as an atypical backed knife (Figure 7.32). It is the presence of the sharp cutting edge (with or without any macroscopic "use" damage) that differentiates a backed knife from an abrupt scraper (type 26—see Chapter 6). If the "backing" occurs on the distal or proximal end, then the piece may be classifiable as a truncation (type 40—see below).

Figure 7.35 illustrates a backed knife from the late Rissian layers of La Chaise (France), which, if found in an Upper Paleolithic context, would easily be typed as a Chatelperron knife.

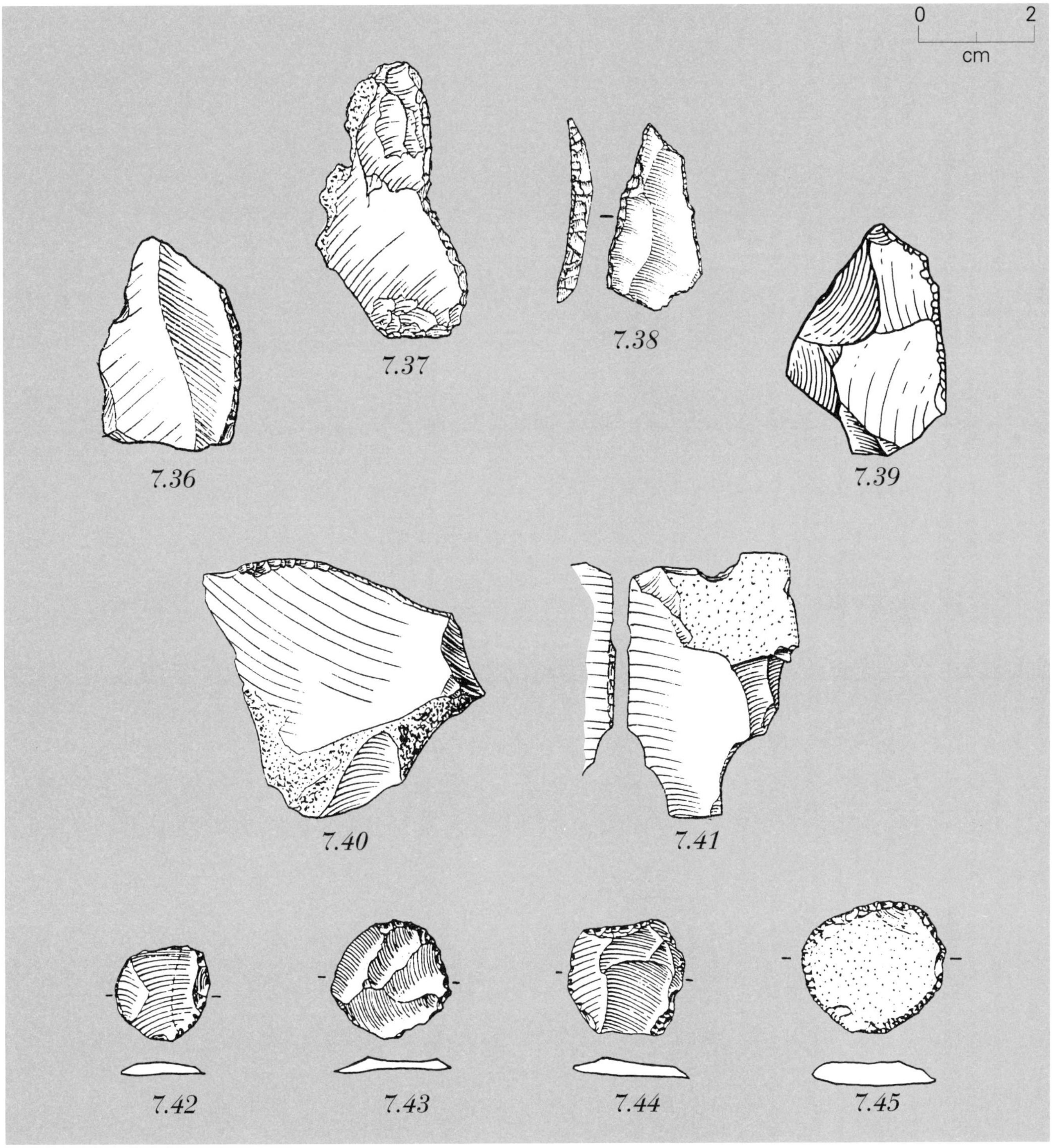

Chapter

7

Raclettes (Type 39; Figures 7.36–7.41). *Raclettes* are thin flakes (usually not blades) which exhibit a fine, continuous retouch, or nibbling, which is usually quite abrupt, often alternate, and sometimes alternating (Bordes 1961:37). The retouch can sometimes be irregular and more or less denticulated. What differentiates these pieces from "utilized" flakes (and from pieces with abrupt and alternating retouch [types 46–49—see Chapter 9]) is the continuous and almost delicate nature of the retouch and the thinness of the flake blanks. However, like types

46–49, some raclettes in Lower and Middle Paleolithic contexts probably most often reflect post-depositional damage (see Kantman 1970a).

Certain tools that resemble raclettes are found in Central and Eastern European contexts; the type is called **Heidenschmiede** (*Umlaufend perlretuschterten Stücke vom Typ Heidenschmiede*) (Figures 7.42–7.45). They are quite small, and are differentiated from raclettes primarily on the basis of their regular and often circular shape.

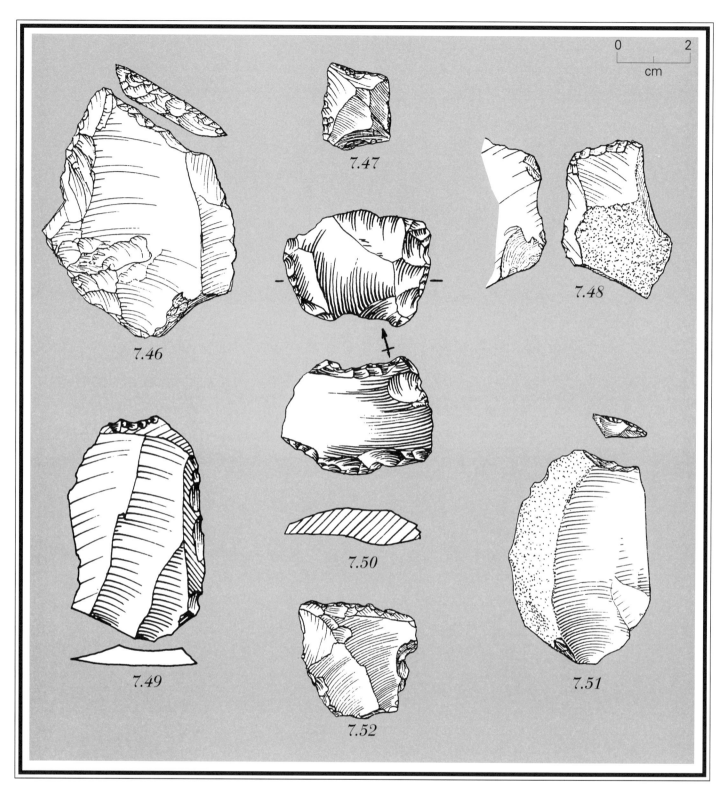

7.47

7.48

7.46

7.50

7.49

7.51

7.52

Truncations (Type 40; Figures 7.46–7.52). Truncations are flakes or blades whose distal ends (or occasionally, both ends) are removed by a very abrupt retouch, more abrupt than is usually seen on endscrapers. The shape of the retouched edge is not important and can be convex, concave, or irregular, though most often it is straight. These pieces can grade into backed knives if the retouch is rather oblique relative to the axis of flaking (Figure 7.46) or if it continues along a lateral margin and is opposite a sharp cutting edge. Sometimes a truncation located on the proximal end of a flake can be mistaken as the original faceted platform of the blank.

The production of a truncation is the first step in the manufacture of Lower and Middle Paleolithic truncated-faceted pieces (see Chapter 9), since the truncated edge serves as a platform for the removal of small flakes from the exterior surface of the blank. Thus, the occurrence of truncations and truncated-faceted pieces are highly correlated with each other in many assemblages. Also, as mentioned above, truncations may serve as platforms for burins.

CHAPTER EIGHT

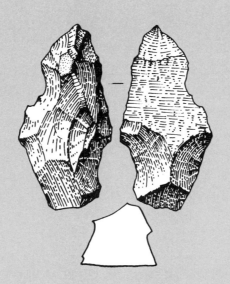

NOTCHED AND DENTICULATED TYPES

NOTCHES AND DENTICULATES REPRE-sent, along with scrapers, the most common-ly occurring types in the Middle Paleolithic and are the principal types represented in Denticulate Mousterian assemblages. However, they are a very amorphous group with few common characteristics. They can occur on virtually any kind of blank, can take any shape, and the retouch can be on the interior as well as the exterior. In spite of this variability, Bordes' typology makes relatively few typological distinctions among them, which is some-what surprising given, for example, the number of scraper types. Even more troubling, however, is that notches and denticulates are fairly often not inten-tional tools, since many different kinds of post-depo-sitional disturbances can produce an uneven, dentic-ulated edge (see Kantman 1970b, 1970c; Verjux 1988) as can heavy utilization of an edge.

Notches (Types 42, 52, 54; Figures 8.1–8.17). A notch can be made with a single blow to the flake surface near an edge or by a series of small contigu-ous removals that hollow out a concavity. Those made with a single blow are often referred to as **Clactonian notches** (Figures 8.2, 8.5, 8.6, and 8.8) and the latter, more complex forms are considered to be **ordinary** or **complex notches** (Figures 8.1, 8.3, 8.4, and 8.7). No typological distinction is usually made between these two techniques, however. The dimensions of the concavity, i.e., its depth and width, are quite variable. Very wide and shallow complex notches will grade into the class of concave scrapers (as in Figure 8.7). Notches can be on either the exte-rior or interior (see Figures 8.3 and 8.7) surface of the blank. Pieces can have multiple concavities and still be considered as one of these types as long as the concavities are not adjacent (resulting in a denticu-late).

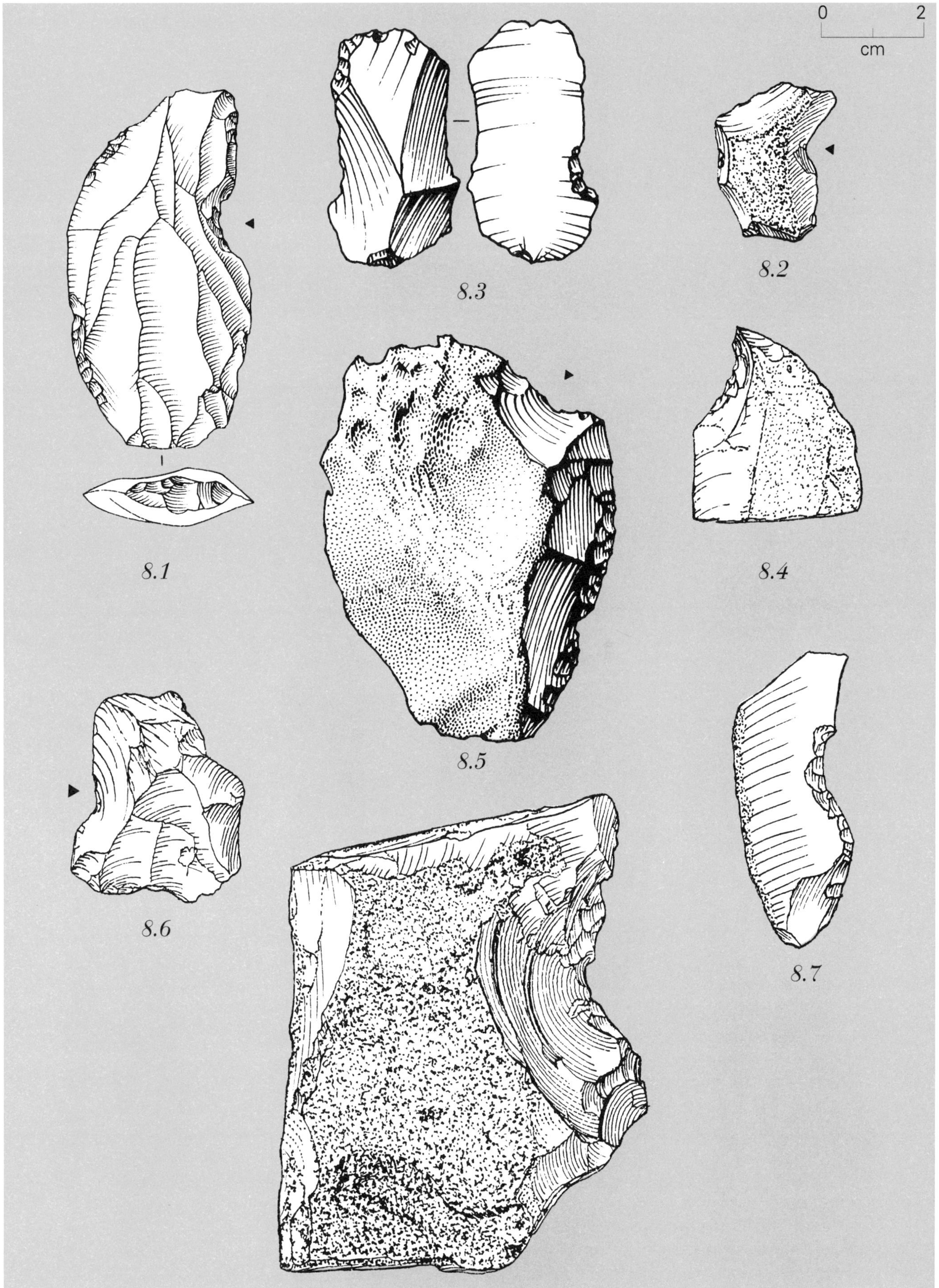

0   2
cm

8.3

8.2

8.1

8.5

8.4

8.6

8.7

Chapter
8

8.8

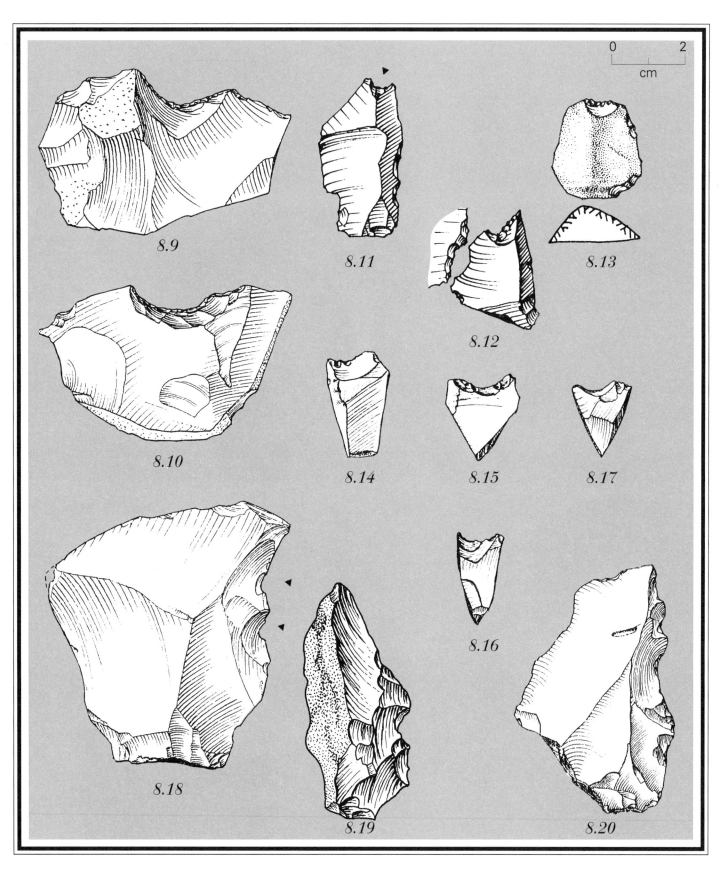

8.9

8.11

8.13

8.12

8.10

8.14

8.15

8.17

8.16

8.18

8.19

8.20

Three types of notches are distinguished by Bordes. **Notches** (Type 42; Figures 8.1–8.8) are as just described. **End-notched pieces** (Type 54; Figures 8.9–8.13) are flakes, or more rarely, blades, with a notch located on their distal end. **Notched triangles** (Type 52; Figures 8.14–8.17), which are quite rare, are triangularly shaped flake fragments with a single notch on one of the sides, usually the side that was part of the original flake edge (Bordes 1961:36).

Denticulates (Type 43; Figures 8.18–8.28). Denticulates, or "tooth-edged" pieces, are blades or flakes which present two or more contiguous notches. The notches themselves can be on the interior or

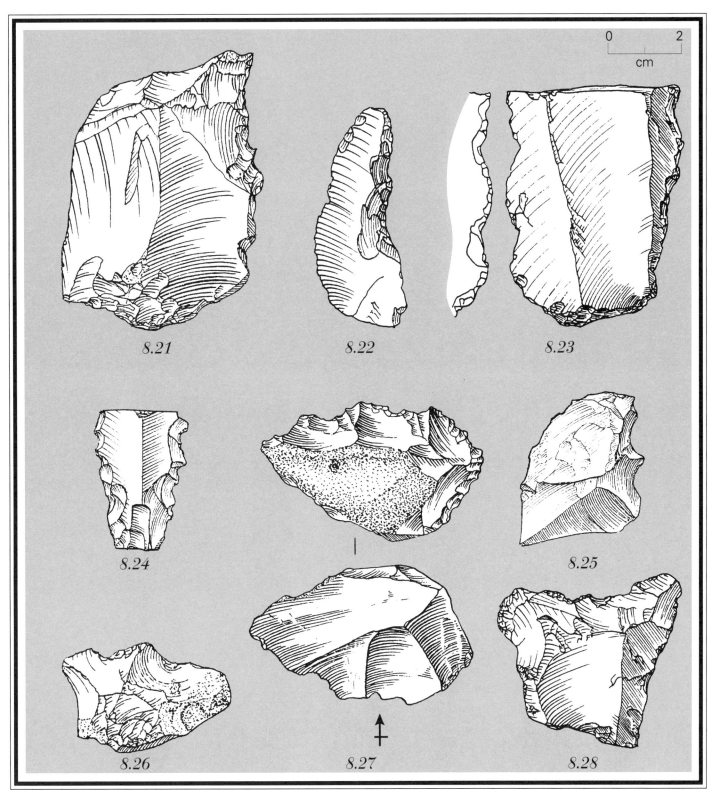

0   2
cm

8.21

8.22

8.23

8.24

8.25

8.26

8.27

8.28

exterior surface, and can be Clactonian or ordinary; their intersection forms a series of "points" or "spines," though these can be fairly rounded. Dibble (1988) has suggested that some denticulates, especially those formed by contiguous Clactonian notches, could be interpreted as multiple notches resulting from notch rejuvenation. It has also been suggested that such pieces may represent a stage in the production of Quina retouch (Lenoir 1986). However, at the other end of a continuum of variability, some

denticulates exhibit a fine retouch, resulting in an almost serrated edge (Figure 8.24). A continuously denticulated edge can also grade into scraper retouch. So it seems that this class of tools is not only highly variable in morphology but also fairly complex in terms of technology and perhaps function as well. Additionally, some of these forms can be the result of heavy utilization or post-depositional damage.

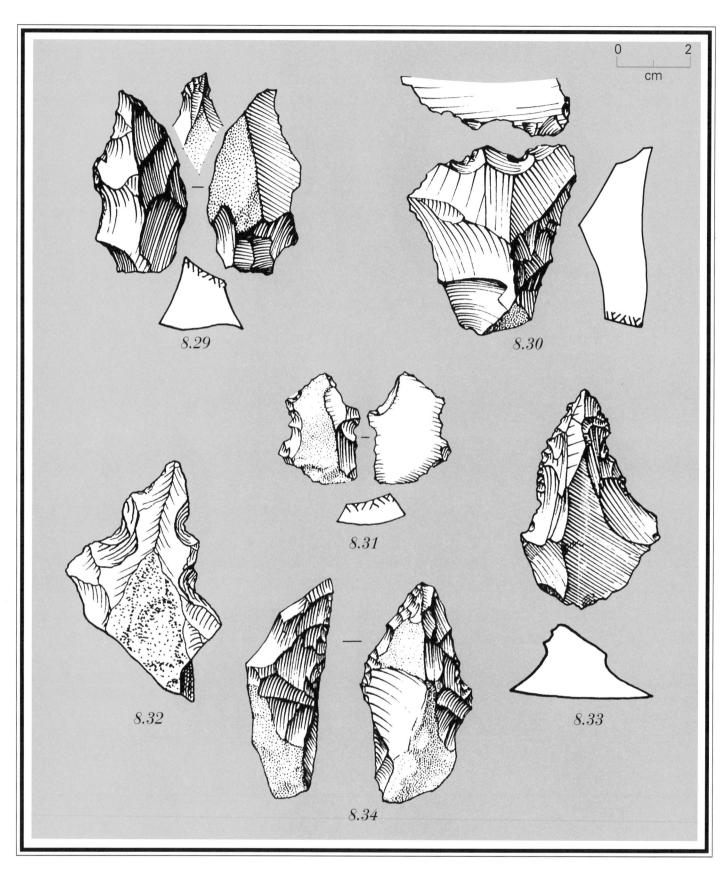

0 2
cm

8.29

8.30

8.31

8.32

8.33

8.34

Alternate retouched becs (Type 44; Figures 8.29–8.31). In general, *becs* ("beaks") are objects that have a sharp, more or less pointed extremity (Brézillon 1968:146), though Bordes (1961:37) reserved this name for objects that have two small contiguous notches, one on the interior *and* one on the exterior, whose intersection produces a spine or point that is somewhat oblique relative to the original flake margin. These pieces are not unlike denticulates (see above) and perçoirs (types 34 and 35— see Chapter 7), except for the alternate nature of the notching. Note that if the bec is formed by a notch and a broken edge, then the piece is typed as a notch (see above).

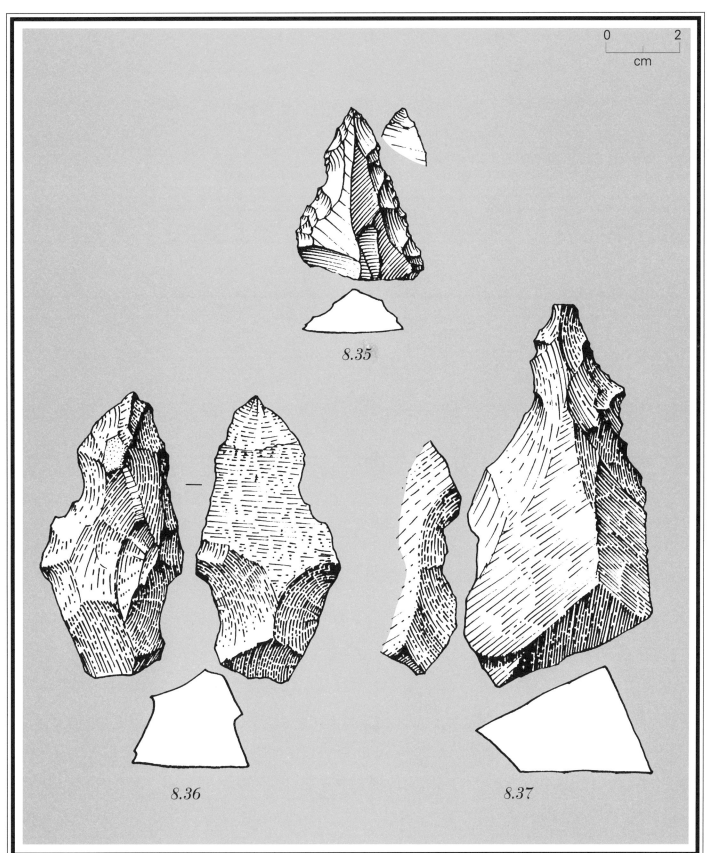

8.35

8.36

8.37

Chapter

8

Tayac points (Type 51; Figures 8.32–8.37). Tayac points are definitely not true projectile points, but rather flakes, often thick, with two denticulated lateral edges which converge toward the (usually distal) end (Bordes 1961). In a sense, they are "convergent denticulates," analogous in some ways to convergent scrapers. Note that the retouched edges can be alternate, as in Figure 8.37. The term *pointe tayacienne* (versus Tayac point or *pointe de Tayac*) was used by de Heinzelin (1962) for pieces retouched by very large notches.

CHAPTER NINE

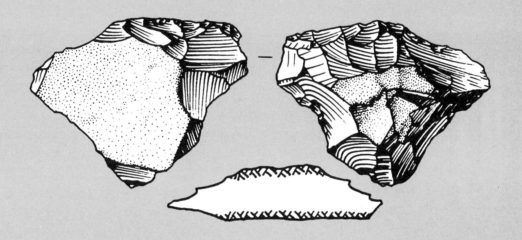

MISCELLANEOUS

IN THIS CHAPTER WE WILL COVER some remaining flake tool types that, while recognizable, are usually rare in Lower and Middle Paleolithic assemblages and which have no real common characteristics. As is true for some other types already covered, some of the types presented here may not be deliberately retouched and so would not represent intentional tools. We will also present two other recognized forms that are not part of Bordes' original typology.

Mousterian tranchets (Type 41; Figures 9.1–9.4). The term *tranchet* was first applied to Lower Paleolithic objects by Commont (1908), and since then has been used by several authors for many different kinds of objects, including cleavers, choppers, and other bifacially retouched objects with sharp, often transverse, cutting edges. Bordes (1961:47) restricted the definition of tranchets to

> flake tools that have a cutting edge, unretouched or with only traces of utilization, located opposite the platform, and which is either oblique or perpendicular to the axis of the flake. The sides of the tool show either an abrupt retouch, are cortical, or are intentionally snapped.

Thus, these pieces are similar to backed and naturally-backed knives, except that the long cutting edge is located on the distal end of the flake. Of course, deciding between an intentional and unintentional snap can be problematic. While these sorts of tools are widespread in the Mesolithic and Neolithic of Europe, they are extremely rare in the Paleolithic.

The term "Mousterian tranchet," as well as the type itself, should not be confused with a "tranchet blow," which is a kind of resharpening technique not unlike a very oblique burin blow, but generally across the distal end of a piece (see Chapter 3). This technique is also commonly found in Europe on bifaces of the type *bout coupé* and *prondniks* or biface cleavers (see Chapter 11). In the Near East, in the Late Levantine Mousterian, such techniques were used for tools on flakes or blades, which are called **chamfered pieces**.

Flakes with irregular retouch on interior (Type 45; Figures 9.5–9.7). These are flakes or blades with restricted amounts of discontinuous and irregular retouch on their interior surfaces. These pieces are distinguished from interior scrapers (type 25—see Chapter 6) by the fact that the retouch is quite irregular and not classifiable as normal scraper retouch; and from other irregularly retouched types (such as types 46–49—see below) by the fact that the interior retouch scars are not abrupt and are fairly large. Note that such retouch could be regarded as thinning if it occurred opposite a scraper edge (cf. type 27, scraper with thinned back—see Chapter 6).

Bifacially retouched pieces (Type 50; Figures 9.8 and 9.9). Like the previously defined pieces with interior retouch (type 45), these are flakes or blades with isolated areas of bifacial retouch, i.e., where the retouch is more restricted than would be true for a bifacial scraper or partial biface (see Chapter 11).

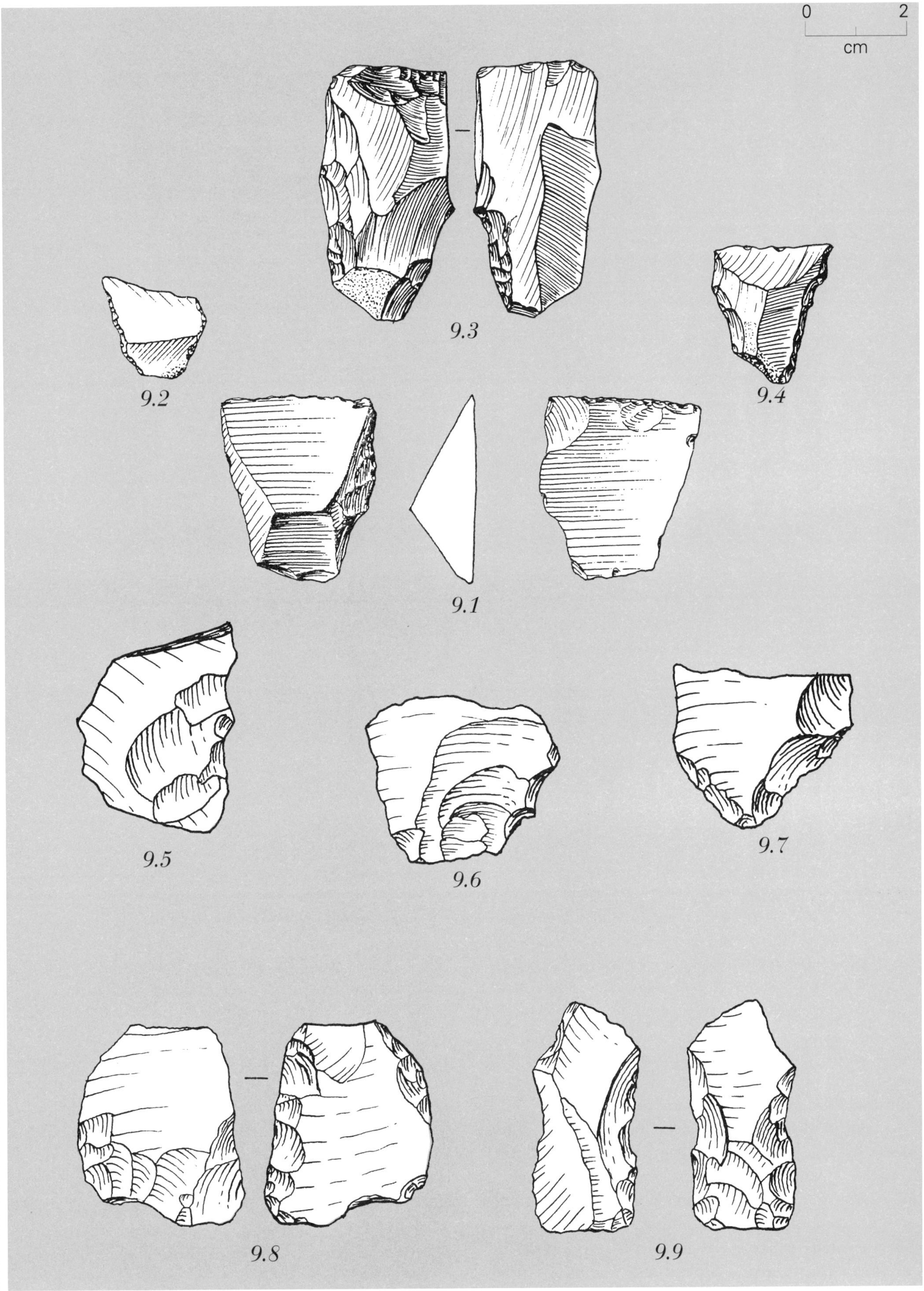

9.2

9.3

9.4

9.1

9.5

9.6

9.7

9.8

9.9

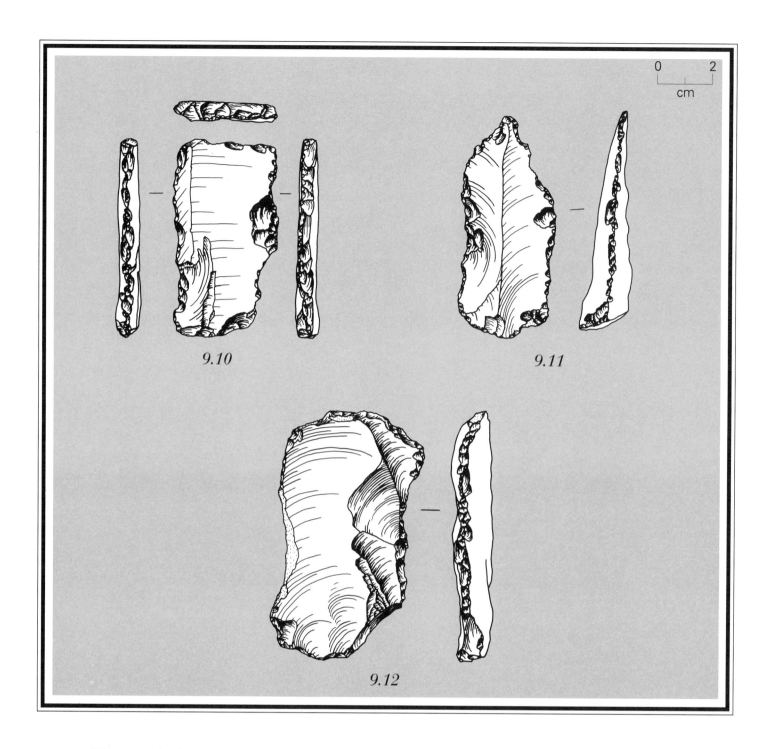

0   2
cm

9.10

9.11

9.12

Pieces with abrupt and alternating retouch (Types 46–49; Figures 9.10–9.12). The four abrupt and alternating retouch types are combined into two groups—types 46 and 47 on thick flakes, and types 48 and 49 on thin flakes. However, since no explicit definitions of "thick" versus "thin" were offered by Bordes, all four types are sometimes combined.

All of them exhibit one or more margins with areas of small, irregular, abrupt and/or alternating retouch. While this may resemble macroscopic traces of utilization (such pieces are sometimes referred to as "utilized flakes") it is probably more true that such damage reflects post-deposition trampling or geological disturbances, such as cryoturbation. In no case should they be interpreted as deliberate tools.

The thinner examples of these types can be confused with raclettes (type 39—see Chapter 7), though the latter are restricted to very small and thin flakes with fine, continuous nibbling retouch which is usually not alternating. Note that the objects illustrated here are much more extensively damaged than is often the case. In fact, even a restricted portion of abrupt and alternating retouch on a flake edge will allow it to be assigned to this type. Note also that abrupt and alternating retouch is ignored (a) if there are other deliberately retouched edges that allow the piece to be assigned to a different retouched type, and (b) if the object is classifiable as one of the technologically defined types (see Chapter 4).

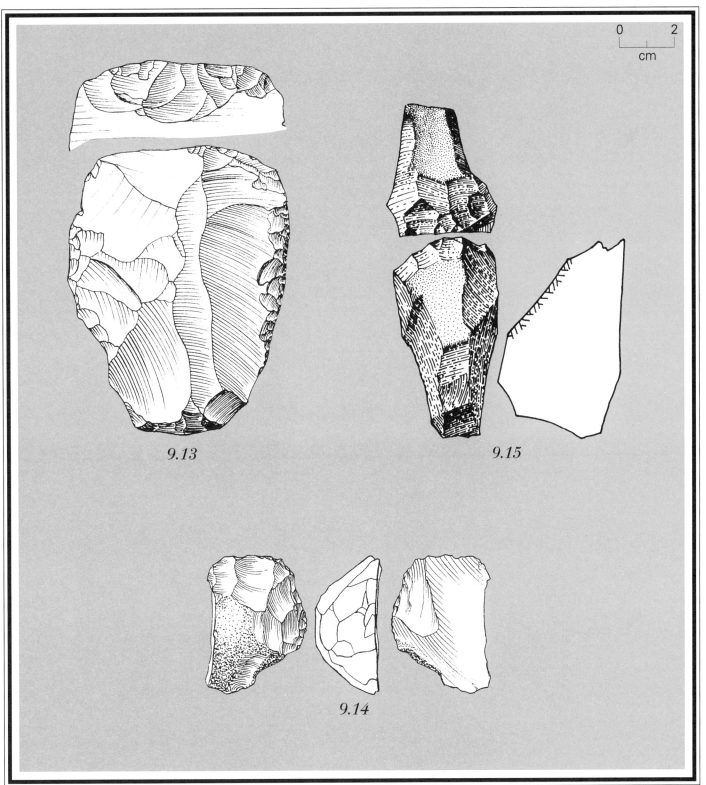

0   2
cm

9.13

9.15

9.14

Hachoirs (Type 55; Figure 9.13). For Bordes (1961:38), *hachoirs* were thick flakes, with a straight or slightly convex bifacially retouched cutting edge at their distal end. Usually the bifacial retouch is more or less irregular. This term covers various objects, from large bifacial scrapers to chopping-tools. In every case, the bifacial retouch is the determining character. In effect, this definition also encompasses truncated-faceted pieces (see below),

though the latter are becoming a recognized type of their own.

Rabots (Type 56; Figures 9.14 and 9.15). *Rabots* ("push planes") are, in effect, extremely large endscrapers, made on a variety of thick blanks or even blocs or cores. The retouch is either abrupt or semi-abrupt. These are very rare in European Lower and Middle Paleolithic contexts, and in some cases may represent cores rather than retouched tools.

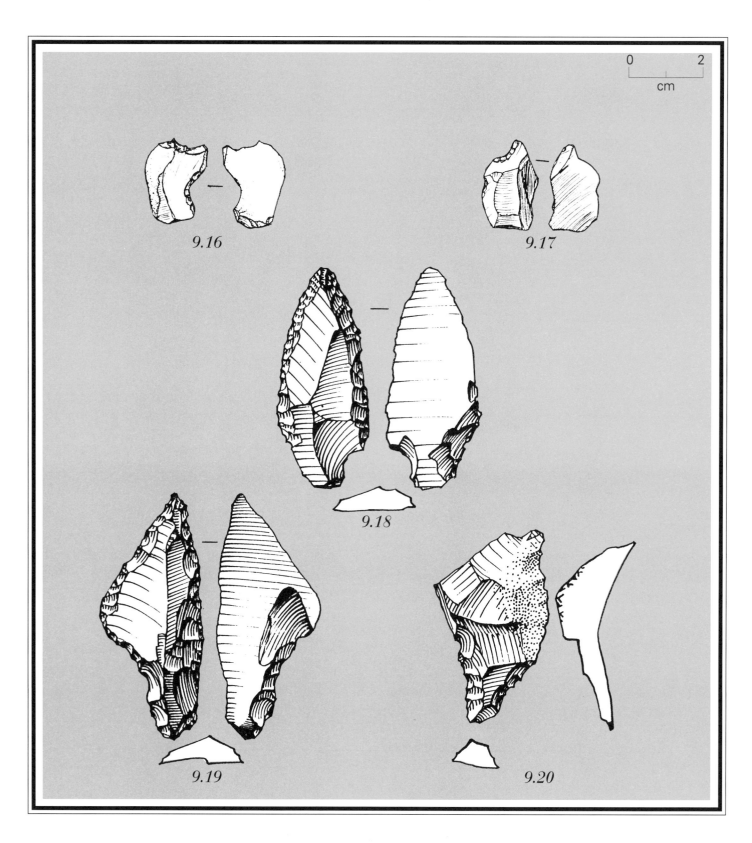

0   2
cm

9.16

9.17

9.18

9.19

9.20

Pseudo-microburins (Type 53; Figures 9.16 and 9.17). So-called **microburin technique**, very characteristic of many microlithic industries, is a way of snapping blades into small segments. First, one or two notches would be made on the lateral margin(s), and then the blade would be struck in the middle of the notch so as to fracture the blade transversely. Pseudo-microburins in the Lower and Middle Paleolithic superficially resemble these, in that they have a notch at the distal end of the piece which is truncated by a transverse snap. However, in the case of pseudo-microburins, the snap does not appear to be intentional and is most likely due to post-depositional breakage (Bordes 1961:38).

Stemmed pieces (Types 57 and 58; Figures 9.18–9.21). Stemmed tools are rare in the European Lower and Middle Paleolithic, but some examples seem so clear that they probably should not be con-

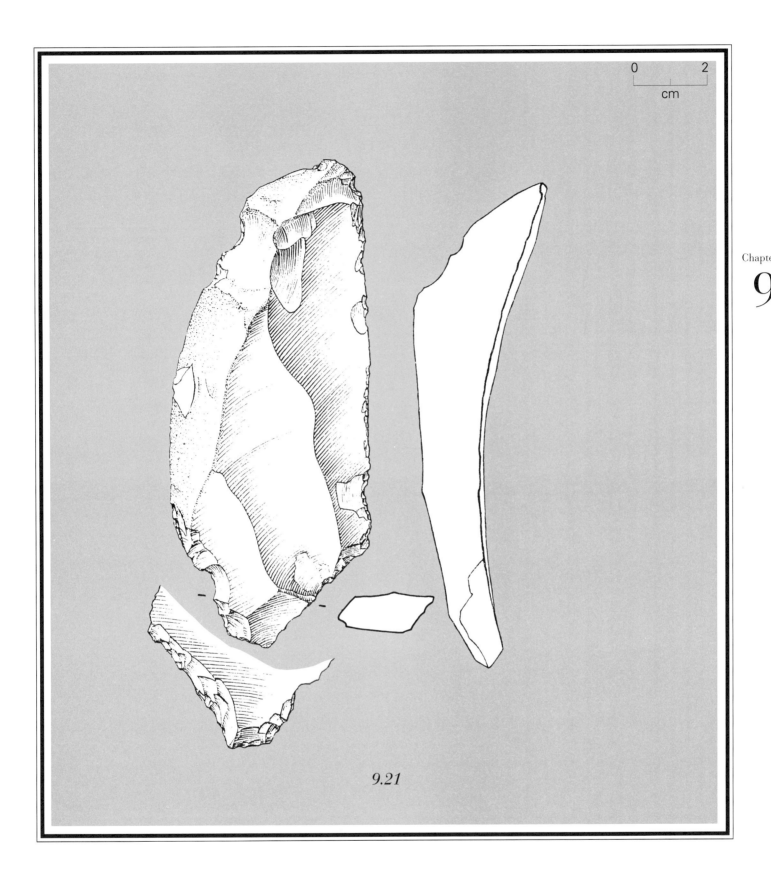

0   2
cm

Chapter
9

9.21

sidered accidents. The stem itself is a more or less isolated protrusion, usually on the proximal part of the flake, formed by direct percussion from either the interior or exterior surface. The retouch forming the stem is not always very regular or continuous, but should be abrupt and bilateral to form both sides of the stem and is often alternate. In his typology, Bordes distinguished between **stemmed points** (type 57; Figures 9.18 and 9.19), and any other piece exhibiting a stem (type 58; Figures 9.20 and 9.21). It is likely that other morphological distinctions could be made within this type, though, again, their infrequent occurrence may make such distinctions unwarranted. Whether or not such stems should be interpreted as hafting modifications has not been conclusively demonstrated.

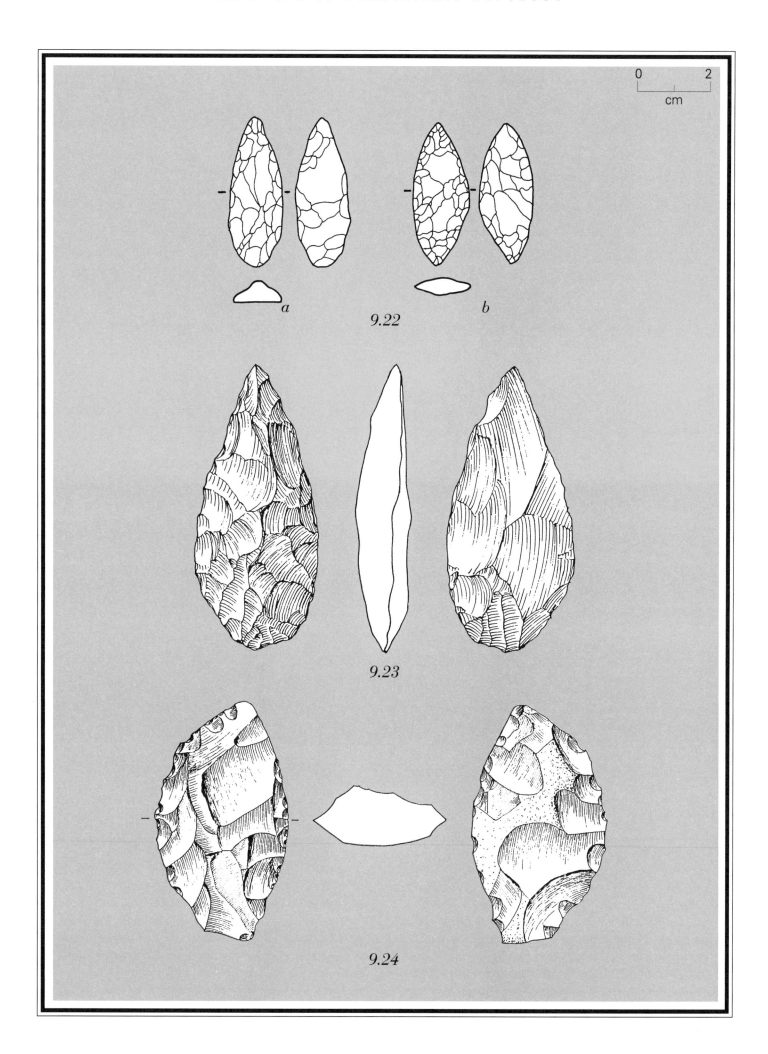

9.22

9.23

9.24

Chapter

9

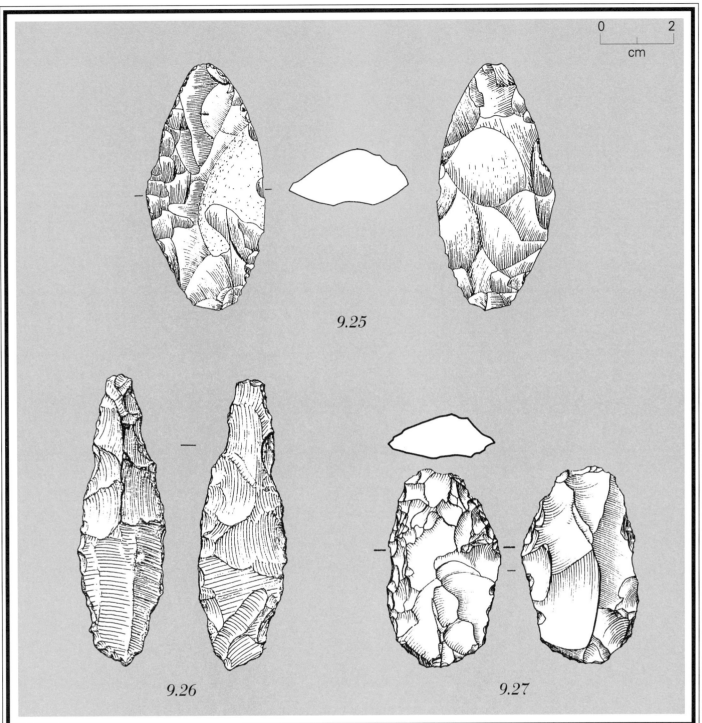

9.25

9.26

9.27

0   2
cm

Bifacial foliates (Type 63; Figures 9.22–9.27). Bifacial foliates ("leaf-shaped" points) are common in Central and Eastern Europe, where they go by the name of *Blattspitzen* (Figure 9.22a and b). They are defined (Ulrix-Closset 1975:25) as elongated and symmetrical leaf-shaped pieces, bifacially retouched, with one end more or less pointed and the other rounded (Figures 9.23–9.25). In Western Europe, bifacial foliates are rare. To be assigned to this type, a piece must be worked over most of its two surfaces and should be reasonably symmetrical (Figures 9.26 and 9.27). They are dis-tinguished from biface scrapers (type 28—see Chapter 11) by the absence of a "back," since their transverse section is more lenticulate (i.e., biconvex or plano-convex) because both lateral edges are bifacially reworked. They also lack the regular and continuous retouch of scrapers. In some cases they are similar in plan form to flat limaces, although the latter are not, of course, bifacially worked, and are usually much thicker. They are generally distinguished from bifaces by their small size and leaf shape, though an explicit distinction between bifacial foliates and other bifaces is not possible.

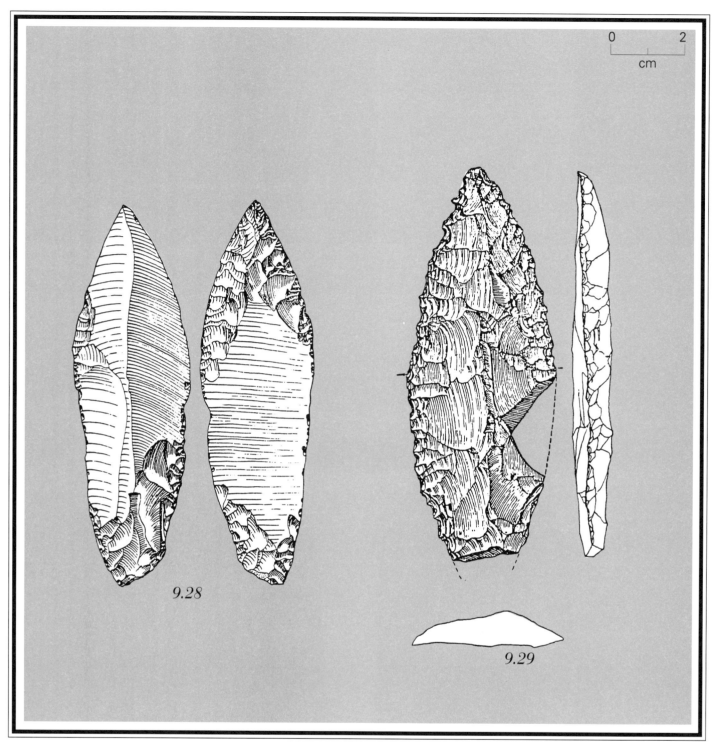

0   2
cm

9.28

9.29

For Central and Eastern Europe, Bosinski (pers. comm.) distinguishes several types of Blattspitzen:

- Incompletely retouched leaf points (*unvoll-ständig flächernretuschierte Blattspitzen*), which clearly reflect the use of the blades as blanks. Such pieces are most often retouched on one face near the medial portion, and on the other side near the proximal and distal ends (Figure 9.28).

- Elongated leaf points (*langgestreckte Blattspitzen*), which have a flat D-shaped cross section (Figure 9.29). Their flat ventral face is usually less well-worked. Others of this type are more regular and have a pointed or ovate cross section.

- Elongated and narrow leaf points with bowed base (*langschmale Blattspitzen mir gebogener Basis*) (Figure 9.30)

- Broad leaf points (*breite Blattspitzen*), which exhibit a D-shaped cross section and a proximal base that is either handle-like (Figure 9.31) or with a basal notch (Figure 9.32)

9.31

9.30

9.32

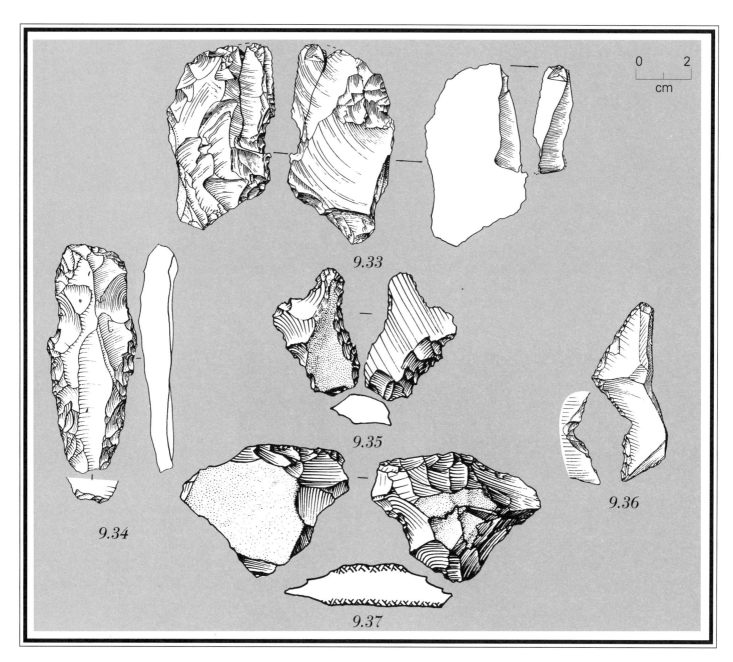

0 2
cm

9.33

9.35

9.34

9.36

9.37

Miscellaneous (Type 62; Figures 9.33–9.37). There are, of course, many examples of intentionally retouched pieces whose morphology does not truly fit any existing categories. Instead of endlessly creating new categories, especially for infrequently occurring forms, Bordes simply created this category of "miscellaneous." Often it includes pieces that are deliberately retouched, for which the original intent is not clear; or pieces that are in some way unique. Depending on the author, this category may also include pieces that are quite distinctive (but do not quite fit an existing category in the typelist) and which occur frequently in a given assemblage. Thus, truncated-faceted pieces (see below), for example, are often designated as type 62 simply because no other type category adequately describes them, and Callow (1986) classified the special resharpened pieces from La Cotte de St. Brelade as type 62 because they represented a distinctive pattern at that

site (Figure 9.33). Although it was Bordes' original intention that such distinctive forms could be the basis of new type categories, no new types have been officially added to the basic list since its final publication in 1961. Illustrated here are a double scraper on a blade with a truncation on the proximal and some exterior retouch on the distal end (Figure 9.34); an alternately retouched piece with a distal notch that isolates an endscraper (Figure 9.35); a piece with a peculiar shape (Figure 9.36); and a bifacially worked fragment of a block (evidenced by the presence of cortex on both surfaces; Figure 9.37).

Type 62 may also include **multiple** or **combination tools**, which can otherwise be a major source of confusion in the typology. These are pieces that exhibit two or more kinds of retouch simultaneously, such as a double scraper and endscraper (Figures 6.112 and 6.113), or a scraper and burin on the

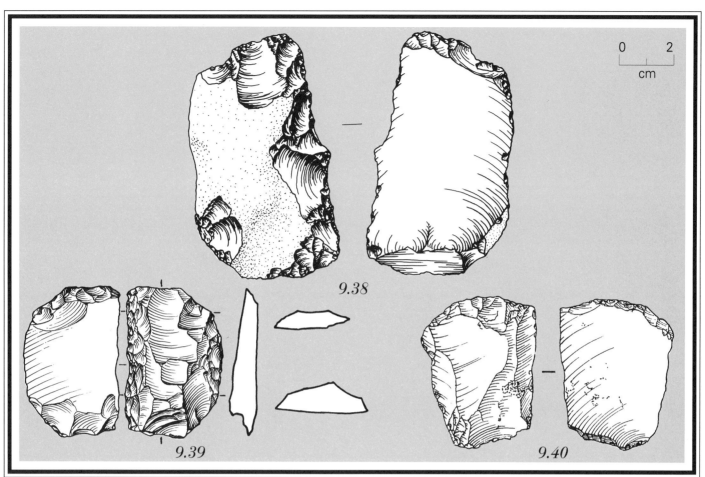

9.38

9.39

9.40

same flake (Figure 6.114). Since Bordes' typology includes no specific combination types, he relied on two criteria to classify them. First, if one of the retouched edges were "better made" than the others, the object would be classified according to that edge. If all of the retouched edges were of the same quality, then the piece would be assigned to the type that was least frequently represented in the assemblage.

Another approach to this problem is to type each retouched edge separately, resulting in a total count of edges, not objects. If this course is taken, it is important to be consistent, even when a type already exists for pieces with more than one retouched edge; convergent scrapers, for example, should be counted as two edges, not one. Most typologists, however, prefer to consider that a single blank can be represented by only one tool, even if it is a multiple tool.

Truncated-faceted pieces (Figures 9.38–9.40) are flakes that exhibit a (usually) inverse truncation (i.e., with retouch originating from the exterior surface) on one or several margins (often the proximal or distal end), which serves as a platform for the removal of one or more small flakes from the (usually) exterior surface. In effect, a truncated-faceted piece is a small core on a flake, though there is no consensus on whether it is a method for producing small flakes, for producing a particular kind

of edge, or even as a hafting modification. The pieces go under a variety of names, including **Kostienki knives** (in Europe), **Nahr Ibrahim cores** (defined by Solecki and Solecki 1970 at the Lebanese site of Nahr Ibrahim), and "sinew-frayers," named by Leakey after observing their manufacture and use in Kenya (Leakey 1935). Since they were not included in Bordes' typelist, they were not consistently recognized until relatively recently. More detailed studies of Near Eastern examples have been published by Nishiaki (1985) and Dibble (1984b).

Because of a lack of understanding of the variability of these pieces, there is some confusion with other types, most readily with truncations (type 40—see Chapter 7), though the latter do not have the secondary removal of the small exterior flakes. Truncated-faceted pieces may also grade into hachoirs, especially if the retouched end is more beveled than abrupt, or they may be confused with burins if the secondary flake removal is close to or along a lateral edge. It should also be noted that a similar technology was employed at the Lower Paleolithic site of La Cotte de St. Brelade (Callow and Cornford 1986), though interpreted there as a technique for rejuvenating the flake edges (Figure 9.33). A similar technique, called **reprise du talon** has been described by Debénath (1974, 1983) for the industries of La Chaise (France).

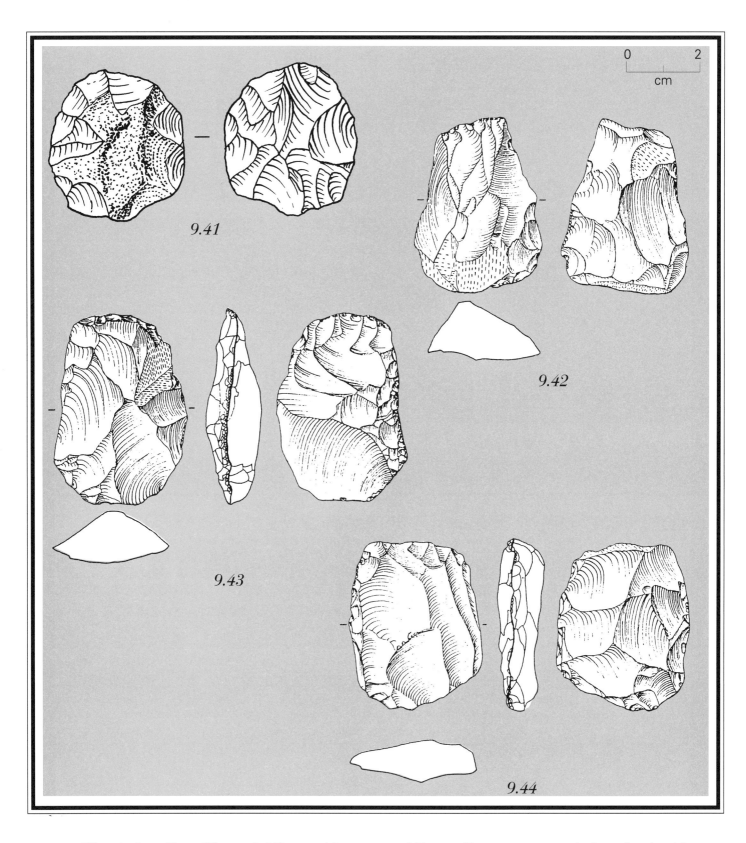

0 2
cm

9.41

9.42

9.43

9.44

Mousterian discs (Figure 9.41), are objects that are generally small, round, and flat, with a flat retouch on both surfaces, though usually one or both surfaces are not completely covered by retouch. Bordes had originally considered them in relation to bifaces, though he did not define them as a particular biface type. It is quite probable that they simply represent completely reduced centripetal cores.

Another bifacial type that is common in Central and Eastern European contexts is that of tools with a wide cutting edge (*Stück mit breiter Scheide*) (Figures 9.42–9.44). These pieces are either rectangular or trapezoidal in shape, with either a flat (Figure 9.44) or an irregular (Figures 9.42 and 9.43) cross section. Some of these also exhibit a lateral retouched edge (Figure 9.43), and may also have lateral tranchet-like removals (Figure 9.44).

CHAPTER TEN

PEBBLE TOOLS

AS THEIR NAME SUGGESTS, PEBBLE tools are often made on more or less fist-sized cobbles or other chunky raw materials, most often with limited retouching along one edge which leaves a large portion of the original cortex. They are typical of the earliest Oldowan-type industries of East Africa, but they also exist in the later European Paleolithic industries (and even up to very recent times in all parts of the world), although much less frequently and with less variability than in the earlier African assemblages.

Although pebble tools in general were first recognized and described by Capitan (1902) and defined systematically by Dalloni (1948), many subsequent authors have introduced new types and new definitions. The principal references for European material are Movius (1957), whose definitions are presented here, as well as Bordes (1961), Collina-Girard (1975), Tavoso (1978), and Debénath (1990). Choppers, chopping-tools, and other pebble tools (such as truncated pebbles and polyhedric balls) are especially well represented in assemblages from North and East Africa. For more information concerning the classification of this material, the reader is advised to consult Debénath (1990), Gobert (1950), and Clark (1970), van Riet Lowe (1952), Dalloni (1948), Ramendo (1963), Biberson (1961, 1967), and Leakey (1966).

Many of these classifications, especially those based on African material, are quite complex, which reflects the tremendous amount of variability among these objects. Another problem is that chopping-tools can grade into partial bifaces and bifaces with unfinished butts (see Chapter 11); or, at the other extreme, it can sometimes be difficult to distinguish choppers and chopping-tools from cores, perhaps in part because that is what some (if not most) of them actually are. In other words, choppers and chopping-tools are right at the boundary between cores and core tools.

While the types presented here must be made on pebbles or blocks (i.e., not on flake blanks), it is important to note that any retouch on a non-flake blank does not result in the classification of that object as a pebble tool. Virtually all of the types presented in the preceding chapters, while usually occurring on flake blanks, can also occur on pebbles or cores, as long as the character or type of retouch is sufficiently clear to warrant such a classification.

Choppers (Type 59; Figures 10.1 and 10.2). These are pebbles or blocks which exhibit an asymmetric cutting edge obtained by the removal of at least two large flakes from one face. According to Movius (1957:151), this type

normally has a round, semi-oval, or almost straight cutting-edge formed by the removal of flakes from the upper surface of the implement only. The cutting edge itself may be either along the side or across the end of the specimen. In certain instances, however, limited flaking is present on the lower surface, but in most cases this appears to be the result of use.

However, if only one flake is removed, then it should not be considered as a chopper, but rather as a piece of raw material that has been "tested," or as a sort of preliminary core, or perhaps as a broken hammerstone. This is also true for a pebble that may have several flakes removed from non-contiguous edges. If the retouch is on a large flake instead of a pebble, then it should be regarded as an endscraper (type 30 or 31—see Chapter 7) or rabot (type 53—see Chapter 9), depending on the thickness of the blank and the size of the retouch scars. There is also the possibility for confusion between choppers and scrapers made on pebbles or cores (instead of flakes). Again, according to Movius (1957:151–152), the essential difference between these two types is size, with the larger pieces typed as choppers. The exact size limit has not been defined, however, and thus the distinction remains subjective.

Chopping-tools (Type 61; Figures 10.3 and 10.4). Following Movius (1957:151–152), chopping-tools

are bifacially worked artifacts in the sense that the cutting-edge has been flaked from both sides. This flaking normally extends either along one side or on only one end of the piece, so that the opposite end or side, as well as the areas of the upper and lower surfaces left unflaked, exhibit the original cortex of the specimen. In most cases the bifacially produced cutting-edge is markedly sinuous, since it is normally worked by alternate flaking, or rather by the intersection of alternating flake scars. In other words, it is the form of a broad "W" in the majority of instances.

Again, we would add that the piece should be made on a cobble or block of raw material, not on a flake.

Inverse Choppers (Type 60). Bordes (1961) defined inverse choppers as split pebbles with unifacial retouch on one of their exterior faces. However, this form can usually be accommodated into the existing types of endscraper (type 30—see Chapter 7) or rabot (type 53—see Chapter 9), depending on its size.

10.1

10.2

Chapter

10

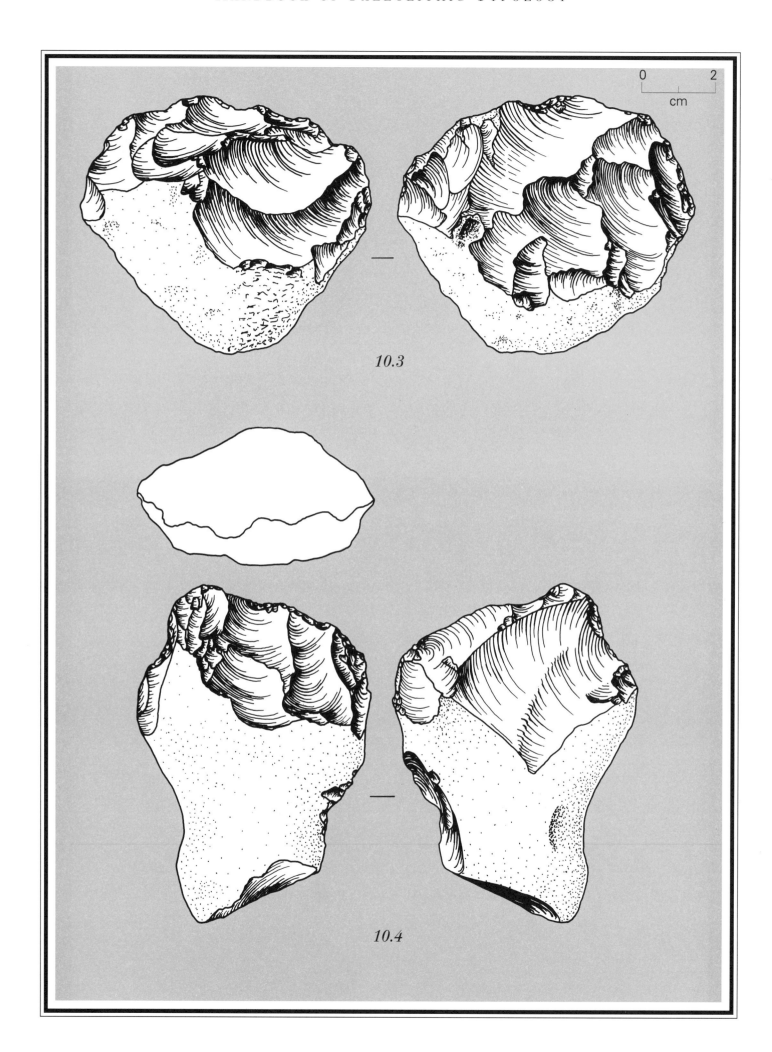

10.3

10.4

CHAPTER ELEVEN

BIFACES AND CLEAVERS

BIFACES WERE THE FIRST PALEOLITHIC artifacts to be recognized as such and were illustrated as early as the end of the eighteenth century by John Frere. Later, in the middle part of the nineteenth century, they were instrumental to the demonstration of the antiquity of man by Boucher de Perthes (1847, 1864). De Perthes also constructed the earliest explicit typology of these forms, distinguishing the older "diluvian" axes (i.e., the Paleolithic variety that were chipped), from the more recent "celtic" axes (i.e., Neolithic ground-stone axes). The diluvian axes consisted of 11 types (see Figure 11.1). Later, de Mortillet (1883) distinguished only two types of these *objets chelléens*: amandes and amygdaloids. He was also the first to refer to them as *coups de poings*, a description which is reflected in English terminology as "handaxe," or in German as *Faustkeil*. Today, the most commonly used term for these objects is "biface," because of its lack of any functional connotations. This term was introduced in the literature by Vayson de Pradenne (1920).

Although bifaces and cleavers are distinguished both technologically and typologically, they will be treated together in this chapter, since they are often associated together in Lower Paleolithic contexts. This is especially true for Africa, but it is true for Europe as well. Bifaces in particular have for some time been considered almost as index fossils of the Acheulian and one facies of the European Mousterian (Mousterian of Acheulian Tradition), and thus show a tremendous spread both in time and space.

Bifaces are usually considered core tools because they are generally produced by the removal of large flakes (biface retouch flakes) from two surfaces of a nodule or cobble. However, they can also be made on large flakes. The retouch often, though not always, appears to have been done with a soft hammer, and generally covers most or all of two opposing surfaces (hence the term "biface"). The edges of the tool are also bifacially worked. Bifaces can have either relatively restricted cutting edges with large areas left unworked, or sharp edges around their entire perimeter (Bordes 1961:49; Tavoso 1978:25; see also Tyldesley 1987). In cross section they are generally lenticular, but can also be triangular or lozenge-shaped. Cleavers, in the strict sense (see below), are made only on flakes and always have a transverse cutting edge on the distal end.

In the case of bifaces made on flakes, the flake blank is often thick and cortical, with a markedly inclined platform. Of course, as reduction continues,

most of the flake characteristics are generally lost, except, perhaps, a platform remnant. What separates these implements typologically from other flake tools (especially bifacial scrapers [type 28—see Chapter 6] or pieces with bifacial retouch [type 50—see Chapter 9]) is the heavily invasive bifacial flaking around at least half of the perimeter. There is also the possibility for confusion with bifacial foliates (type 63—see Chapter 9), which are generally much smaller, thinner, and more leaf-shaped than bifaces. Thus defined, bifaces exhibit quite a bit of variability in form and it is such variability that forms the basis of Bordes' typology. However, this approach to biface typology is much different than that for the flake tools, as will be shown. For other typological approaches besides Bordes', the reader should consult Neuville (1931), Gruet (1945), Ulrix-Closset (1975), Tavoso (1978), and especially Roe (1968).

THE METRICAL BASIS FOR BIFACE CLASSIFICATION

In Bordes' typology, three particular aspects of biface form are most important: thickness relative to width, length relative to width (or "elongation"), and the shape of the lateral and distal edges. These are based on a series of standardized measurements and calculated ratios. As defined by Bordes (1961:49), these measurements are as follows (see Figure 11.2):

- Biface **length**, which Bordes defined as the maximum distance parallel to the long axis of symmetry of the piece.

- **Maximum width**, measured perpendicularly to the length axis.

- **Distance from the base to the maximum width** along the length axis.

- **Width at midpoint** of the length axis.

- **Width at three-quarters** of the length from the base.

- **Thickness**, which is maximum thickness on the object.

The greatest difficulty in taking these measurements comes from problems of orientation. A biface that is symmetrical poses few problems, unless it is symmetrical along two axes (an ovate, for example). In this case it is oriented so that length is taken along the longest of the two axes. Most bifaces have one end that is either more pointed or thinner, and this end is considered the distal end, or tip, which is opposite the proximal end (the base or butt).

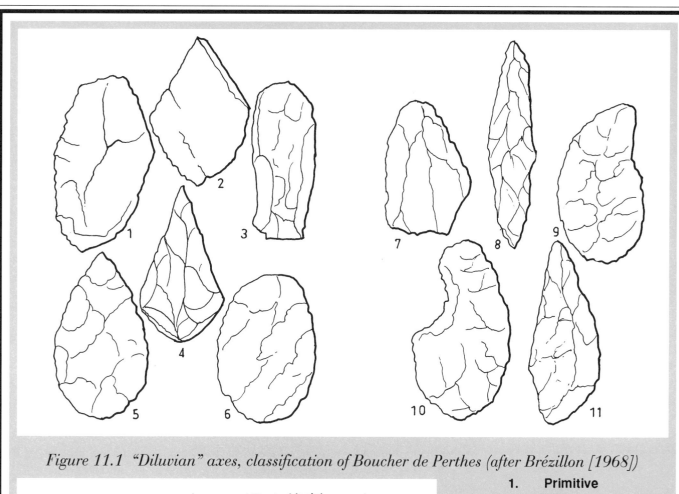

Figure 11.1 "Diluvian" axes, classification of Boucher de Perthes (after Brézillon [1968])

1. Primitive
2. Flat
3. Curved
4. Teardrop
5. Almond
6. Oval
7. Half-axe
8. Double-pointed axe
9. Comma-shaped axe
10. Hook
11. Lanceolate

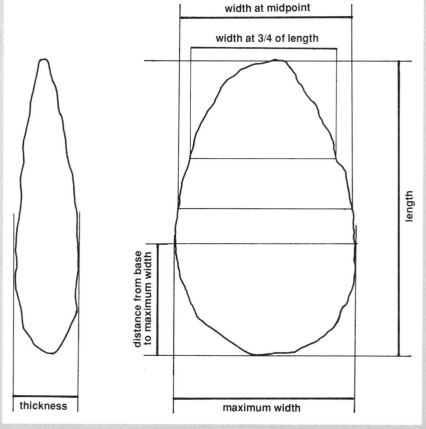

Figure 11.2 Biface measurements (after Bordes [1961])

Chapter

11

However, in the case of cleavers, the distal end is the end with the sharp, unworked, cutting edge and is often the widest end. If a piece is asymmetrical, then length simply follows the longest axis.

Based on these measurements, the following ratios are computed:

- The **location of the maximum width**, which is calculated by dividing length by the distance to the maximum width.

- The **roundness of the edges**, expressed as the width at midpoint divided by the maximum width.

- An index of **pointedness**, which is width at three-quarters divided by maximum width.

- The **Elongation Index**, defined as the ratio of length to maximum width. A biface is considered **elongated** when this ratio is greater than 1.5.

- The **Flatness Ratio**, which is the result of dividing maximum width by maximum thickness. Bordes more or less arbitrarily decided that if this ratio is greater than 2.35, then the biface is considered to be **flat**; otherwise it is **thick**.

The distinction between flat and thick bifaces serves as the first criterion for biface classification, defining two major classes. Within each of these, flat versus thick, most type classes are differentiated on the basis of the other ratios, principally the location of the maximum width and the roundness of the edges. This is shown in Figure 11.3, which is a scatter diagram of bifaces plotted against these two ratios. The four zones separated by the plotted lines (defined by the equations in the figure) are arbitrary divisions proposed by Bordes to distinguish four classes of flat bifaces, namely the triangulars (Zone I), subtriangulars (Zone II), cordiforms (Zone III), and a diverse group in Zone IV that includes the ovate, discoidal, and limande types. For the thick bifaces, lanceolates fall into Zones I and II, amygdaloids in Zone III, and fusiformes in Zone IV. Thus, classification proceeds by computing these ratios and plotting the results onto Figure 11.3 to see in which zone a piece falls. Note, however, that Bordes relied on additional criteria to differentiate among other major classes of bifaces, including partial bifaces, "Abbevillian" bifaces, pics, and core-like bifaces.

While the zones of Figure 11.3 provide explicit metric criteria for distinguishing several of Bordes' major types, a simpler and more heuristic way of expressing biface typological variability is shown in Figure 11.4. Here the vertical axis reflects overall shape variation from triangular to oval, which corresponds more or less to Bordes' location of maximum width. The horizontal axis represents elongation, which, unlike the roundness ratio, is completely independent of the location of maximum width. Neither of these axes is defined numerically, since the intention of this figure is only to show that much of the variability important for Bordes' typological categories rests on only two variables: how triangular versus ovate the object is in plan form and the degree of elongation of that shape. All of these types will be more explicitly defined below.

Another metrical approach to biface typology was developed by Roe (1968), which is essentially similar to Bordes' but with two new width measurements, one taken at one-fifth of the distance from the base and another at four-fifths of that distance (versus Bordes' measurement at three-quarters width). The major difference between these two approaches is, however, the presentation of biface variability within an assemblage. Bordes chose to use the measurements as criteria for classification into several types (which were then presented as type counts), while Roe developed a tripartite graphical means of showing biface variability, separating cleaver forms from ovate and pointed ones and presenting overall variability within these three classes. The reader is urged to consult Roe's work for more details of his method.

FLAT BIFACES

Again, flat bifaces are those that have a Flatness Ratio of greater than 2.35. A total of six types (some with additional subtypes) are defined in this class based primarily on plan form, and especially on the ratios of the relative location of the maximum width and the midpoint width to maximum width. Triangular, subtriangular, and cordiform bifaces generally have distinctly pointed distal ends and maximum width near the base. On the other hand, discoid, ovate, and limande types have bases and tips that are generally rounded and a maximum width closer to the middle of the length axis. The bifaces are increasingly elongated as one moves from discoids through ovates to limandes.

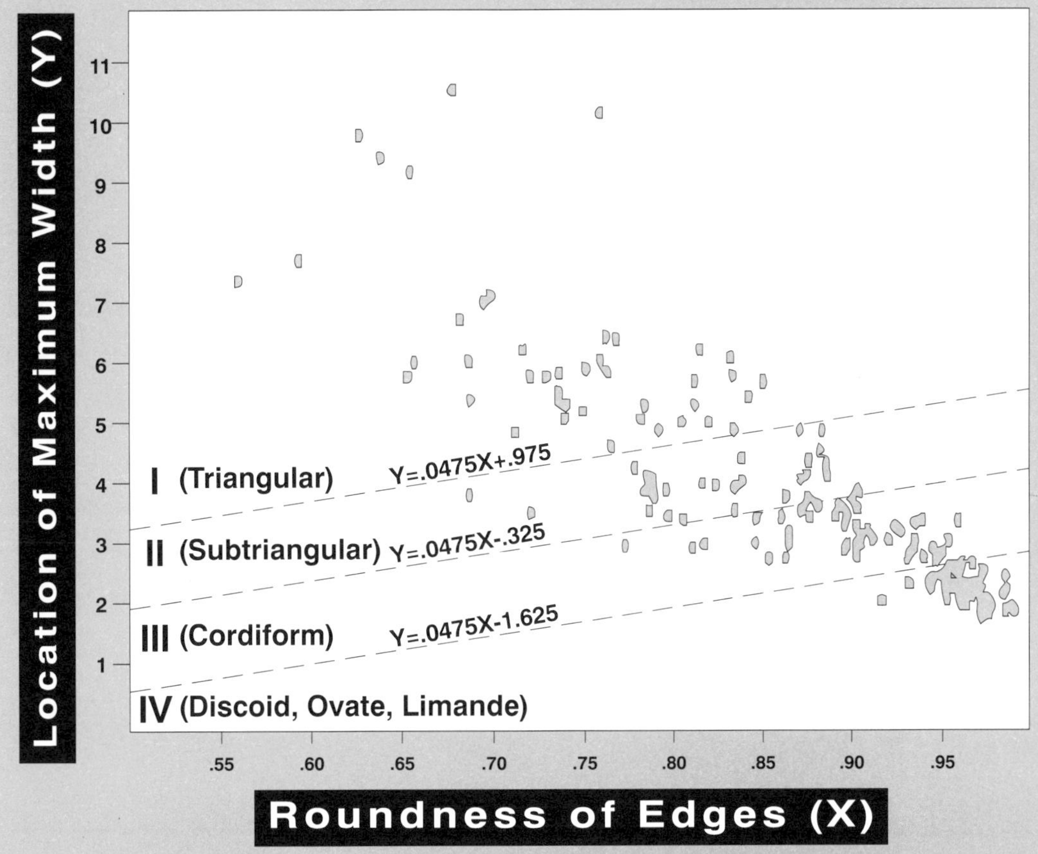

Figure 11.3 Scatter diagram of bifaces, redrawn after Bordes 1961

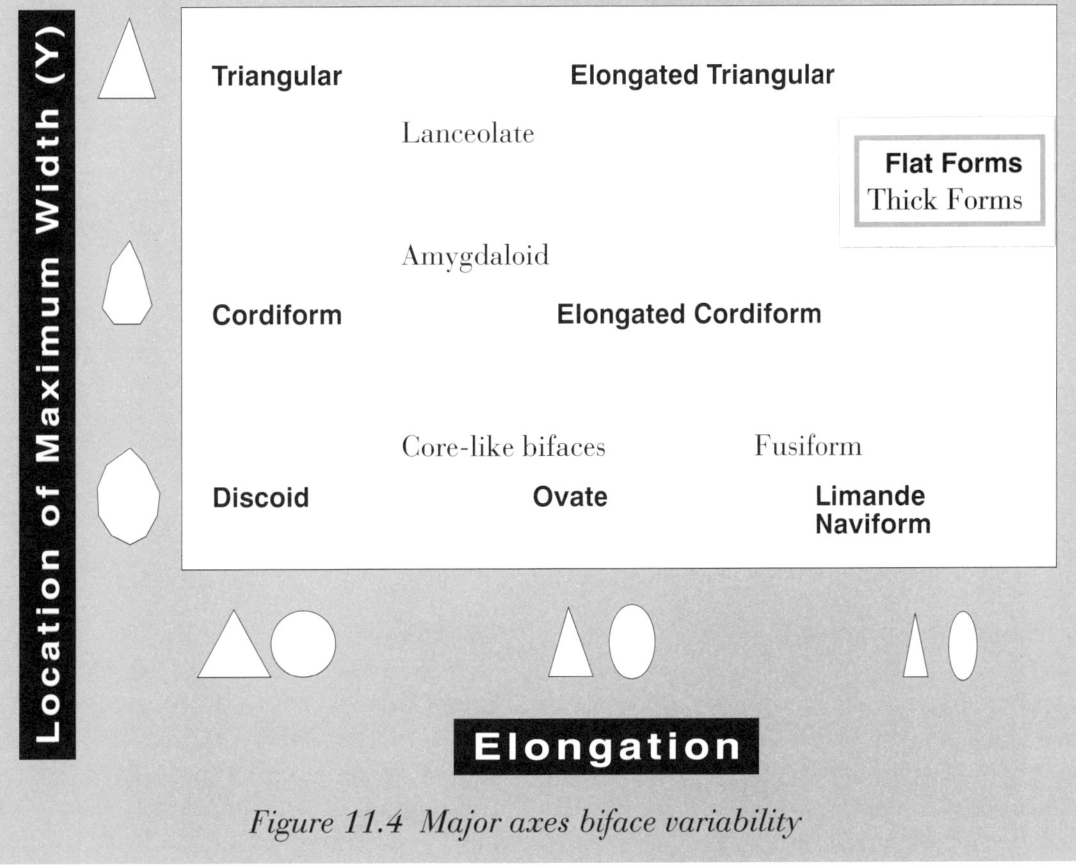

Figure 11.4 Major axes biface variability

Chapter

11

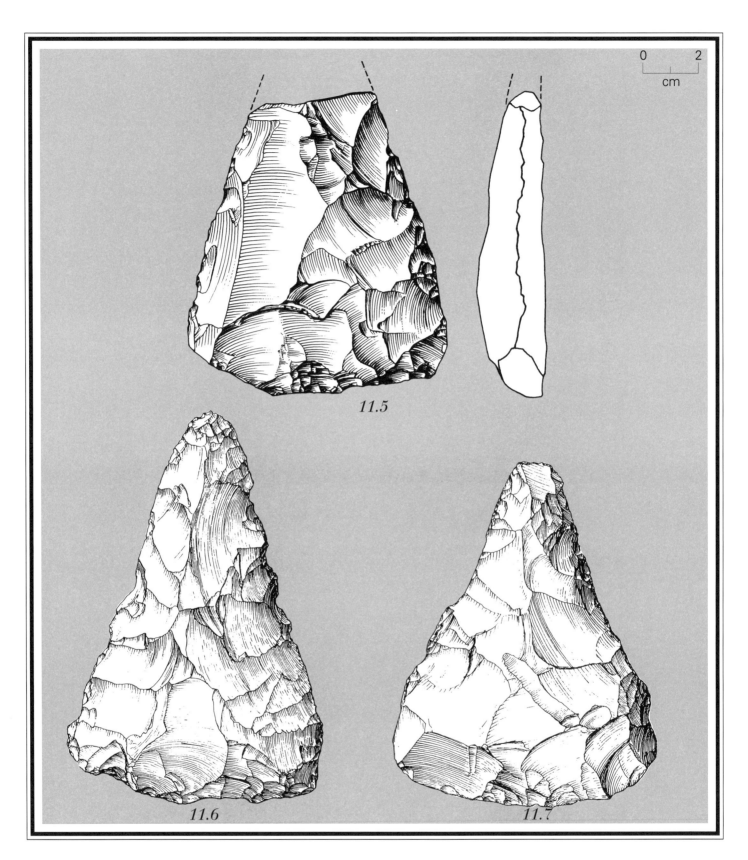

0 [__] 2
cm

11.5

11.6

11.7

Triangular bifaces (Figures 11.5 and 11.6). These have lateral edges that are either straight or only lightly convex, and generally a straight base. The base is often retouched to be sharp, but it can also retain a certain amount of cortex or be naturally blunt. In the case of a biface made on a flake blank, the base of the biface may retain a remnant of the striking platform. The Elongation Index of triangu- lar bifaces is less than 1.5; if it is greater than this, then the biface is considered an **elongated triangular biface**. When the lateral edges of a triangular biface are markedly concave (with either a lightly convex, straight, or lightly concave base), it is sometimes called a "**shark's tooth**," because the silhouette is similar to the teeth of a *Carcharodon megalodon* (Figure 11.7).

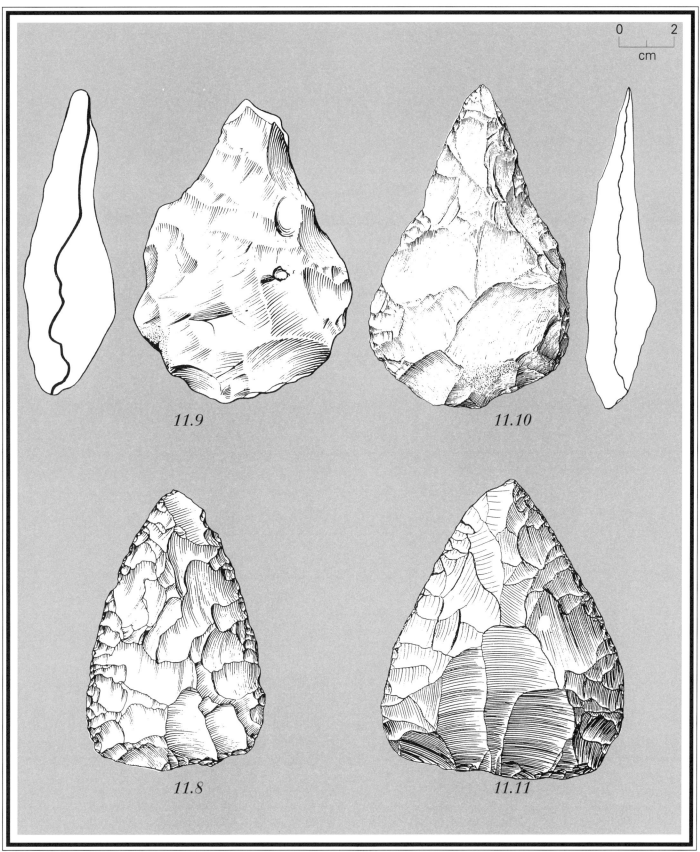

0   2
cm

11.9

11.10

Chapter

11

11.8

11.11

Subtriangular bifaces (Figure 11.8). These objects have bases that are definitely rounded, though their lateral edges are slightly convex, straight, or very slightly concave. The base can be sharp or not. Similar to these are the **pélécyformes** (from the Greek *pelekus*, or "axe") (Figures 11.9 and 11.10), which have rounded bases and more markedly concave edges. Bordes also included in this group **ogivo-triangulaire** forms (such as Figure 11.11) that have straight bases but markedly convex lateral edges.

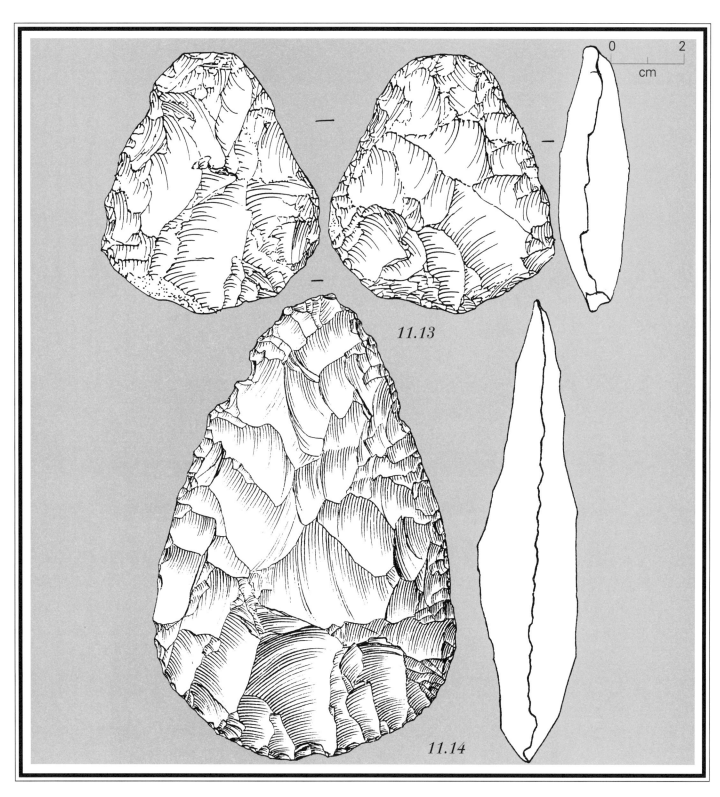

11.13

11.14

Cordiform bifaces. Bordes (1961:59) defines cordiforms ("heart-shaped") as flat bifaces with rounded bases (with the edge of the base either sharp or not) *and* markedly convex edges, and distal extremities that are pointed or slightly rounded. Bordes also distinguished between regular and irregular cordiforms. In the former are the **typical cordiforms** (Figures 11.12–11.14), which have an Elongation Index of less than 1.5, and the **elongated cordiforms** (Figure 11.15), whose Elongation Index is greater than 1.5. The typical cordiforms are often made on large flakes, and sometimes, notably in the Mousterian of Acheulian Tradition, retain a lateral blunt area near the base representing the platform remnant (similar to that seen in some triangular bifaces). Among the irregular cordiforms are those called **sub-cordiforms** (Figure 11.16) and **elongated sub-cordiforms**, which are distinguished from the regular cordiforms by being thicker and sometimes retaining significant amounts of cortex on their bases; and from each other by the index of elongation (greater than 1.5 for elongated forms).

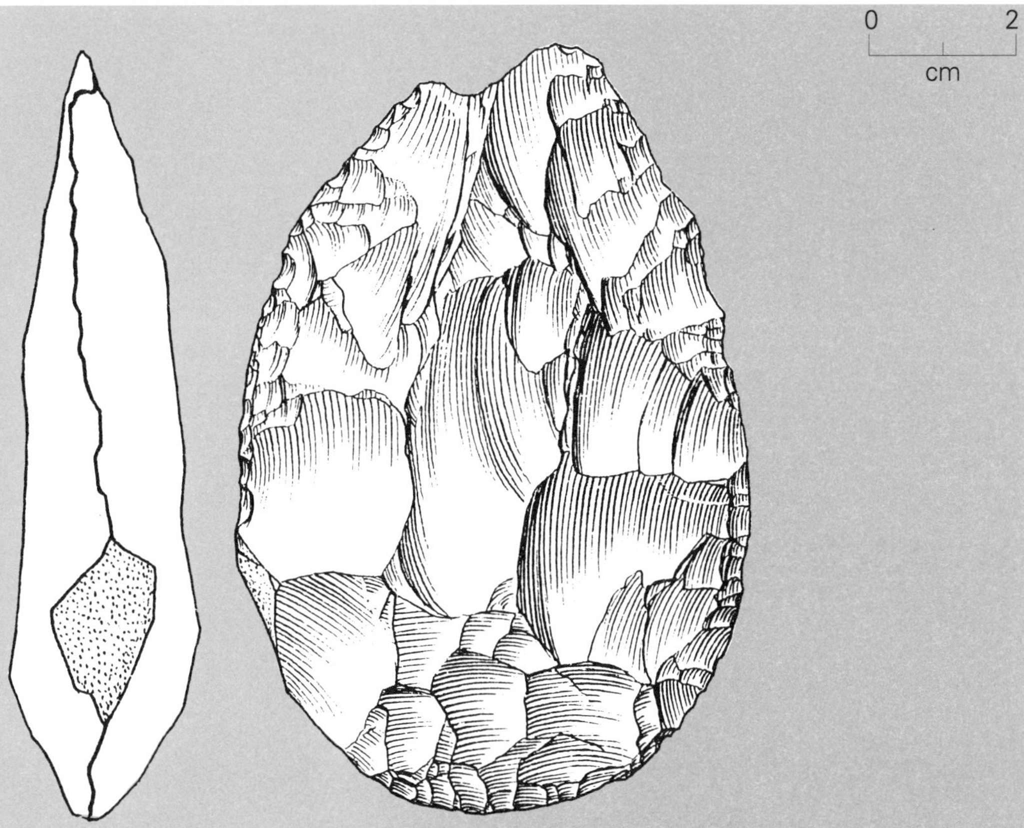

0 2
cm

11.12

Chapter
11

11.15

11.16

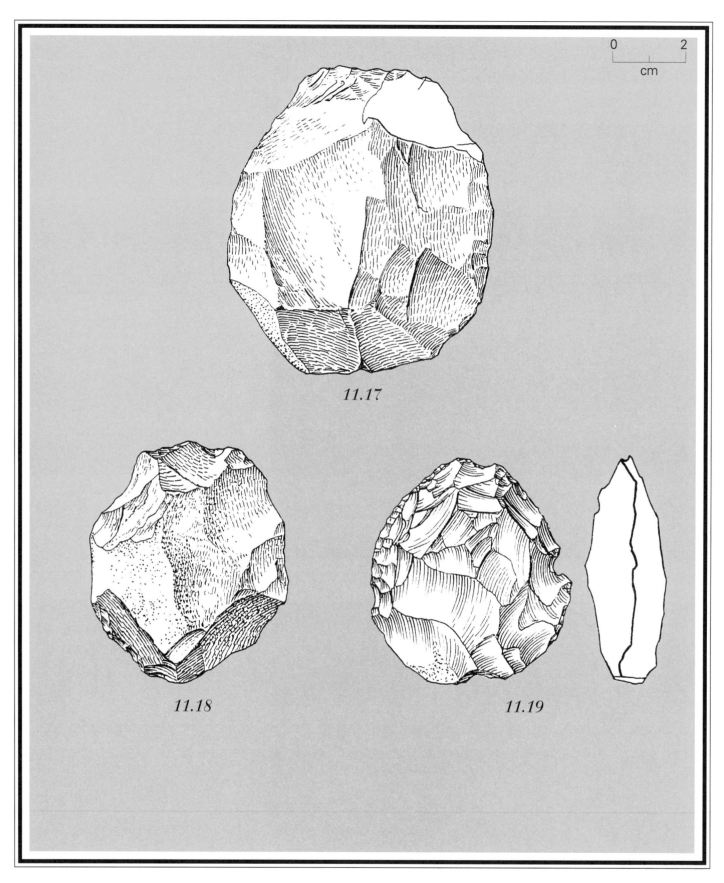

0 — 2
cm

11.17

11.18   *11.19*

Discoidal bifaces (Figures 11.17–11.19). Situated in Zone IV of Figure 11.3, these bifaces have a more or less circular contour and their index of elongation is, therefore, very low, generally with a value less than 1.3. Bordes distinguished **typical discoids** (whose entire circumference is sharp) from **discoides à talon**, which exhibit a blunt portion on one edge (e.g., Figure 11.19). These should not be confused with Mousterian discs (see Chapter 9), which are much smaller and usually have one surface that is not entirely covered by retouch.

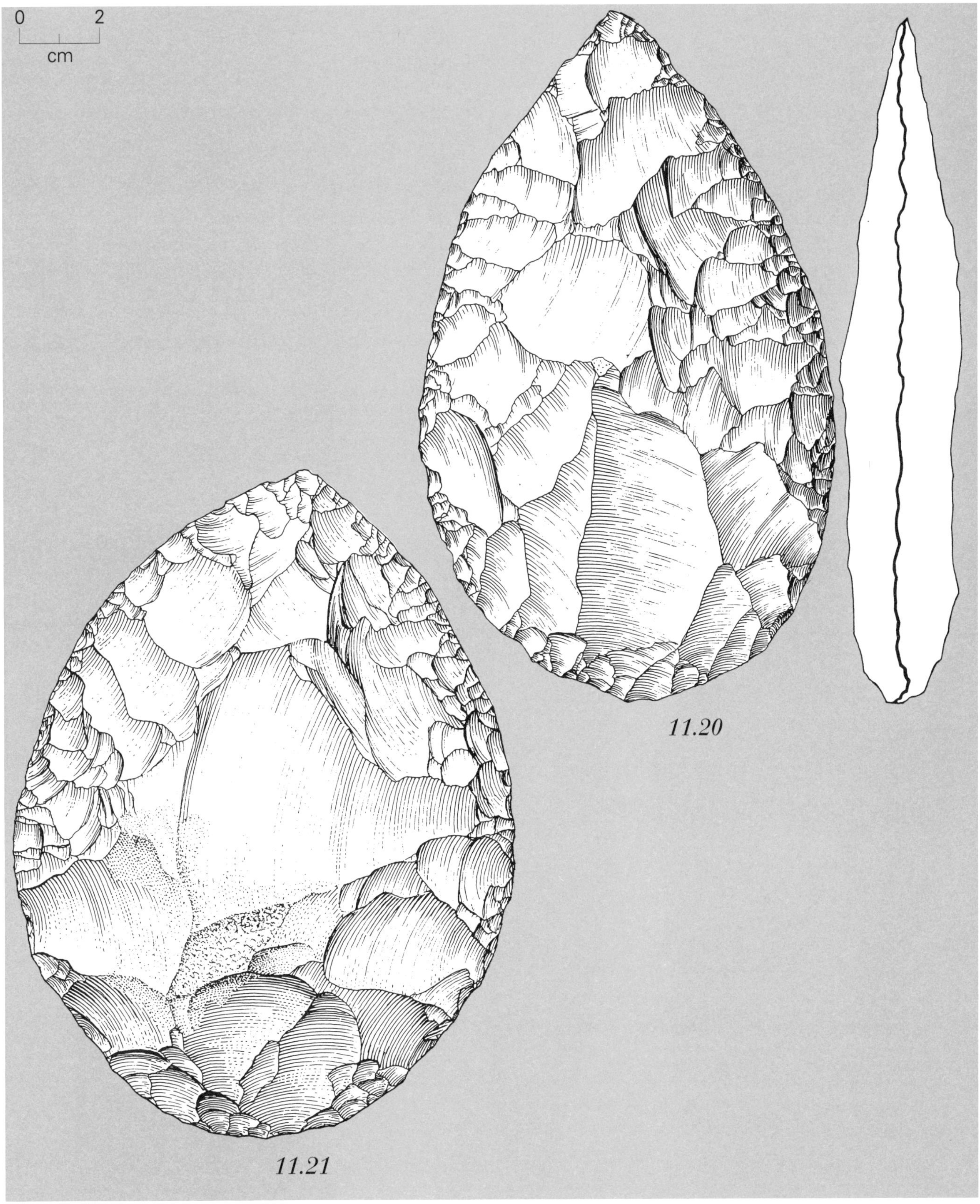

0
2
cm

11.20

Chapter

11

11.21

Ovate bifaces (Figures 11.20 and 11.21). Similar to the discoidal bifaces, ovate bifaces are also found in Zone IV of Figure 11.3 and they have sides that are clearly convex. Their index of elongation is between 1.3 and 1.6. Again, a distinction can be made between **typical ovate bifaces,** which have a sharp cutting edge around their entire perimeter, and **ovalaires à talon**, which exhibit a blunt or cortical portion along an edge. There are some forms intermediate between ovates and cordiforms, depending primarily on the position of the maximum width along the length axis.

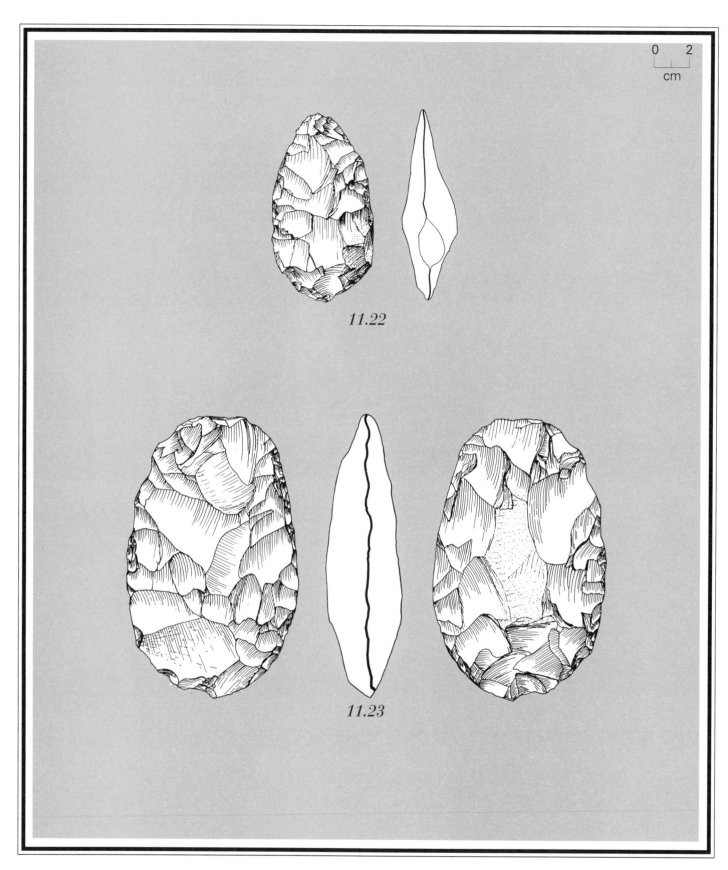

0   2
cm

11.22

11.23

Limandes (Figures 11.22 and 11.23). This type was first named by Commont in 1906, and its flat character was emphasized by Vayson de Pradenne (1920) and by Gruet (1945). Bordes (1961) distinguished limandes from ovates by their Elongation Index, which is greater than 1.6 and can even exceed 2.0. Both ends are rounded, usually equally so, and the edges are generally straight, though sometimes twisted. Certain similar forms of the Lower Acheulian were considered by Bordes to be **proto-limandes,** because they were thicker than would be normally accepted in the definition (i.e., a Flatness Ratio less than 2.35).

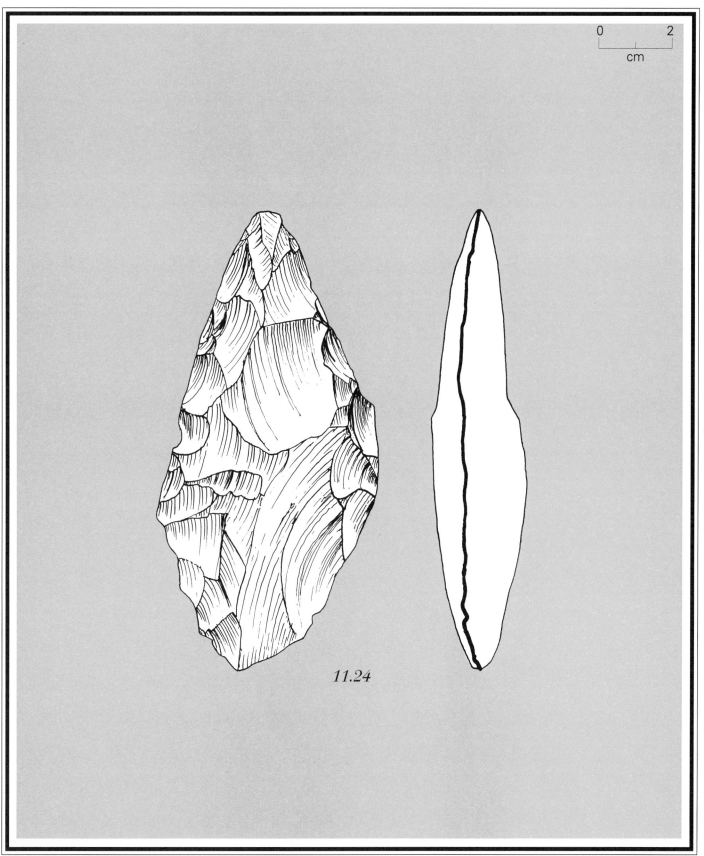

0   2
cm

Chapter
11

11.24

Naviform bifaces (Figure 11.24). This type, which is fairly rare in Europe but more common in Africa, also falls in Zone IV of Figure 11.3. Such bifaces are "elongated and pointed at both ends, with the form of a ship's hull" (Bordes 1961:68). They are thus similar to limandes, except for being pointed instead of rounded, with an Elongation Index greater than 1.5. It is also possible, though very rare, to have **bifaces naviformes à talon**. Also very rare are thick varieties of this shape, which Bordes termed **fusiform bifaces**.

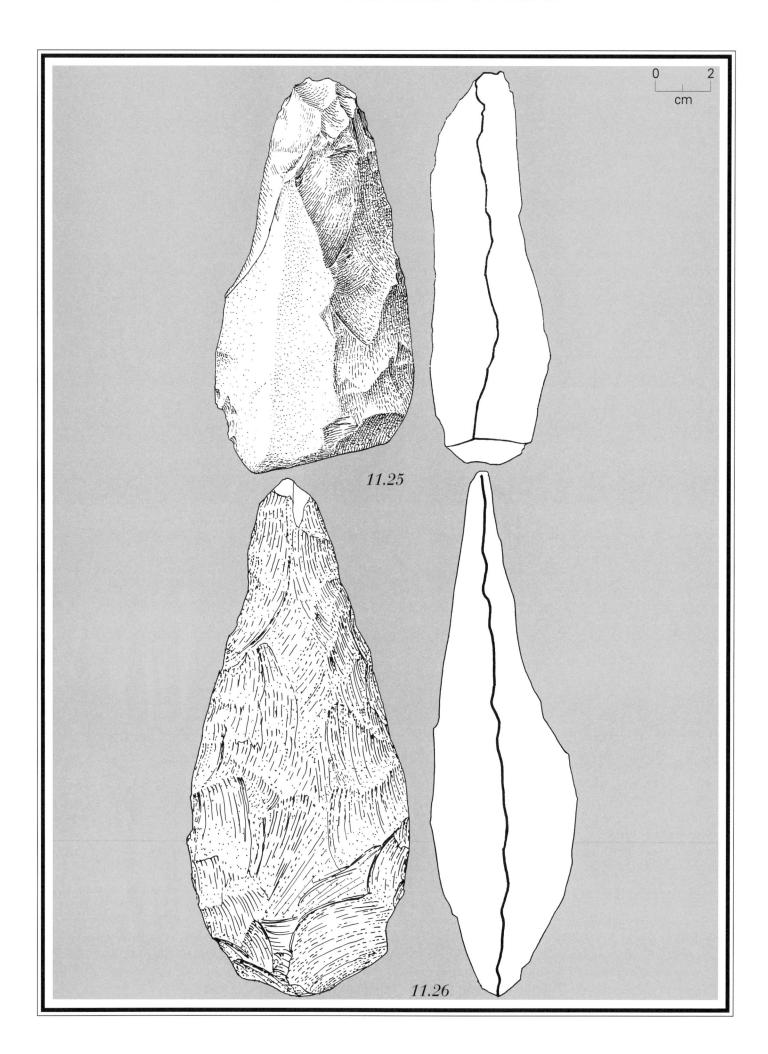

0 2
cm

11.25

11.26

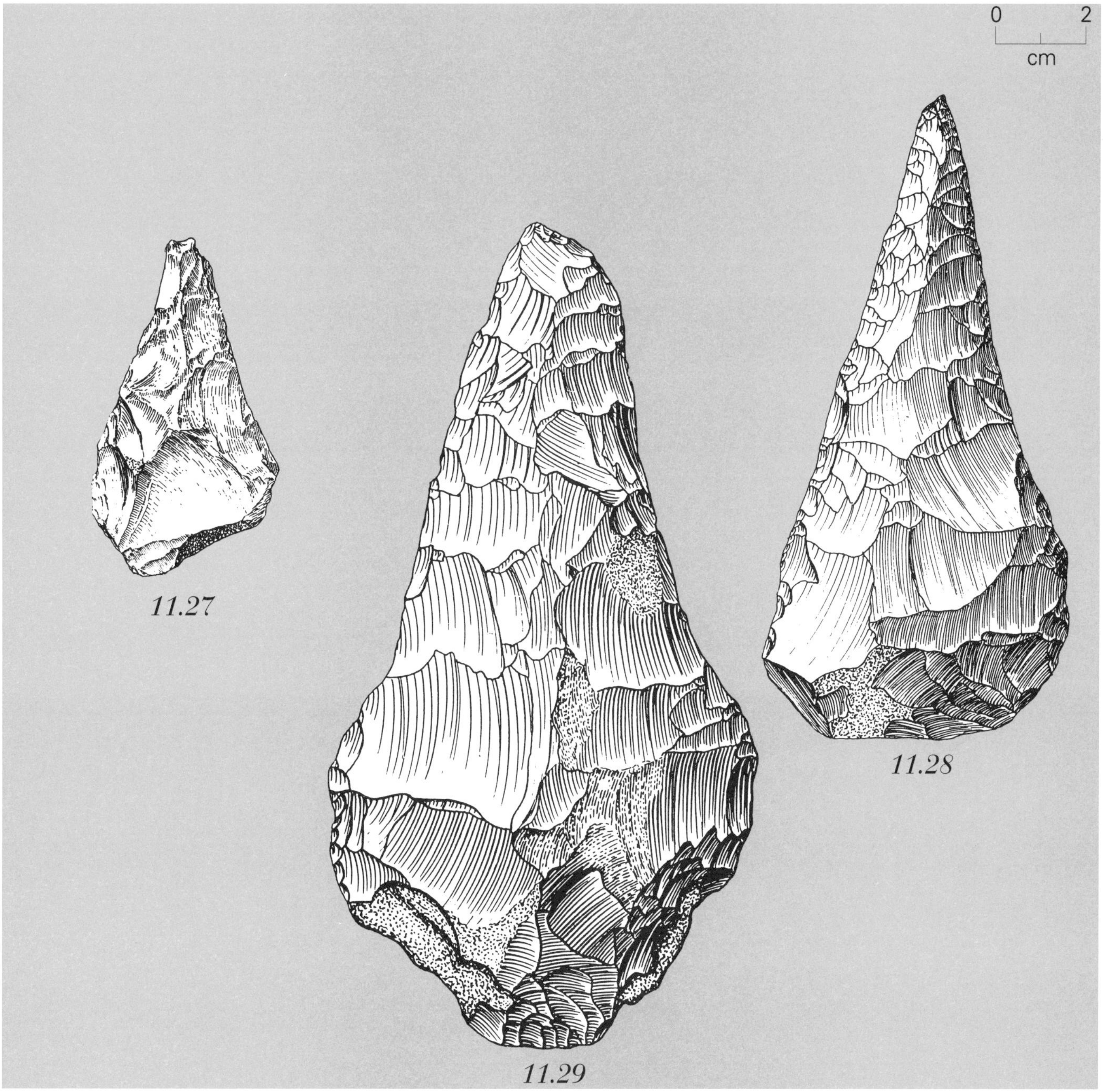

11.27

11.28

11.29

Chapter

11

THICK BIFACES

Thick bifaces (with a Flatness Ratio that is less than 2.35) are separated into three groups: (1) those with a lanceolate ("lance-like") aspect; (2) those with a cordiform aspect (amygdaloids); and (3) those which are pointed at both ends (fusiformes). As described above, the last group just includes the thick naviforms.

BIFACES WITH A LANCEOLATE ASPECT: There are three principal types of lanceolate bifaces, all of which have in common "a thick butt which is sometimes globular and often with some cortex retaining, and a long, slender point" (Bordes 1961:57), making them all generally triangular in form, and usually quite elongated.

Typical lanceolate bifaces (Figures 11.25 and 11.26) have edges that are straight or very slightly convex and a distal point that has a cross-section that is either triangular (more or less like an isosceles triangle) or lenticular. **Naturally-backed lanceolate bifaces** have a distal point which has one or both sides flat, but in these cases the base itself should not be thick.

Typical Micoquian bifaces and **naturally-backed Micoquian bifaces** are differentiated from the lanceolate bifaces only by the concave aspect of their edges (Figures 11.27–11.29).

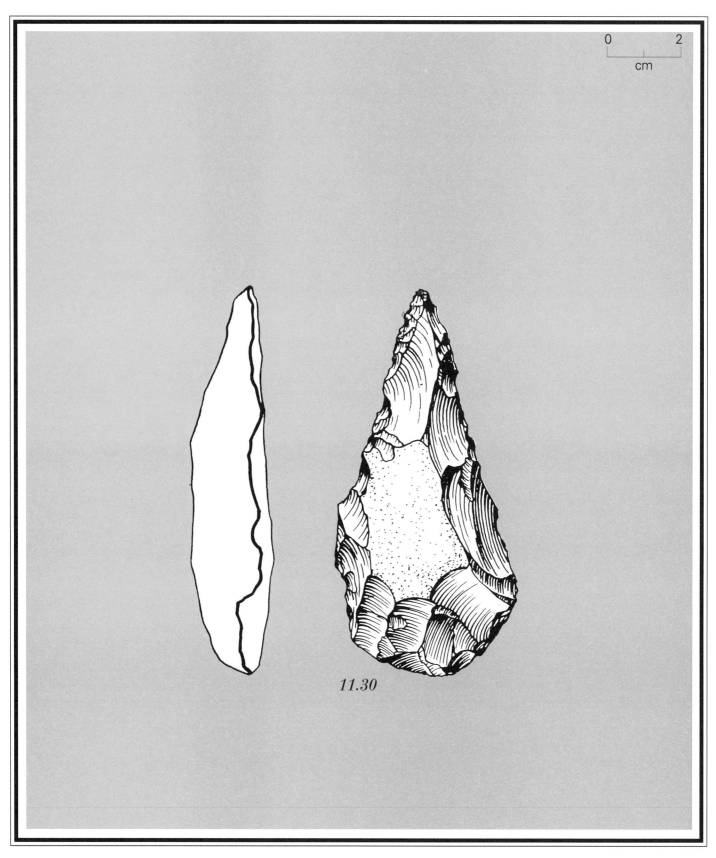

0   2
cm

11.30

Ficrons (Figures 11.30–11.33) "have the same form as typical lanceolate or micoquian bifaces, but the formation of the edges is less careful" (Bordes 1961:58). In other words, ficrons tend to be less well made. **Lanceolate ficrons** have edges that are lightly convex, while **Micoquian ficrons** have lightly concave edges, in plan view. The term *ficron* origi-

nally referred to the iron tip on the end of rafting poles used on canals of the Somme basin (France).

The term *biface lagéniforme* (Figures 11.34 and 11.35) was employed by Bordes for elongated bifaces, with a long and thickish butt, with a distal extremity that has more or less parallel edges, like the neck of a bottle. Typical **lagéniformes** are those

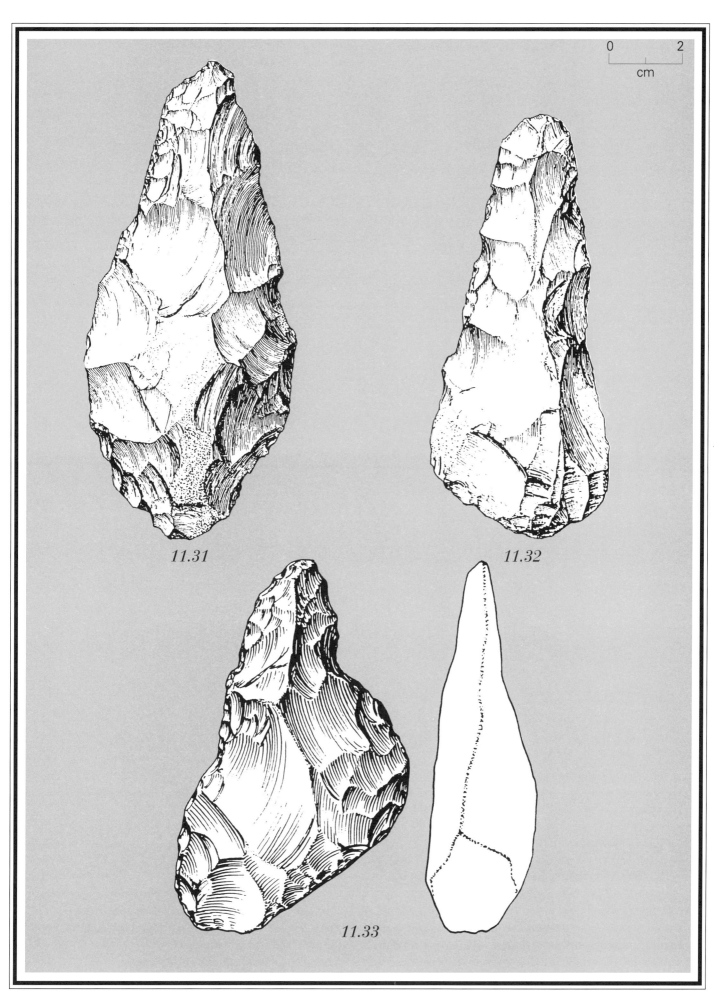

0   2
cm

11.31

11.32

11.33

Chapter
11

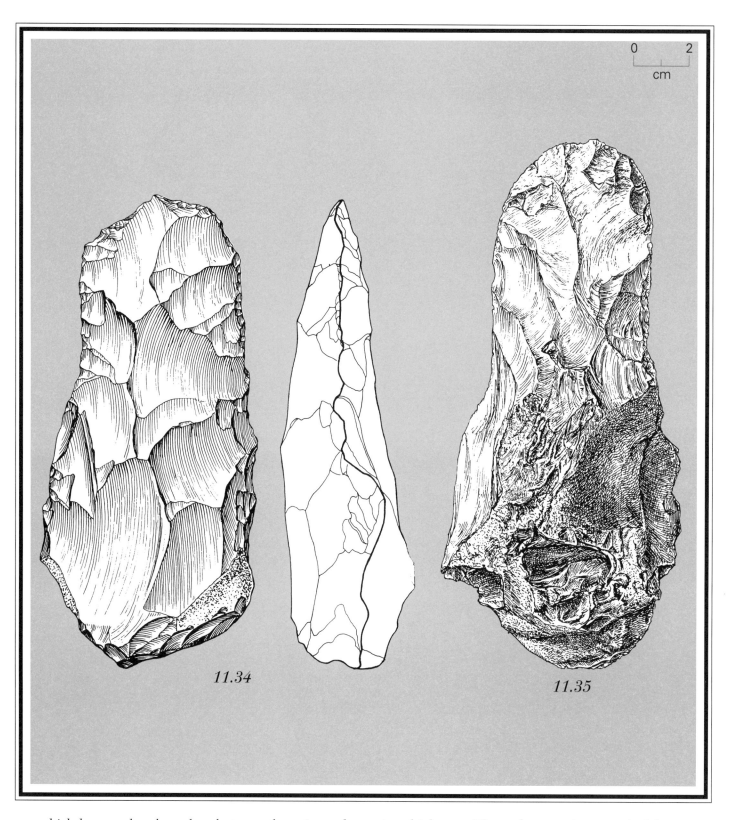

11.34

11.35

which have a clear boundary between the point and the base, while this boundary is less clear for atypical lagéniformes. As remarked by de Heinzelin (1962:44), the distal extremity is lightly rounded and not at all pointed.

BIFACES WITH A CORDIFORM ASPECT: These types, generally referred to as amygdaloid bifaces, are similar in plan form to the cordiform bifaces described earlier but differ from them in terms of their greater relative thickness. They often retain a cortical base. Bordes (1961) distinguished between **typical amygdaloids** (Figures 11.36 and 11.37) and **amygdaloides à talon** (Figures 11.38 and 11.39) depending on whether or not the edge of the base is sharp. In either case, both types have an Elongation Index greater than 1.5, while **short typical amygdaloids** or **short amygdaloids à talon** have an index that is less than 1.5.

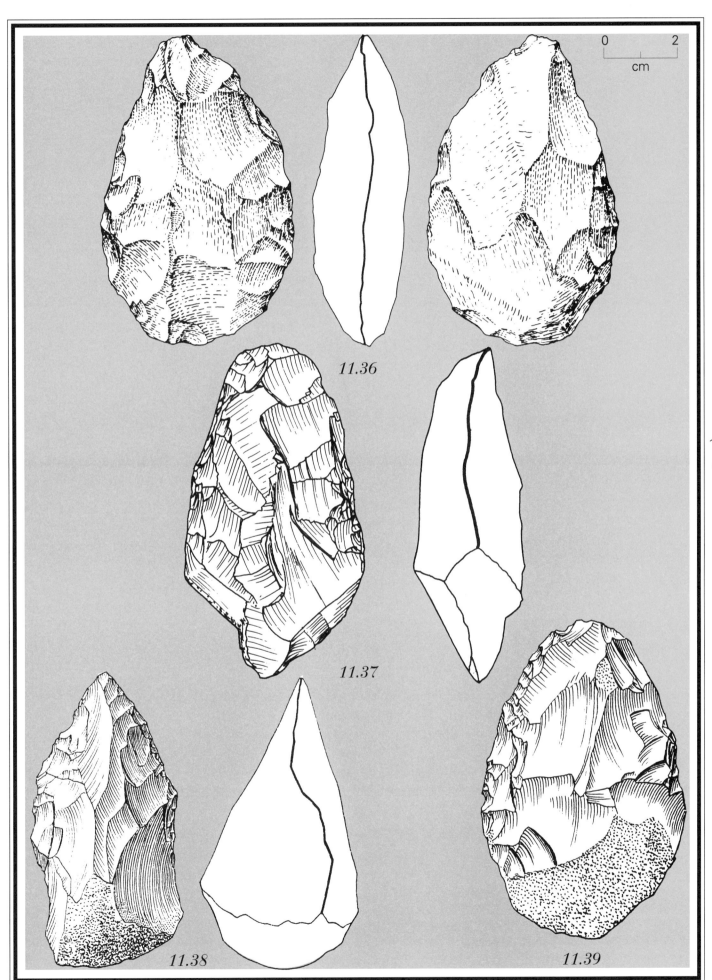

0
2
cm

11.36

Chapter
11

11.37

11.38

11.39

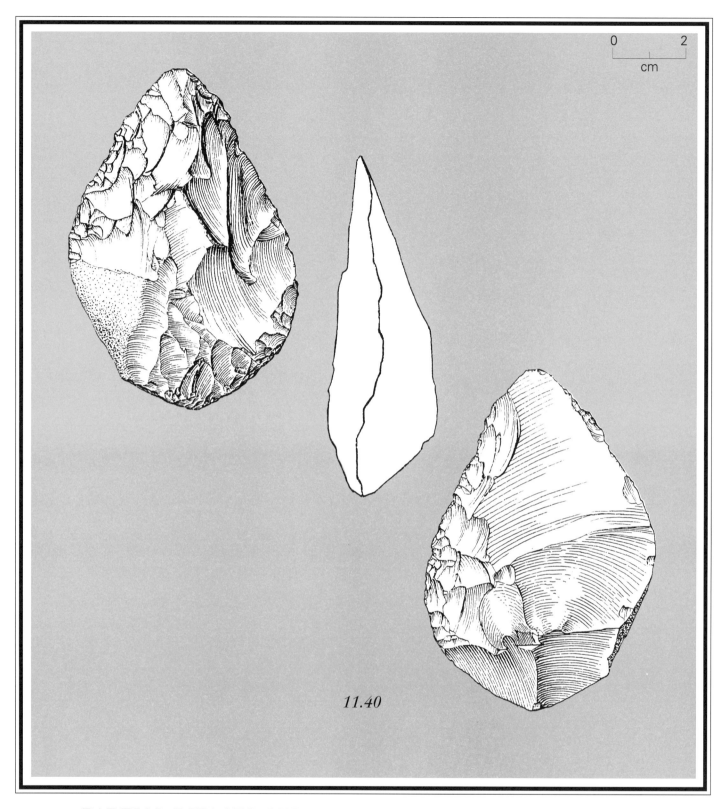

0   2
cm

11.40

PARTIAL BIFACES AND BIFACES WITH UNRETOUCHED BASES

Partial bifaces are not broken or fragmentary bifaces, but rather bifaces that have significant unretouched areas on one or both of their surfaces. They are often found on flakes and, in fact, there are examples of these where the former interior of the flake is completely devoid of retouch, but the exteri-

or face is retouched completely (after the removal of the flake blank itself, of course) as in other bifaces. Such **unifaces** are also called **unifacial bifaces** or **pseudo-bifaces** by Ulrix-Closset (1975). What separates unifaces made on flakes from other flake tools is that, in the former, the flaking covers one of the flake surfaces almost entirely and the shape is modified into a classifiable form, such as a partial cordiform (Figure 11.40), partial triangular, etc.

Related to partial bifaces are pieces whose

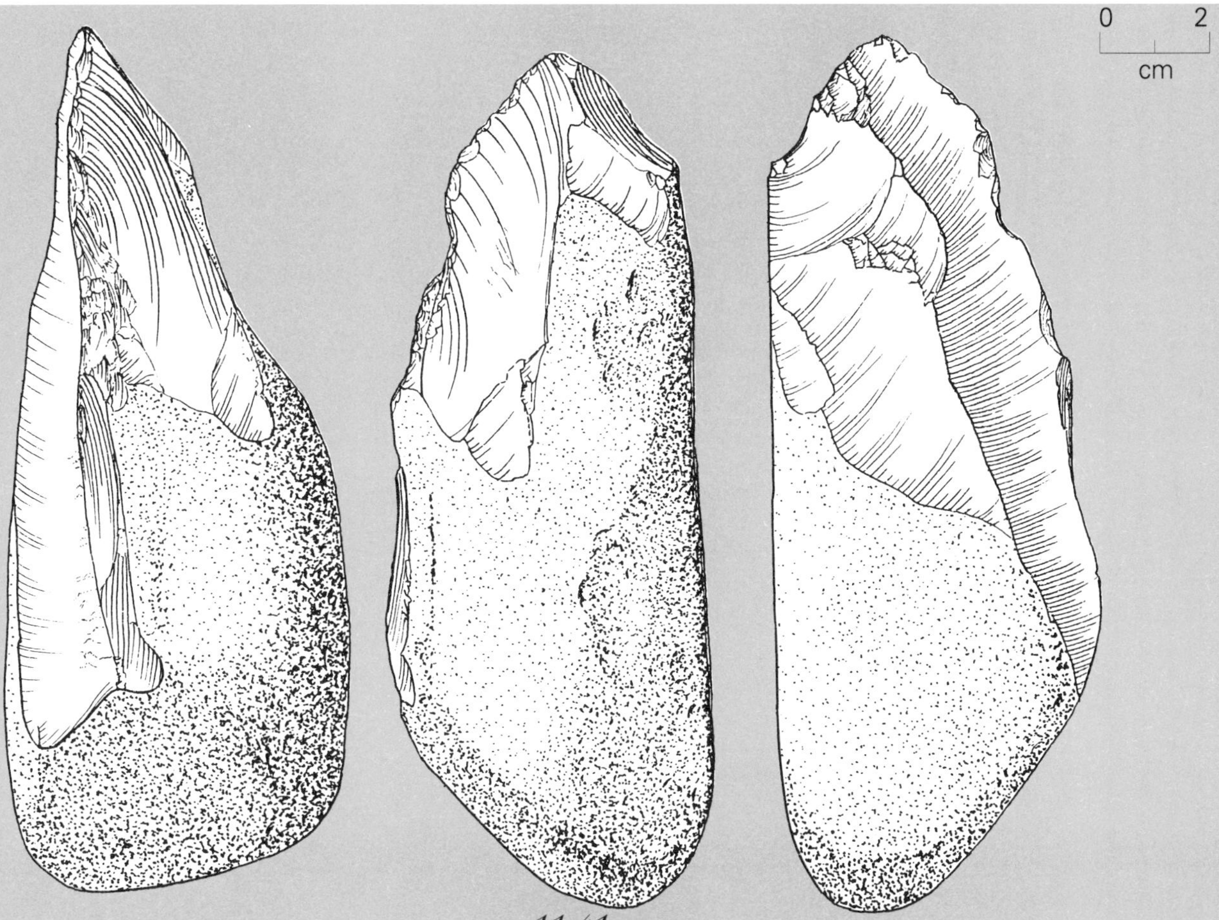

11.41

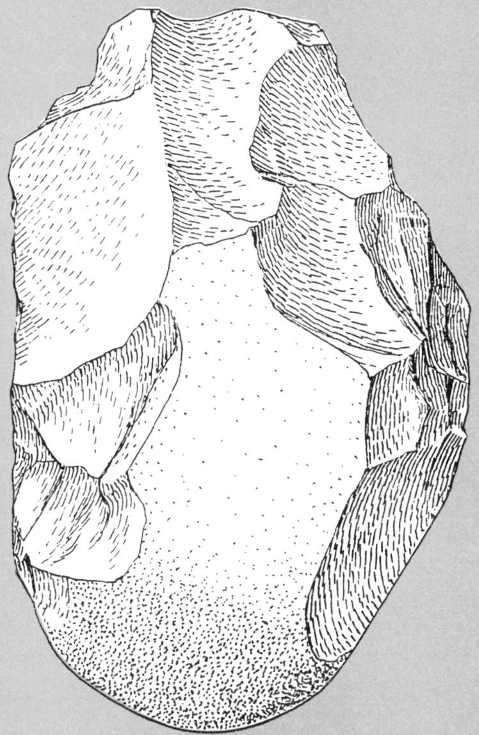

11.42

entire proximal end is left completely unretouched (in comparison to the other types, which may have small areas of cortex remaining). Such **bifaces à talon réservé** (Figures 11.41 and 11.42) can be of variable dimensions and shapes without their classification being affected.

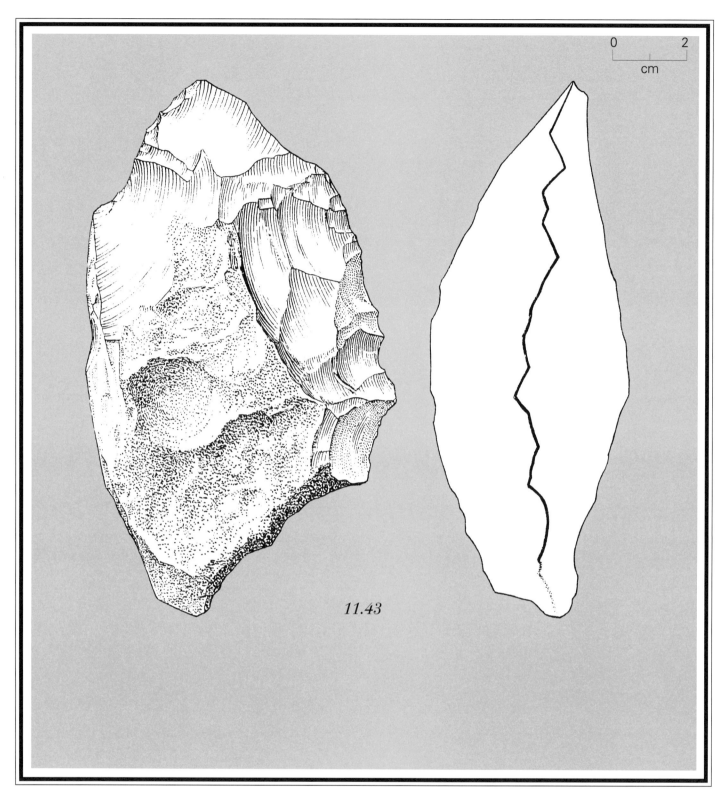

11.43

ABBEVILLIAN BIFACES

Known to earlier prehistorians as Chellean handaxes, **abbevillian bifaces** have an air of being very primitive (Figure 11.43). They are thick, with sinuous or S-shaped edges (as viewed from the side), and they have tips that are markedly triangular or even rectangular in section. In general, they appear to have been manufactured with direct, hard-hammer percussion. Their overall form is not highly pat-

terned, and often a significant area of the base is left cortical or only summarily modified. They are very core-like and often grade into core-like bifaces (see below), or even cores.

This type of biface is not particularly well named since it is not a unequivocal index fossil for the Abbevillian period (which itself has not yet been defined in terms of its overall typological or technological characteristics). As Bordes (1961) points out, this type can also be found in Late Acheulian and even Mousterian contexts.

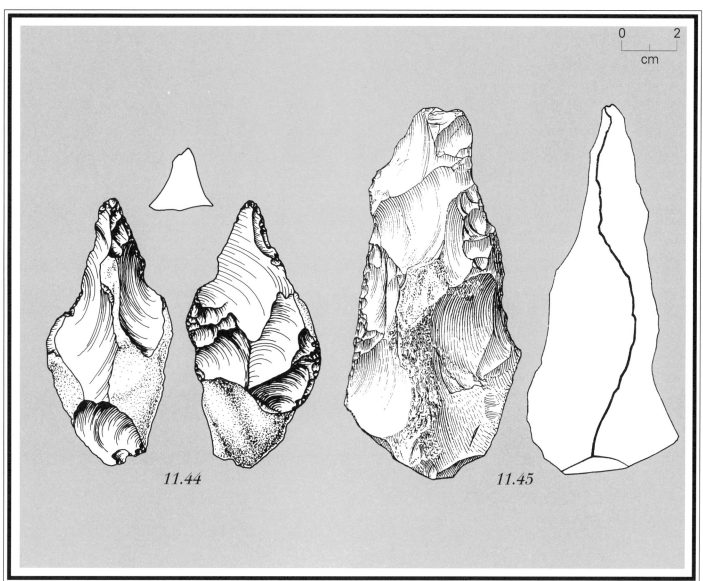

0   2
cm

11.44   *11.45*

Chapter
11

OTHER TYPES OF BIFACES

Besides the "classic" handaxe forms described above, one finds many other varieties in various European Paleolithic contexts.

PICS: Pics were first described at the end of the last century, for Neolithic flint mines, and were only later recognized in Paleolithic contexts. For Bordes (1961:69), they are typically "very elongated bifaces, with a thick section that is more or less quadrangular, or sometimes triangular." It is thus the cross-section form that is most characteristic of these pieces (Figures 11.44 and 11.45). Tavoso (1978:28) refers to pics as unifaces with a trihedral point, of which the triangular section is obtained by the flaking of an angular pebble (or flake) from two faces. This definition is somewhat ambiguous since, because two of three sides of the pebble are retouched, it is difficult to consider this kind of tool as a uniface, and it can easily create confusion with

pointes de Quinson (see Chapter 5).

A triangular-formed pic termed the **Chalossian pic** (Figure 11.46) was for some time considered characteristic of the Chalossian industry of southwest France (Thibault 1970), though the distinction of this particular industry is in doubt. Although this type may show some development in the Middle Acheulian of the Pyrenean region of France, these forms cover a broad chronological range.

CENTRAL AND EASTERN EUROPEAN FORMS: There are many forms of bifaces that are specific to the Central and Eastern European "Micoquian" industries (Bosinski 1967). One of these is the **Micoquekeile** type (Figures 11.47–11.50). As their name suggests, these forms resemble the classic Micoquian types, but often exhibit one lateral edge that is preferentially retouched giving rise to a general asymmetry in their plan form. The base is often either unworked (Figures 11.48 and 11.49) or crudely worked, and so is often left blunt.

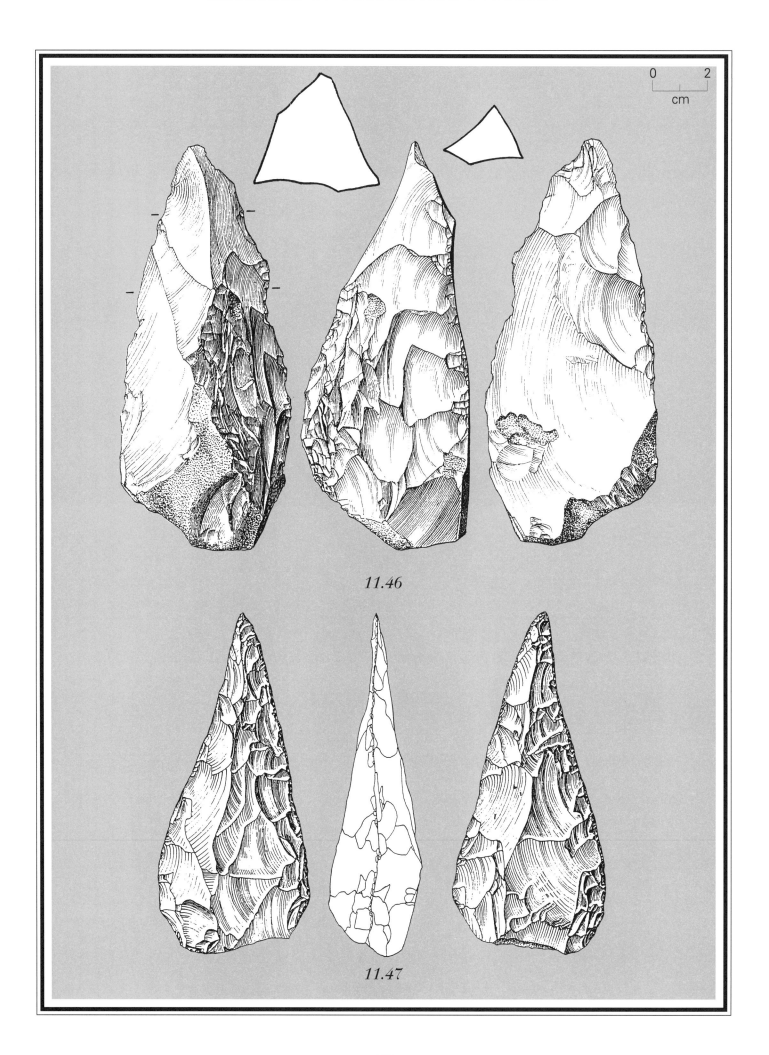

11.46

11.47

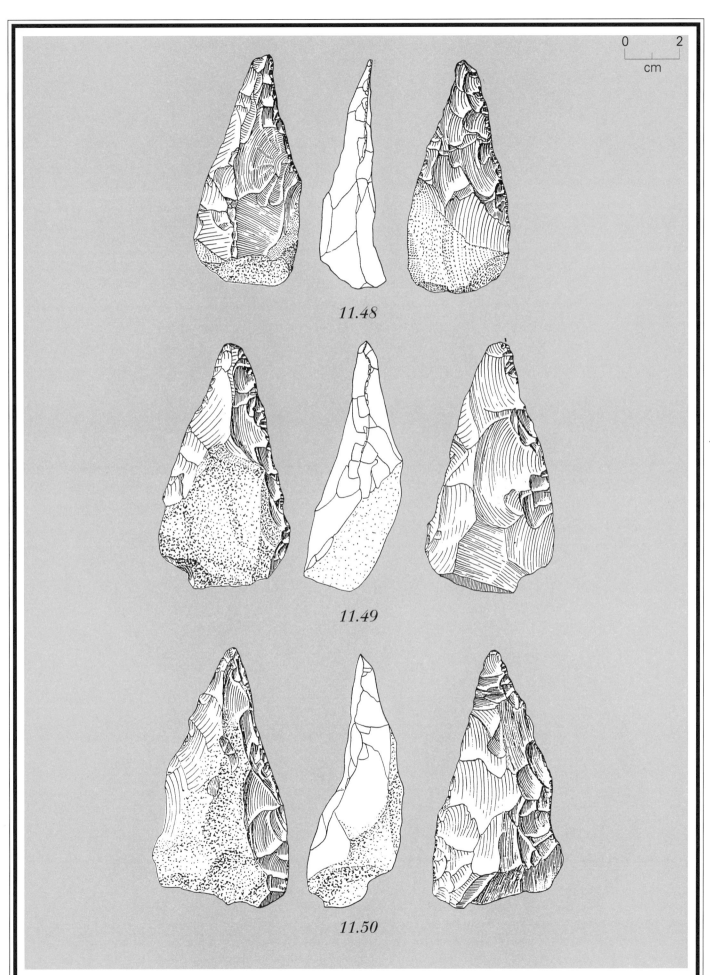

0   2
cm

11.48

11.49

11.50

Chapter
11

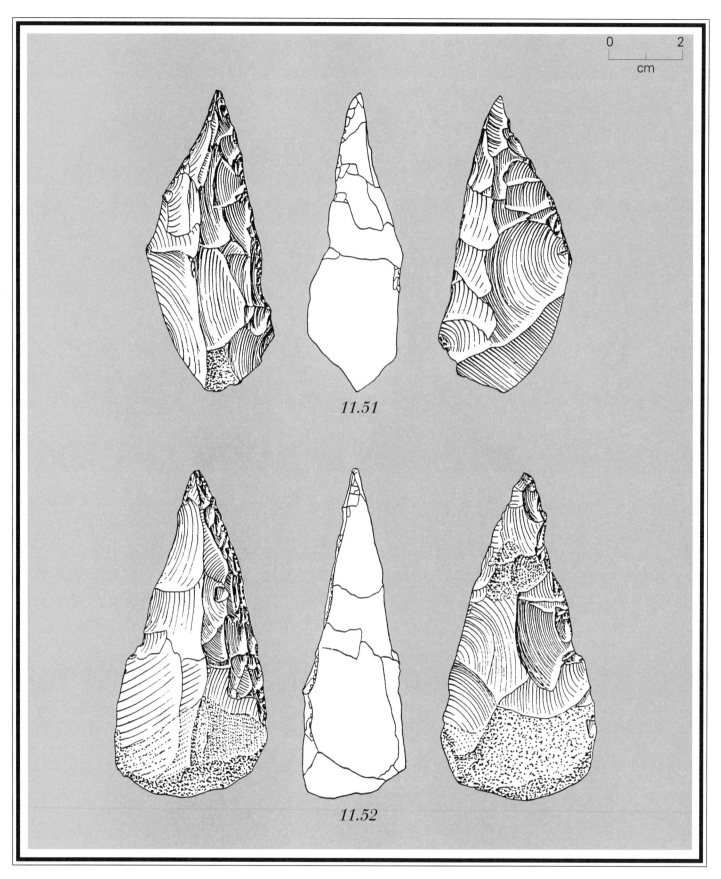

0   2
cm

11.51

11.52

There are also a number of types that occur here which are collectively termed **backed bifaces**, or **scraper bifaces**, though it is important not to confuse these with scrapers with bifacial retouch (type 28—see Chapter 6) or with pointes de Quinson (see Chapter 5). The first of these is the **Halbkeile** (Figures 11.51–11.54). Their flat, or sometimes concave ventral face is only roughly worked, while the opposite face is vaulted. The distal points and lateral edges are retouched, though one edge is usually preferentially treated. The base is either left cortical or only minimally retouched.

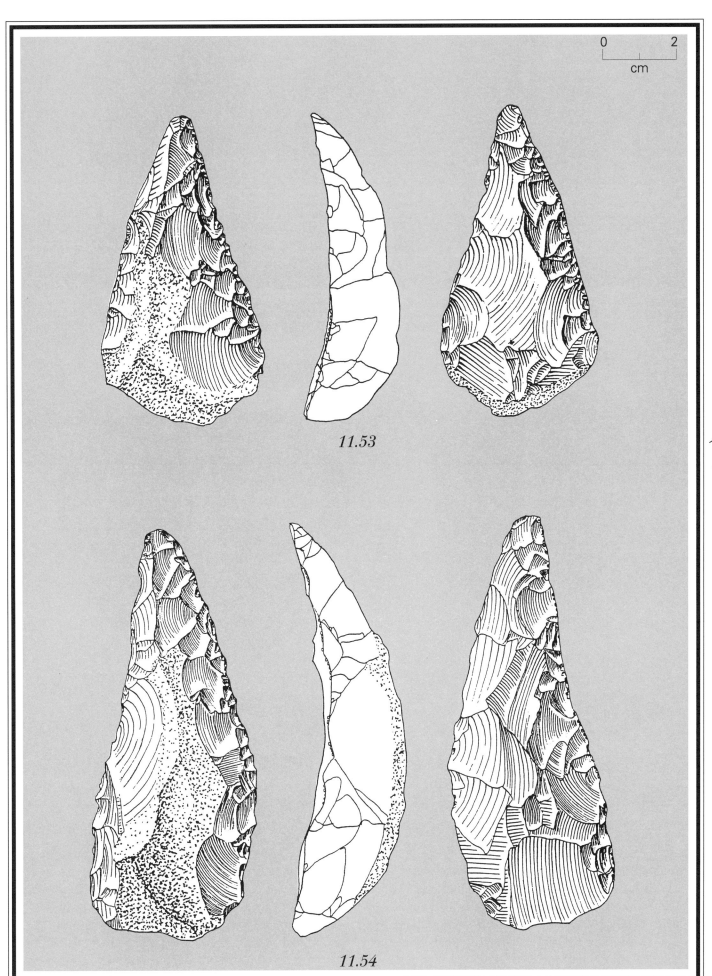

0   2
cm

11.53

11.54

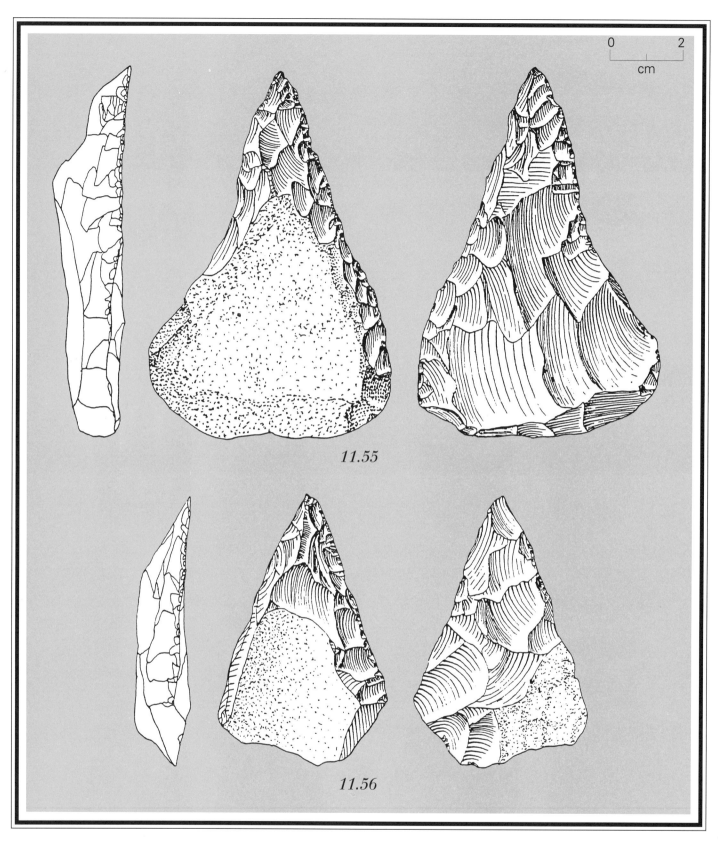

11.55

11.56

Faustkeilblätter (Figures 11.55–11.60) are thin and markedly flat in section. The point is generally well made while the base is, again, blunt and usually unworked. One of the faces is completely worked over the entire surface and is generally quite flat. Retouch on the opposite face is often confined to the distal point and the lateral edges. There are several subtypes, including the **large** (*breite*) (Figures 11.55 and 11.56) and **narrow** (*schmale*) *Faustkeilblätter* (Figures 11.57 and 11.58), the latter of which sometimes exhibit marked longitudinal asymmetry. There are also **small** and **asymmetric** (*kleine, asymmetrische*) *Faustkeilblätter* (Figures 11.59 and 11.60), whose distal points often resemble leaf points (type 63—see Chapter 9) but whose bases are oblique.

11.57

11.59

11.60

11.58

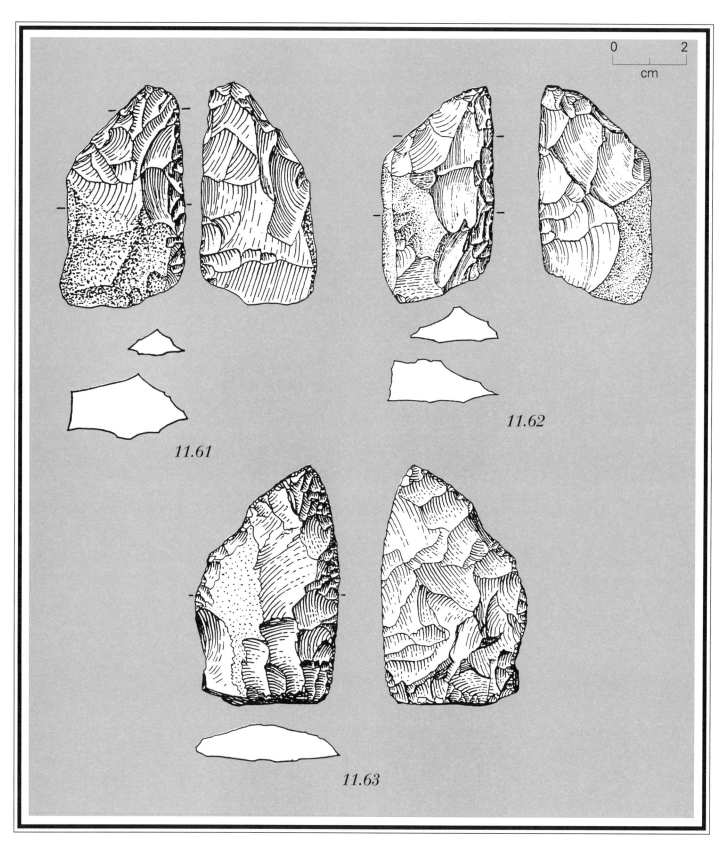

0   2
cm

11.61

11.62

11.63

Keilmesser (Figures 11.61–11.66) represent another class of backed bifaces which have only one well-retouched straight lateral edge opposite a blunt or backed edge (which can be either straight, convex, or concave). They are typically wedge-shaped in cross section. The **Klausennische** subtype (Figures 11.61–11.63) exhibit a backed (or naturally blunt) edge that is roughly parallel to the retouched work-

ing edge, while the distal end is more oblique to the axis of the piece and retouched in a manner similar to the straight lateral working edge. They are thus reminiscent of déjeté scrapers (type 21—see Chapter 6), except that they are bifacially worked. Another important subtype is the **Bocksteinmesser** (Figures 11.64–11.66), which has a straight backing that extends to the distal extremity.

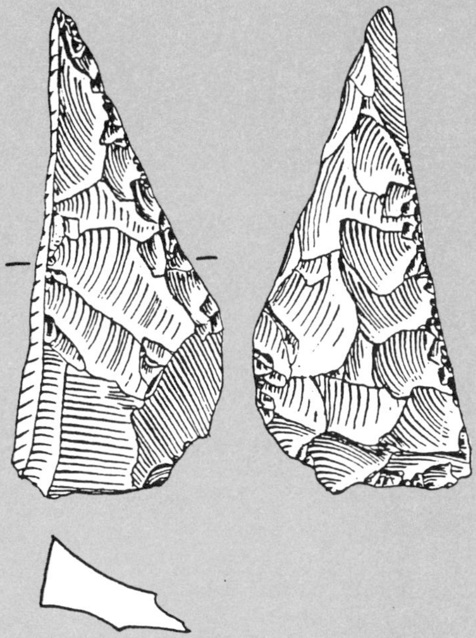

0 2
cm

11.64

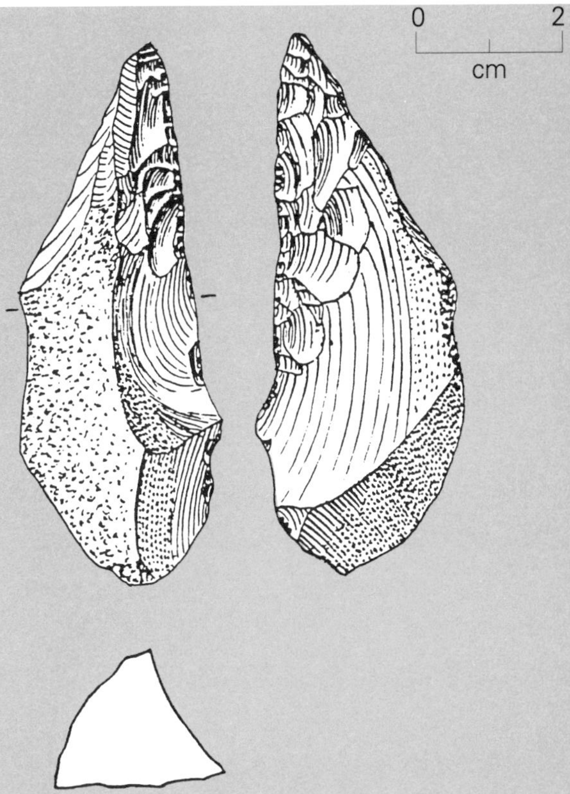

11.65

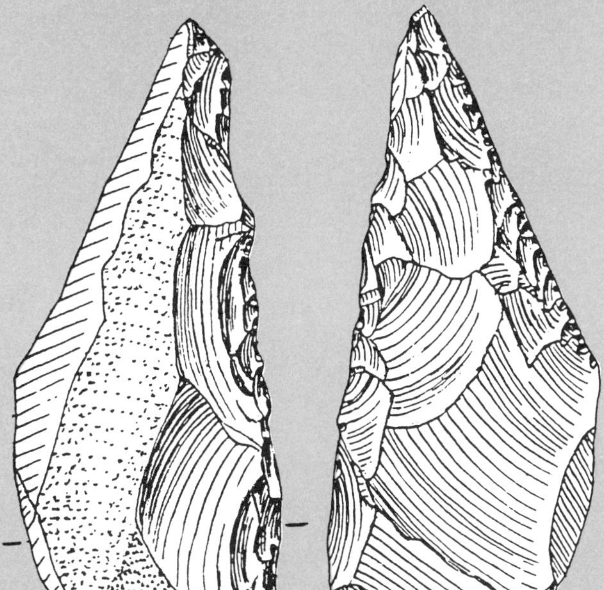

11.66

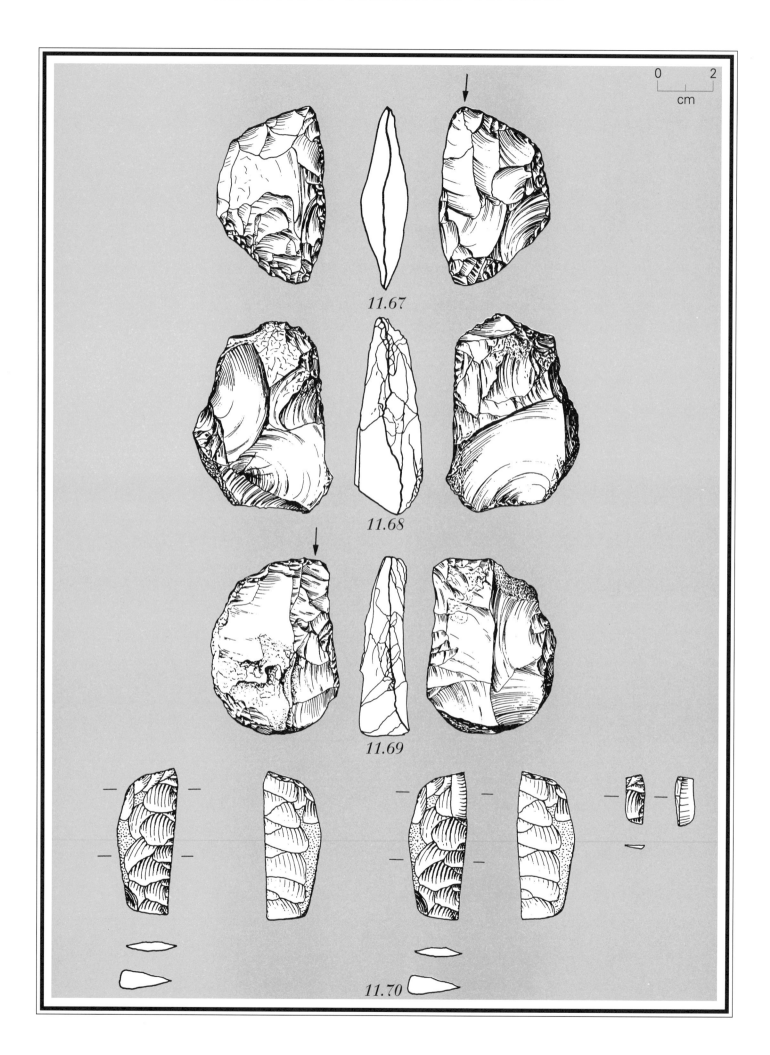

11.67

11.68

11.69

11.70

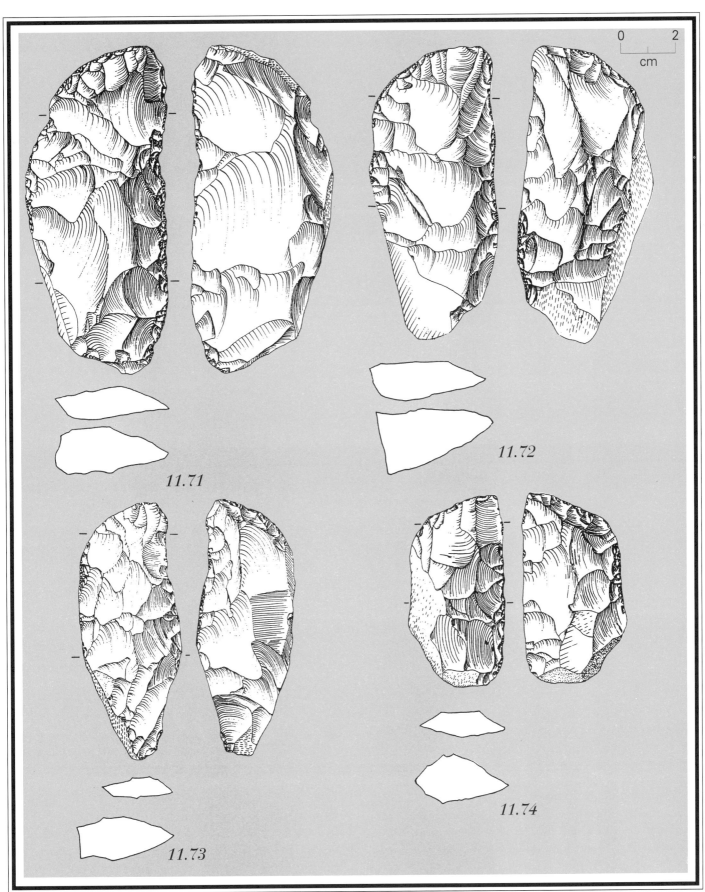

0   2
cm

11.71

11.72

Chapter

11

11.73

11.74

Prondniks (Figures 11.67–11.78). *Prondniks* (or *Pradnik messer* in German) were first recognized by Krukowski (1924) in Poland. Chmielewski (1969) was the first to formally define them, as hav- ing a flat bifacial retouch, which is sometimes partial if the piece is on a flake blank. For him, prondniks exhibit one lateral margin that is straight (or rarely slightly concave), a slightly convex tip, and a lateral

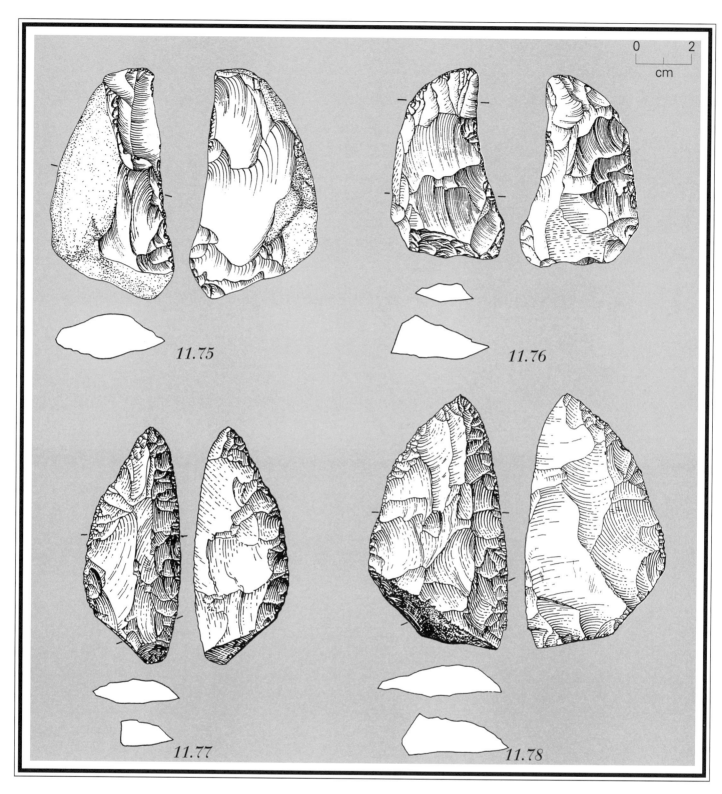

11.75

11.76

11.77

11.78

tranchet that originates from the distal end. The opposite edge is most often convex and thick (Figures 11.67–11.69), attaining its maximum thickness at about the middle or proximal two-thirds of the piece. In plan form, prondniks are generally D-shaped, with a base that is usually large and often cortical (Figure 11.69). However, Desbrosse et al. (1976) note that, as a group, prondniks are quite variable and that they may or may not be made on flakes and may or may not exhibit the lateral tranchet blow. Bosinski (1967) considers them gen-

erally under the subtype *Keilmesser*, and notes that the working edge may exhibit repeated resharpening through the use of the tranchet "prondnik technique" (Figure 11.70), which is reminiscent of the use of tranchet blows to retouch unifacial scrapers at La Cotte de St. Brelade (Callow and Cornford 1986). He does distinguish a special form, the **Königsaue A** type of Keilmesser (Figures 11.77 and 11.78), which is characterized by a small backing in the proximal one-third of the piece, while the distal end resembles a leaf point.

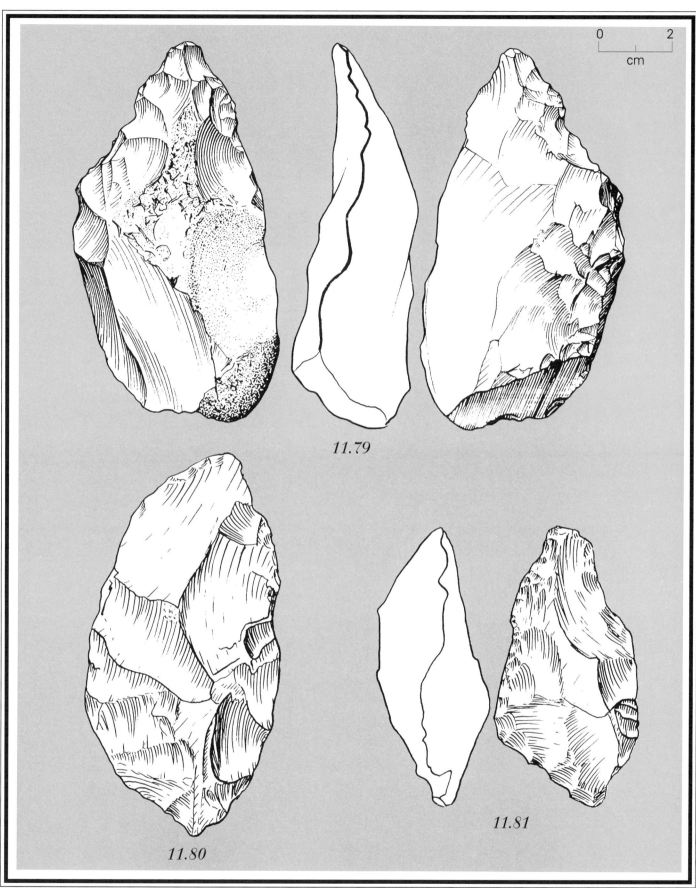

0 ——— 2
cm

11.79

Chapter

11

11.80

11.81

BERGERAC FORMS: In the Perigord region of France, around the modern city of Bergerac, a number of particular biface types have been defined by Guichard (1965, 1976). Bifaces of the type **Les** **Pendus** (Figures 11.79–11.81) are relatively long, with subparallel edges, a base that is either unworked or slightly rounded, and a twisted profile.

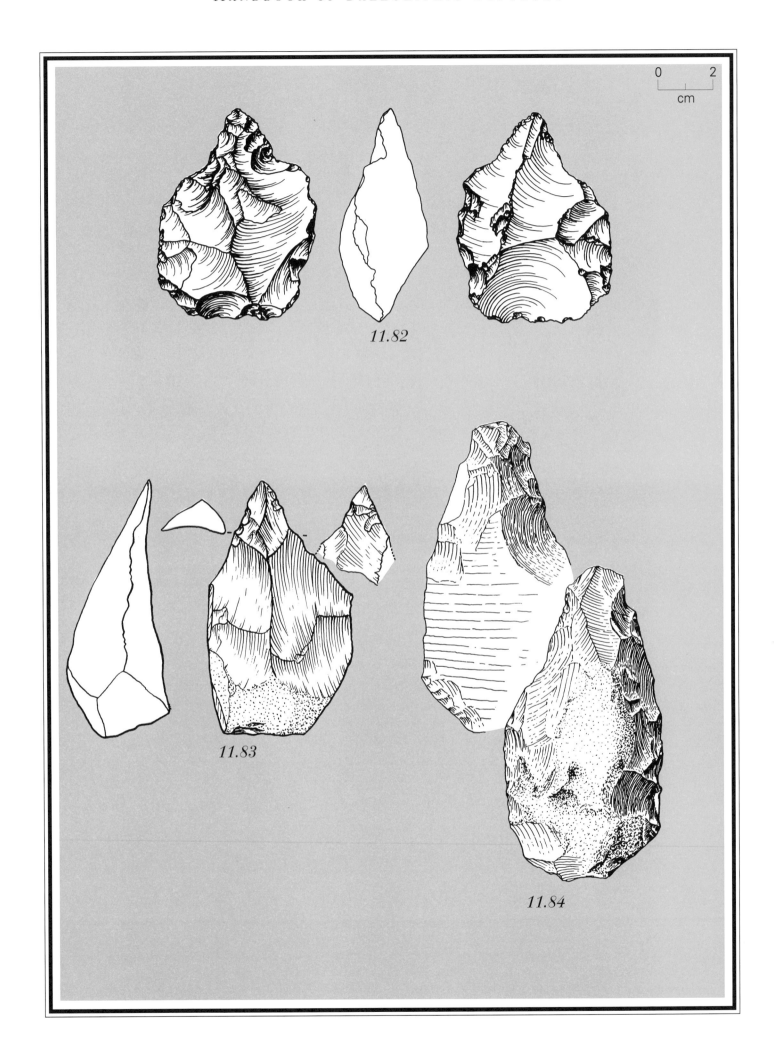

11.82

11.83

11.84

11.85

Chapter

11

Bifaces à rostre aplati (Figures 11.82 and 11.83) are partial bifaces with dorsal surfaces worked by large, flat flake removals that are more or less convergent and which isolate or form a wide-angle point. The contour of the base of these forms is globular and more or less convex. **Carinated bifaces** (Figure 11.84) are described by Guichard as having a partial contour which in plan view describes the "hull of a ship." The dorsal surface is strongly convex while the ventral surface is clearly concave, which, according to Guichard, thins the cutting edge. Bifaces of the type **Cantalouette** (Figure 11.85) have more or less a lanceolate form, but with a longitudinal profile that is clearly curved, resulting in a ventral face that is strongly concave.

CLEAVER-LIKE BIFACES: Some totally or partially bifacially-worked implements exhibit a thin, transverse cutting edge at the distal end, analogous to a cleaver edge. This cutting edge, which is made by intentional unifacial or bifacial retouching, is usually straight, but can be somewhat convex, concave, or twisted. Varieties of such pieces have been called many names, including **cleaver-biface** (Bordes 1961:63), **biface-cleaver** (Guichard and Guichard 1966; Guichard 1976:919), **biface à biseau oblique**, or **biface à biseau transversal** (Gruet 1945), **biface à biseau terminal** (Chavaillon 1964), **biface à bout droit** (de Heinzelin 1962), **biface à bout tranchant** (Leroi-Gourhan 1964), and more recently, **biface à bout coupé** (Roe 1968; Mellars 1974; Tyldesley 1987). Generally, such pieces are symmetrical and often thick (with the exception of typical *bout coupé* bifaces, which are thin).

In order to reduce the multiplicity of names, we would suggest (following Guichard and Guichard

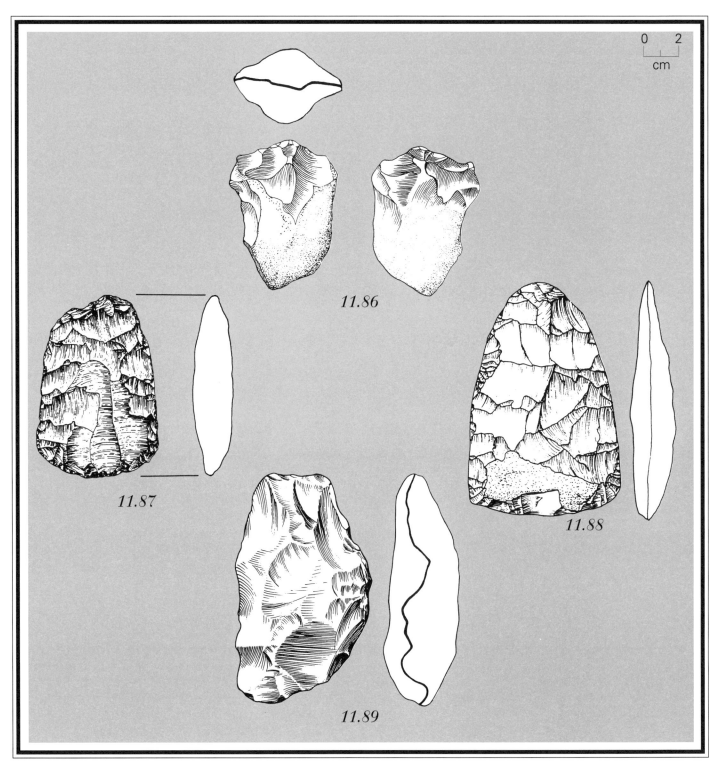

0 2
cm

11.86

11.87

11.88

11.89

1966) that the major distinction among most of these types be made on the basis of the *technique* used for producing the distal cutting edge, and not on its shape (cf. Tavoso 1978:25). For those cleaver-like objects whose distal cutting edge is produced by multiple flake scars (whether bifacial or unifacial and from whatever directions) we suggest that the term **beveled biface** be applied (Figures 11.86 and 11.89). The term **biface cleaver** should be used only for those forms whose distal cutting edge is produced by a lateral tranchet blow that extends across the surface at the tip, thus leaving a sharp cutting

edge (Figures 11.90–11.93). If the transverse edge of the piece is not retouched, that is, if it is made on a flake whose distal end is left unworked (but not cortical), then it should be regarded as a cleaver (what is sometimes referred to as a **flake cleaver**), regardless of the presence of other retouch around the proximal and lateral peripheries (see below). It could be that the distinction of the *bout coupé* type (Figures 11.87 and 11.88) should be retained because of its distinct form and refinement of flaking, and because of its restricted distribution in

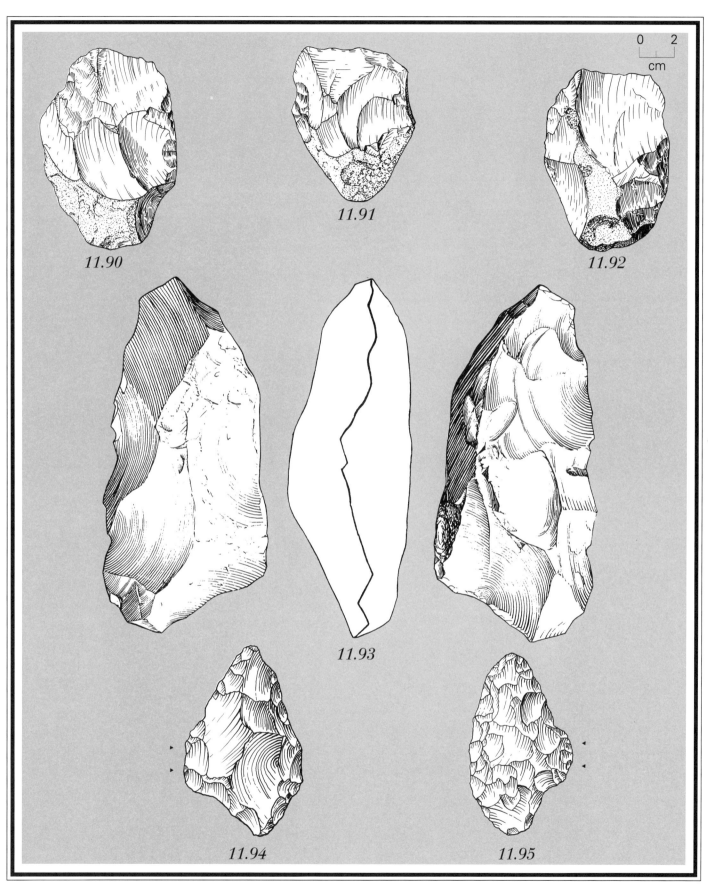

11.90

11.91

11.92

11.93

11.94

11.95

Chapter

11

space (southeast England) and industrial affiliation (Mousterian). On the other hand, many of the examples of this type could be subsumed under existing types, such as cordiforms or beveled bifaces as defined here (see Tyldesley 1987).

BIFACES À GIBBOSITÉ: We propose to use the term **bifaces à gibbosité** (i.e., with a protuberance: Figures 11.94 and 11.95) for bifaces of various plan forms but which have a deliberately shaped protuberance on one edge.

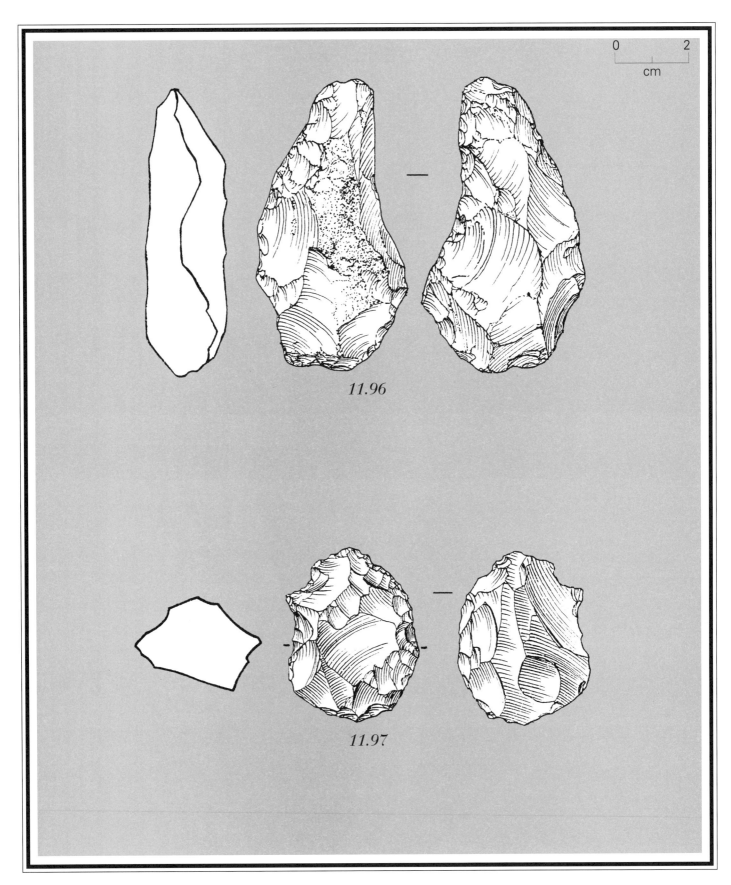

0   2
cm

11.96

11.97

CORE-LIKE BIFACES: As noted by Brézillon (1968), a major problem in defining this type is that their only common characteristic is the difficulty they present to typologists trying to differentiate them from cores. The only criterion which allows one to make a distinction is that the **core-like bifaces** have an edge which "seems to have been functional" (de Heinzelin 1962), while cores do not. Two examples of core-like bifaces are shown in Figures 11.96 and 11.97). Whether or not these edges were actually used remains an open question.

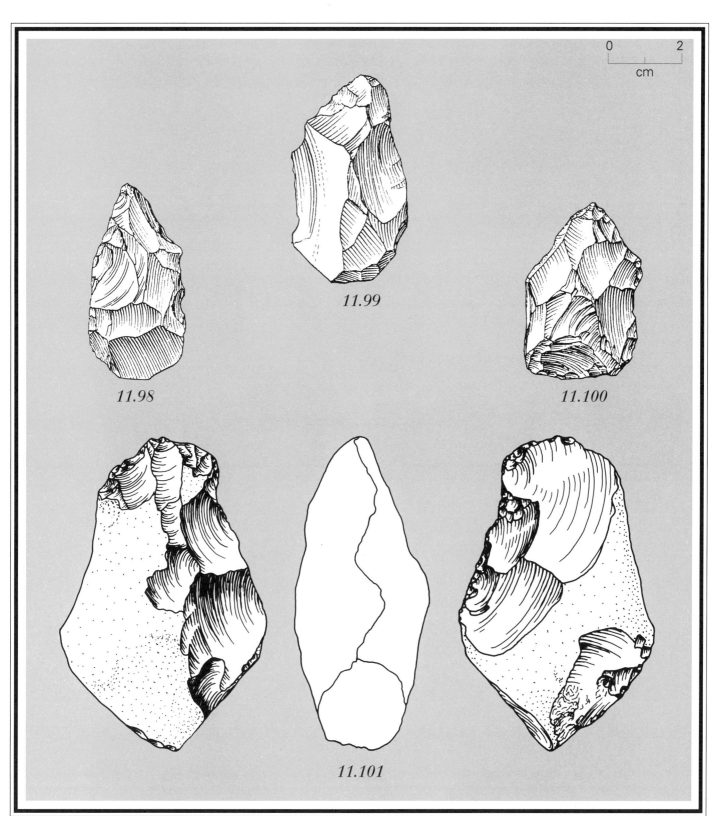

0   2
cm

11.99

11.98

11.100

Chapter

11

11.101

MISCELLANEOUS: Finally, there are some bifaces which simply cannot be placed into a well-defined typological category, and so they should be put into the category of "miscellaneous" (see Figures 11.98–11.101). Although by definition such bifaces have few characteristics in common, they are, in general, often rather large and thick, and often only partially worked, what Ulrix-Closset (1975) refers to as "degenerated bifaces." Often they come from assemblages that are relatively poor in handaxes, such as the "Tayacian" or Quina-type Mousterian. Bordes (1961:68) also included in this category some forms that are well shaped, but which are found only rarely, such as square bifaces, biface-borers, etc. Note, however, that a partial biface that is classifiable into a recognized form should be typed as such (e.g., the partial cordiform shown in Figure 11.40.

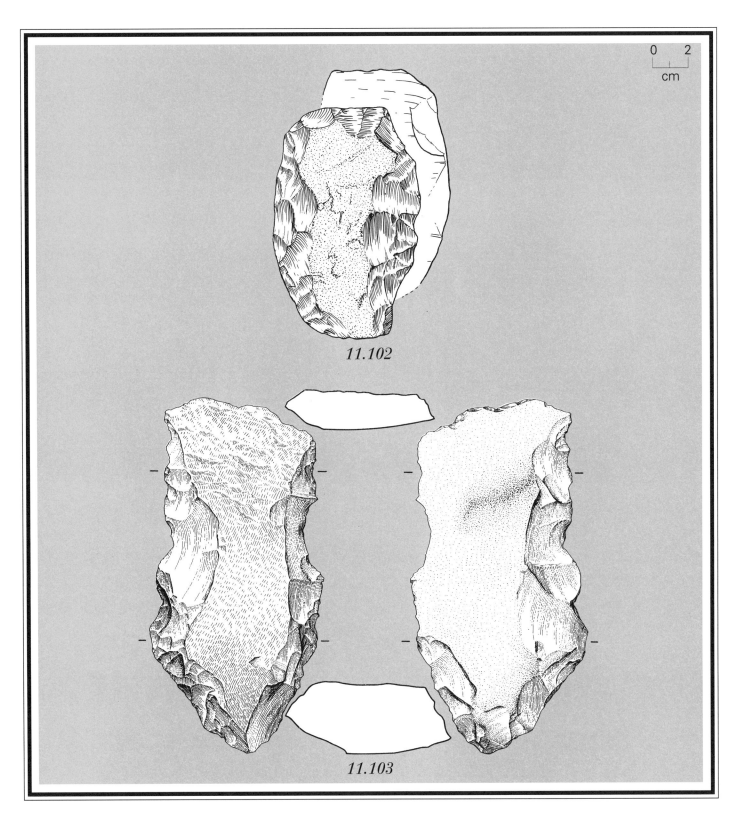

0 2
cm

11.102

11.103

CLEAVERS

For a long time **cleavers** (Figures 11.102–11.107) were regarded as a specifically African form. In North Africa, for example, they are frequently found in the oldest industries of Algeria and continue until the Upper Acheulian of Morocco, the Sahara, and Central Africa. They are found in Lower Paleolithic industries in Europe as well, however, particularly in the southwest. But there they are limited to the Upper Acheulian and Mousterian and thus they do not appear to be strictly contemporaneous with the African forms.

For Tixier (1956:916), cleavers are tools made on flakes that have an unworked distal cutting edge that is the original distal edge of the flake. While some cleavers present some bifacial retouch on other edges (Figures 11.103 and 11.106), such retouch should not occur on the distal cutting edge. For Biberson (1954), as for Bordes (1961) and Guichard

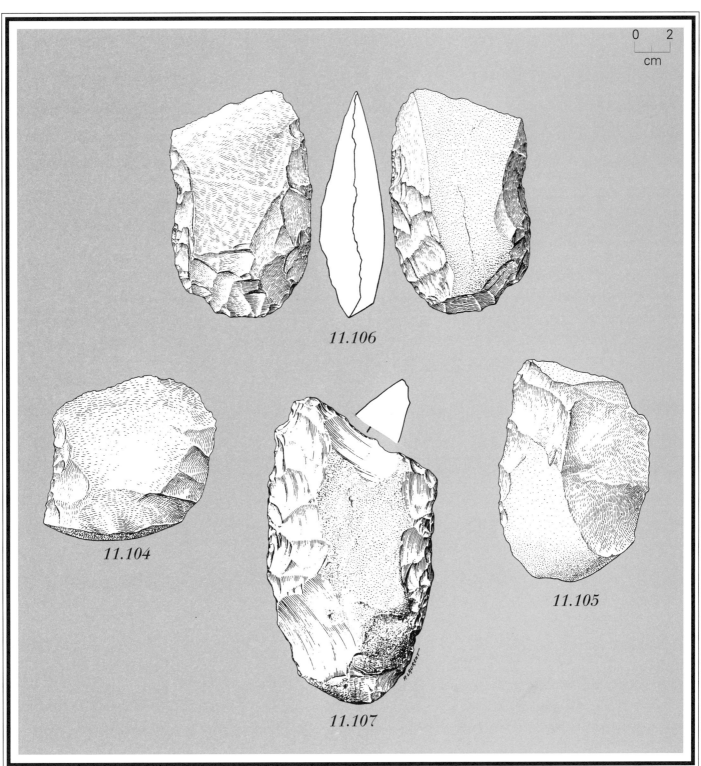

0 2
cm

11.106

11.104

11.105

11.107

Chapter

11

and Guichard (1966), cleavers can be either unifacial (i.e., cleavers on flakes) or bifacial, except for the distal cutting edge. Of course, bifacial cleavers should not be confused with chopping-tools (type 61—see Chapter 10), beveled bifaces, or biface cleavers (see above), all of which are bifacially worked at the tip. For Chavaillon (1964), cleaver classification is based on their relative thickness (i.e., the ratio of maximum width to thickness, following the same dimensions presented by Bordes [see above]), with a series of morphological subtypes

then defined for thick and flat cleavers.

Based on their work in the Bergerac region of France, Guichard and Guichard (1966) propose a more detailed classification of cleavers which includes fourteen types. These are distinguished on the basis of different kinds of retouch on the edges and the morphology of the lateral chisel edges thus formed. Tixier (1956) also distinguishes six types of cleavers, based essentially on technological criteria. These latter types are relevant primarily to African material, however, and so do not concern us here.

APPENDIX
I

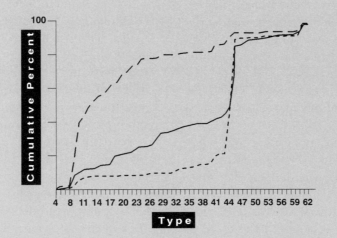

THE BORDIAN METHOD

SINCE ITS DEVELOPMENT IN THE 1950s, Bordes' approach to Lower and Middle Paleolithic assemblage description (Bordes 1953b; Bourgon 1957) has been widely used in Europe, the Near East, and northwest Africa, and so it is important to present the basic outlines of it here. The **Bordian Method**, as it is called, was originally intended to provide a statistical and graphical means of comparing assemblages on the basis of their entire lithic composition. It thus was intended to eliminate the "index fossil" approach used by earlier prehistorians, where one or two diagnostic types were all that were required for the classification of assemblages (see Sackett 1982). It also served as the basis for the definition of Bordes' various assemblage groups (or **facies**) of the Mousterian (see Bordes 1950; Bordes and Bourgon 1951).

Bordes felt that in order for the method to be effective, three principals must be respected. First, the number of objects in an assemblage should be sufficiently large—minimally, around one hundred. Second, the assemblage should be intact, that is, not affected by any biases in recovery or curation (which is a real problem in dealing with older excavations or museum collections that have been broken up and distributed among several institutions). Third, the assemblage should represent a homogeneous depositional unit.

For his principal typology, Bordes assigned a number to each type (Table I.1). For the most part, these numbered types represent the common tools made on flakes, as well as unretouched but characteristic technological products, such as Levallois flakes and points. However, some of these types, such as choppers and chopping-tools, are not on flakes. The various biface types are not usually numbered, since for the most part, Bordes excluded the biface types from his statistical and graphical representations.

For some of his indices, primarily the so-called technological indices, Bordes utilized the entire non-biface component. For the other indices and graphs that were designed to show typological variation, he relied on two separate populations: the **real count** of the entire number of objects classified into his types 1–63; and the **essential count**, which excludes the unretouched Levallois pieces (types 1–3), pieces with interior retouch (type 45); the abrupt and alternating retouched pieces (types 46–49); and the pieces with isolated bifacial retouch (type 50). Thus, the essential count retained only those tools that were truly characterized by deliberate retouch. Recently, and for the same reason, many Paleolithic archaeologists have begun to eliminate pseudo-Levallois points (type 5) and naturally-backed knives (type 38) from the essential counts.

For a visual representation of assemblage variability, Bordes relied on the use of cumulative graphs. The horizontal axis of these graphs represents the ordered type numbers (for either the essential or real counts), while the vertical axis represents the cumulative percentages as one proceeds along the typelist. The graph allows one to view the contribution of the percentage of each type relative to the others for a single assemblage, as well as to compare the typological makeup of several assemblages simultaneously. Figure I.1a displays cumulative graphs of the real count for three examples of Middle Paleolithic assemblage groups: a Ferrassie Mousterian rich in Levallois flakes and scrapers; a Quina Mousterian rich in scrapers but without many Levallois products; and a Denticulate Mousterian rich in notches and denticulates. Notice that there is a fair degree of separation of all three assemblage groups. Figure I.1b displays these same three assemblages on the basis of their essential counts, which serves to eliminate much of the separation between the Quina and Ferrassie assemblages since they differ primarily in the higher presence of Levallois pieces in the latter.

Type # Description

1.......Typical Levallois flake
2.......Atypical Levallois flake
3.......Levallois point
4.......Retouched Levallois point
5.......Pseudo-Levallois point
6.......Mousterian point
7.......Elongated Mousterian point
8.......Limace
9.......Single straight scraper
10.......Single convex scraper
11.......Single concave scraper
12.......Double straight scraper
13.......Double straight-convex scraper
14.......Double straight-concave scraper
15.......Double convex scraper
16.......Double concave scraper
17.......Double convex-concave scraper
18.......Straight convergent scraper
19.......Convex convergent scraper
20.......Concave convergent scraper
21.......Déjeté scraper
22.......Straight transverse scraper
23.......Convex transverse scraper
24.......Concave transverse scraper
25.......Scraper on interior surface
26.......Abrupt scraper
27.......Scraper with thinned back
28.......Scraper with bifacial retouch
29.......Alternate scraper
30.......Typical endscraper
31.......Atypical endscraper
32.......Typical burin
33.......Atypical burin
34.......Typical perçoir
35.......Atypical perçoir
36.......Typical backed knife
37.......Atypical backed knife
38.......Naturally-backed knife
39.......Raclette
40.......Truncation
41.......Mousterian tranchet
42.......Notch
43.......Denticulate
44.......Alternate retouched bec
45.......Flake with irregular retouch on interior
46–49..Flake with abrupt and alternating retouch
50.......Bifacially retouched flake
51.......Tayac point
52.......Notched triangle
53.......Pseudo-microburin
54.......End-notched flake
55.......Hachoir
56.......Rabot
57.......Stemmed point
58.......Stemmed tool
59.......Chopper
60.......Inverse chopper
61.......Chopping-tool
62.......Miscellaneous
63.......Bifacial foliate

Table I.1 Bordes' (1961) typelist

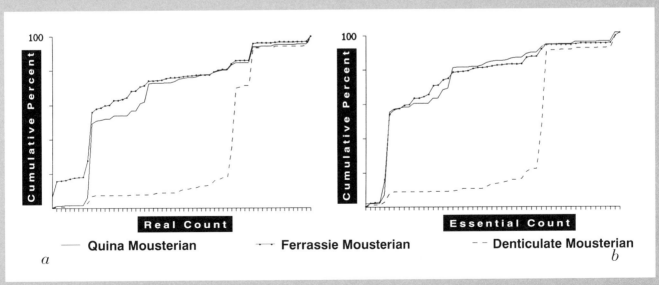

Real Count

Essential Count

—— Quina Mousterian   ⊷ Ferrassie Mousterian   – – Denticulate Mousterian

a

b

Appendix

I

Figure I.1a, b Real and essential cumulative graphs for selected Mousterian variants

Recently, certain authors, (e.g., Turq 1979) have begun to abandon the use of cumulative graphs in favor of a simplified circular or star diagram which represents the relative contribution of eight major classes of tools from the essential list (Table I.2).

Each tool class is then represented by one of eight axes in a circular diagram, with the percentages of the classes expressed as the length its axis. The Denticulate and Quina assemblages used in Figures I.1a and b are reproduced in the star diagrams of Figures I.2a and I.2b, respectively.

Bordes defined five *technological* indices based on the total of objects with recognizable features. These are:

- **Levallois Index** (IL): The number of Levallois flakes, blades and points (retouched or not) divided by the total of the non-biface assemblage.

- **Faceting Index** (IF): The percentage of faceted or dihedral platforms relative to the total number of recognizable platforms.

- **Strict Faceting Index** (IFs): The percentage of faceted platforms (excluding dihedrals) relative to the total number of recognizable platforms.

- **Blade Index** (Ilam): The number of blades (flakes whose length is at least twice their width) divided by the total number of complete flakes, blades, and points, regardless of technology (i.e., Levallois or not). Debénath and Duport (1986) consider this index a "strict" Blade Index, in contrast to a more encompassing one proposed by them that also considers bladey flakes with a length between 1.5 and 2 times their width.

- **Quina Index** (IQ): The number of objects in types 6–29 which exhibit Quina retouch, relative to the total number of these types. A broader index (Debénath and Duport 1986) also considers pieces with atypical Quina retouch.

Bordes also defined a number of *typological* indices, based on either the real or essential count:

- **Typological Levallois Index** (ILty): The number of types 1–4 divided by the total type count of types 1–63. If the index is to be based on the essential count, then it is the number of type 4 only divided by the essential type count.

- **Scraper Index** (IR): The percentage of types 9–29 relative to the total type count.

- **Total Acheulian Index** (IAt): The number of bifaces and backed knives (types 36 and 37) divided by the total type count plus bifaces.

- **Unifacial Acheulian Index** (IAu): The number of backed knives (types 36 and 37) relative to the total type count. Note that this "backed knife index" does not consider uniface bifaces.

- **Biface Index** (IB): The number of bifaces divided by the total type count plus bifaces.

- **Charentian Index** (IC): The percentage of single convex scrapers (type 10) and transverse scrapers (types 22–24) relative to the total type count.

Bordes also defined a number of typological indices that he called *groups*, which he often presented as a series of histograms accompanying the cumulative graphs:

- **Group I** (Levallois group): This is defined exactly as the Levallois Typological Index.

- **Group II** (Mousterian group): The percentage of types 5–29 relative to the total type count. It thus differs from the Scraper Index by the inclusion of pseudo-Levallois points, Mousterian points, and limaces.

- **Group III** (Upper Paleolithic group): The total of types 30–37 plus type 40 divided by the total type count. Note that raclettes (type 39) are excluded in the numerator.

- **Group IV** (Denticulate group): The number of denticulates divided by the total type count. Many authors have modified this to include the notched types as well as denticulates.

It should be pointed out that it is becoming increasingly clear that these indices alone are not sufficient to interpret or describe many aspects of assemblage variability. In part this is because of the addition of several new tool types defined since the time that Bordes developed his typology and defined these indices. Thus, several new indices have been defined to cover other descriptive or analytical needs. The reader should take care to note how each index is defined in the context of a particular report. Moreover, there is increasing attention being paid to more detailed technological aspects of Lower and Middle Paleolithic industries, most of which are not covered adequately in Bordes' method.

Class	Description	Type #
I	Points	4, 6, 7
II	Simple lateral and double scrapers	9–17, 25–27, 29
III	"Quina" scraper types	8, 22–24, 28, 55, 56
IV	"Mousterian of Acheulian Tradition" types	36, 37, and bifaces
V	"Ferrassie" Mousterian types	18–21 and discs
VI	Denticulates and notches	42–44, 51, 52, 54
VII	Miscellaneous	39, 41, 53, 57–61, pics and cleavers
VIII	Upper Paleolithic types	30–35, 40

Table I.2 Eight major classes of tools from Bordes' list of essential tools (Turq 1979)

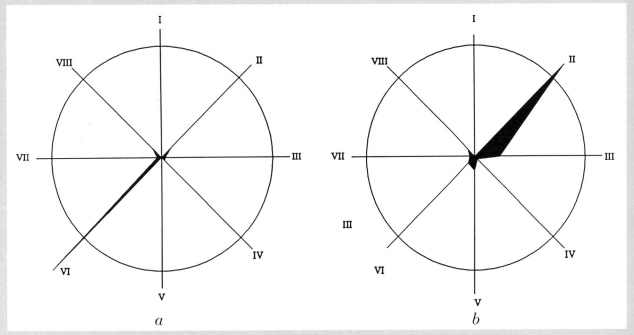

Figure I.2a, b Star diagrams of selected Mousterian variants

Appendix

I

APPENDIX
II

LIST OF FIGURES

Except where otherwise noted, the sites are located in France. Unsourced material is from the collections of The University Museum of Archaeology and Anthropology, University of Pennsylvania.

Appendix

II

5.14:   Mousterian point with thinned base and point, Nantet, Acheulian (Thibault 1970)

5.15:   Mousterian point retouched on the interior surface, Bouheben, typical Mousterian (Thibault 1970)

5.16:   Mousterian point with thinned base and point, La Chaise de Vouthon, Rissian Mousterian (Debénath 1974)

5.17:   Elongated Mousterian point, on a Levallois blade, Champ Paillard, Mousterian (Ricard 1989)

5.18:   Thick elongated Mousterian point, Bouheben, Acheulian (Thibault 1970)

5.19:   Elongated Mousterian point, Bouheben, Acheulian (Thibault 1970)

5.20:   Elongated Mousterian point, Bouheben, typical Mousterian (Thibault 1970)

5.21:   Elongated Mousterian point, Bouheben, Acheulian (Thibault 1970)

5.22:   Elongated Mousterian point whose morphology approaches a foliated point, La Règle, Mousterian (Ricard 1989)

5.23:   Fontmaure point, Fontmaure, Mousterian of Acheulian Tradition (Pradel and Pradel 1970)

5.24:   Quinson point, Fontmaure, Mousterian of Acheulian Tradition (Pradel and Pradel 1970)

5.25–5.28: Quinson points, La Crouzade, Charentian Mousterian (de Lumley 1971)

5.29:   Quinson point truncated by scalar retouch, Baume des Peyrards, Ferrassie Mousterian (de Lumley 1971)

5.30:   Quinson point truncated by abrupt retouch, L'Hortus, Mousterian (de Lumley 1971)

5.31–5.35: Typical limaces, Baume des Peyrards, Ferrassie Mousterian (de Lumley 1971)

5.36:   Typical limace, Genay, Mousterian (Pautrat 1985)

5.37:   Atypical limace, Baume des Peyrards, Ferrassie Mousterian (de Lumley 1971)

5.38:   Atypical limace, La Vauzelle, Quina Mousterian (Debénath 1968)

5.39:   Atypical limace, Grossen Grotte (Germany), German Micoquian (Wagner 1983)

5.40:   Atypical limace, Nantet, Mousterian (Thibault 1970)

5.41:   Atypical limace, Trou Magrite (Belgium), Mousterian (Ulrix-Closset 1975)

5.42:   Atypical limace, Spy (Belgium), Mousterian (Ulrix-Closset 1975)

6.1:   Single straight sidescraper, Combe-Capelle bas, Mousterian (excavations H. Dibble and M. Lenoir)

6.2:   Single straight sidescraper, Pillon, Mousterian (Thibault 1970)

6.3:   Single straight sidescraper, Bouheben, Mousterian (Thibault 1970)

6.4:   Single sidescraper, Grossen Grotte (Germany), Mousterian (Wagner 1983)

6.5:   Single straight sidescraper, Combe-Capelle bas, Mousterian (excavations H. Dibble and M. Lenoir)

6.6:   Single straight sidescraper with thinned base, La Chaise, Mousterian (Debénath 1974)

6.7:   Single sidescraper, on a Levallois blade, La Chaise de Vouthon, Rissian Mousterian (Delagnes 1992)

6.8:   Single straight sidescraper, La Quina, Mousterian

6.9:   Single straight sidescraper, Les Peyrards, Ferrassie Mousterian (de Lumley 1971)

6.10:   Single straight sidescraper with Quina retouch, Chateauneuf-sur-Charente, Quina Mousterian (Debénath 1970)

6.11:   Single convex sidescraper with atypical Quina retouch, Bouheben, Acheulian (Thibault 1970)

6.12:   Single convex sidescraper, Cotencher (Switzerland), Alpine Micoquian (Jequier 1975)

6.13:   Single convex sidescraper, Genay, Mousterian (Pautrat 1985)

6.14:   Single convex sidescraper, Bouheben, Acheulian (Thibault 1970)

6.15:   Single convex sidescraper, on a blade, Gare de Couze, Mousterian

6.16:   Single convex sidescraper, Bouheben, Acheulian (Thibault 1970)

6.17:   Single convex sidescraper, La Chaise de Vouthon, Rissian Mousterian (Delagnes 1992)

Appendix

II

6.57:   Double convex scraper, Bouheben, upper Acheulian (Thibault 1970)

6.58:   Double convex-concave scraper, Nantet, upper Acheulian (Thibault 1970)

6.59:   Double convex-concave scraper, La Cote de Saint Brelade (Jersey), Acheulian (Callow and Cornford 1986)

6.60:   Double straight-concave scraper, Bouheben, upper Acheulian (Thibault 1970)

6.61:   Double straight-concave scraper, Gare de Couze, Mousterian

6.62:   Convergent straight scraper, on a truncated blade, Bouheben, upper Acheulian (Thibault 1970)

6.63:   Convergent straight scraper, Bouheben, upper Acheulian (Thibault 1970)

6.64:   Convergent straight scraper with thinned base, Bouheben, upper Acheulian (Thibault 1970)

6.65, 6.66: Convergent convex scrapers, La Chaise de Vouthon, Rissian Mousterian (Delagnes 1992)

6.67, 6.68: Convergent convex scrapers, La Chaise de Vouthon, Rissian Mousterian (Delagnes 1992)

6.69:   Déjeté scraper, La Chaise de Vouthon, Rissian Mousterian (Delagnes 1992)

6.70:   Convergent convex scrapers, La Chaise de Vouthon, Rissian Mousterian (Delagnes 1992)

6.71:   Convergent convex scraper, Chateauneuf-sur-Charente, Quina Mousterian (Debénath 1974)

6.72:   Déjeté scraper, La Chaise de Vouthon, Rissian Mousterian (Delagnes 1992)

6.73:   Convergent concave scraper, Combe-Grenal, Quina Mousterian (Bordes 1961)

6.74:   Déjeté scraper, La Vauzelle, Quina Mousterian (Debénath 1968)

6.75:   Déjeté scraper, La Vauzelle, Quina Mousterian (Debénath 1968)

6.76:   Déjeté scraper, Chateauneuf-sur-Charente, Quina Mousterian, (Debénath 1974)

6.77:   Déjeté scraper, Gonderans les Moulins, Alpine Micoquian (Jequier 1975)

6.78:   Déjeté scraper, Pelanne, upper Acheulian (Thibault 1970)

6.79:   Triple déjeté scraper, typical Mousterian, Bouheben (Thibault 1970)

6.80:   Scraper with interior retouch, Ruisseau de Gravier, Mousterian (Lenoir 1983)

6.81:   Convex-concave scraper with interior retouch, on a blade, La Chaise de Vouthon, Rissian Mousterian (Delagnes 1992)

6.82:   Scraper with interior Quina retouch, La Quina, Quina Mousterian

6.83:   Scraper with interior retouch, La Chaise de Vouthon, Mousterian (Debénath 1974)

6.84:   Scraper with interior retouch, Baume des Peyrards, Ferrassie Mousterian (de Lumley 1971)

6.85:   Abrupt scraper, La Vauzelle, Quina Mousterian (Debénath 1968)

6.86:   Abrupt scraper, Les Artigaux, Mousterian (Lenoir 1983)

6.87:   Scraper with thinned back, Ruisseau de Gravier, Mousterian (Lenoir 1983)

6.88:   Scraper with thinned back, Castagens, Mousterian (Lenoir 1983)

6.89:   Transitional between scraper with thinned back and denticulated scraper form, La Quina, Mousterian

6.90:   Scraper with a thinned back, Combe-Capelle bas, Mousterian

6.91:   Scraper with thinned back and base, La Chaise de Vouthon, Rissian Mousterian (Delagnes 1992)

6.92:   Scraper with thinned back, La Chaise de Vouthon, Rissian Mousterian (Delagnes 1992)

6.93:   Scraper with thinned back, partially bifacial, La Quina, Quina Mousterian

6.94:   Scraper with thinned back and base, La Quina, Mousterian

6.95:   Scraper with bifacial Quina retouch, Jouanmartin, Mousterian (Thibault 1970)

6.96:   Scraper with bifacial Quina retouch, Chateauneuf-sur-Charente, Quina Mousterian (Debénath 1974)

6.97:   Scraper with bifacial retouch, Grand Darremont, Mousterian (Thibault 1970)

Appendix

II

7.20:   Burin/inverse denticulate, La Chaise de Vouthon, Rissian Mousterian (Delagnes 1992)

7.21:   Atypical burin, Ruisseau de Gravier, Mousterian (Lenoir 1983)

7.22:   Typical perçoir, La Chaise de Vouthon, Rissian Mousterian (Delagnes 1992)

7.23:   Billhook perçoir, Les Trécassats, Evenosian (de Lumley 1971)

7.24:   Trihedral perçoir, Engihoul, Denticulate Mousterian (Ulrix-Closset 1975)

7.25:   Lateral perçoir, Engihoul, Denticulate Mousterian (Ulrix-Closset 1975)

7.26:   Atypical perçoir, Ruisseau de Gravier, Mousterian (Lenoir 1983)

7.27:   Typical perçoir, Denticulate Mousterian, Nantet (Thibault 1970)

7.28:   Backed knife, Cornemps, Mousterian (Lenoir 1983)

7.29:   Typical backed knife, Pennon, Mousterian (Thibault 1970)

7.30:   Backed knife, Cornemps, Mousterian (Lenoir 1983)

7.31:   Typical backed knife, Ruisseau de Gravier, Mousterian (Lenoir 1983)

7.32:   Atypical backed knife, Pech de Bourre, Mousterian

7.33, 7.34: Typical backed knives, Cros de Peyrolles, typical Mousterian (de Lumley 1971)

7.35:   Chatelperron knife, La Chaise de Vouthon, Rissian Mousterian (Debénath 1974)

7.36:   Raclette, La Chaise de Vouthon, Mousterian (Debénath 1974)

7.37:   Raclette, Cornemps, Mousterian (Lenoir 1983)

7.38:   Raclette on a backed flake, Pennon, late Mousterian (Thibault 1970)

7.39:   Raclette, Genay, Mousterian (Pautrat 1985)

7.40:   Raclette, Jouanmartin, upper Acheulian (Thibault 1970)

7.41:   Raclette, Bouheben, typical Mousterian (Thibault 1970)

7.42–7.44: *Heidenschmiede*, Heidenschmiede bei Heidenheim (Baden-Württemberg), "Micoquian" (excavations H. Mohn and E. Peters, drawing H. Bosinski and E. Peters)

7.45:   *Heidenschmiede*, Hohler Stein bei Schambach (Bayern), "Micoquian" (excavations K. Gumpert, drawing W. Taute)

7.46:   Truncation, Castagens, Mousterian (Lenoir 1983)

7.47:   Truncation, Chateauneuf-sur-Charente, Denticulate Mousterian (Debénath 1974)

7.48:   Truncation, Camiac, Mousterian (Lenoir 1983)

7.49:   Truncation, Cros de Peyrolles, typical Mousterian (de Lumley 1971)

7.50:   Truncated flake, Fonseigner E, Mousterian (Geneste 1985)

7.51:   Truncated backed flake, La Vauzelle, Quina Mousterian (Debénath 1968)

7.52:   Truncation, Chateauneuf-sur-Charente, Denticulate Mousterian (Debénath 1974)

8.1:   Ordinary notch, La Chaise de Vouthon, Rissian Mousterian (Delagnes 1992)

8.2:   Clactonian notch, Chateauneuf-sur-Charente, Denticulate Mousterian (Debénath 1974)

8.3:   Interior notch, Esquicho Grapaou, Quina Mousterian (de Lumley 1971)

8.4:   Ordinary notch: Le Gua Mort, Mousterian (Lenoir 1983)

8.5:   Clactonian notch, Ioton, Charentian Mousterian (de Lumley 1971)

8.6:   Clactonian notch, Ruisseau de Gravier, Mousterian (Lenoir 1983)

8.7:   Interior notch, Pennon, late Mousterian (Thibault 1970)

8.8:   Clactonian notch, Ruisseau de Gravier, Mousterian (Lenoir 1983)

8.9, 8.10: End-notched pieces, Nantet, Denticulate Mousterian (Thibault 1970)

8.11, 8.12: End-notched pieces, L'Hortus, Denticulate Mousterian (de Lumley 1971)

8.13:   End-notched piece, Fenillot, Evenosian (de Lumley 1971)

Appendix

II

Appendix

II

BIBLIOGRAPHY

Addington, R.
1986 *Lithic Illustration: Drawing Flaked Stone Artifacts for Publication.* Chicago: University of Chicago Press.

Ahler, S.
1989 Mass Analysis of Flaking Debris: Studying the Forest Rather than the Trees. Pp. 85–118 in *Alternative Approaches to Lithic Analysis,* eds. D. Henry and G. Odell. Archaeological Papers of the American Anthropological Association No. 1.

Anderson-Gerfaud, P.
1990 Aspects of Behaviour in the Middle Palaeolithic: Functional Analysis of Stone Tools from Southwest France. Pp. 389–418 in *The Emergence of Modern Humans: An Archaeological Perspective,* ed. P. Mellars. Ithaca: Cornell University Press.

Barton, C. M.
1990 Beyond Style and Function: A View from the Middle Paleolithic. *American Anthropologist* 92:57–72.

Baumler, M.
1988 Core Reduction, Flake Production, and the Middle Paleolithic Industry of Zobiŝte (Yugoslavia). Pp. 255–274 in *Upper Pleistocene Prehistory of Western Eurasia,* eds. H. Dibble and A. Montet-White. University Museum Monograph 54. Philadelphia: University Museum, University of Pennsylvania.

Bertouille, H.
1989 *Théories physiques et mathématiques de la taille des outils préhistoriques.* Cahiers du Quaternaire 15. Paris: Centre National de la Recherche Scientifique.

Beyries, S.
1984 Approche fonctionelle de la variabilité des faciès du Moustérien. Thesis, Université de Paris.
1988 Functional Variability of Lithic Sets in the Middle Palaeolithic. Pp. 213–224 in *Upper Pleistocene Prehistory of Western Eurasia,* eds. H. Dibble and A. Montet-White. University Museum Monograph 54. Philadelphia: University Museum, University of Pennsylvania.

Biberson, P.
1954 Le hachereau dans l'Acheuléen du Maroc atlantique. *Libyca* 2:39–61.
1961 *Le Paléolithique inférieur du Maroc atlantique.* Publications du Service des Antiquités du Maroc 17. Rabat.
1967 *Galets aménagés du Maghreb et du Sahara.* Fiches Typologiques Africaines, 2ème cahier, fiches 33–64. Paris: Arts et Métiers Graphiques.

Boëda, E.
1990 De la surface au volume: analyse des conceptions de débitages Levallois et laminaire. Pp. 63–68 in *Paléolithique moyen récent et Paléolithique supérieur ancien en Europe,* ed. C. Farizy. Mémoires du Musée de Préhistoire d'Ile de France 3.

Boëda, E.; Geneste, J.-M.; and Meignen, L.
1990 Identification de chaînes opératoires lithiques du Paléolithique ancien et moyen. *Paléo* 2:43–80.

Boëda, E., and Pelegrin, J.
1983 Approche technologique du nucléus Levallois à éclat. *Etudes préhistoriques* (1979–1980) 15:41–48.

Bonnichsen, R.
1977 *Models for Discovering Cultural Information from Stone Tools.* Archaeological Survey of Canada Paper 60. Ottawa: National Museum of Canada.

Bordes, F.
1947 Etude comparative des différentes techniques de taille du silex et des roches dures. *L'Anthropologie* 51:1–29.
1950 Principes d'une méthode d'étude des techniques de débitage et de la typologie du Paléolithique ancien et moyen. *L'Anthropologie* 54:19–34.
1953a Notules de typologie paléolithique, II: Pointes levalloisiennes et pointes pseudo-levalloisiennes. *Bulletin de la Société Préhistorique Française* 50:311–313.
1953b Essai de classification des industries "moustériennes." *Bulletin de la Société Préhistorique Française* 50:457–466.
1961 *Typologie du Paléolithique ancien et moyen.* 2 vols. Mémoires de l'Institut Préhistoriques de l'Université de Bordeaux 1. Bordeaux: Delmas.
1965 A propos de typologie. *L'Anthropologie* 69:369–377.
1968 *Le Paléolithique dans le monde.* Paris: Hachette, l'Univers des Connaissances.
1969 Reflections on Typology and Techniques in the Paleolithic. *Arctic Anthropology* 6:1–29.

1980　Le débitage levallois et ses variantes. *Bulletin de la Société Préhistorique Française* 77:45–49.

Bordes, F., and Bourgon, M.
1951　Le complexe moustérien: Moustérien, Levalloisien et Tayacian. *L'Anthropologie* 55:1–23.

Bordes, F., and Crabtree, D.
1969　The Corbiac Blade Technique and Other Experiments. *Tebiwa* 12:1–21.

Bordes, F., and Fitte, P.
1953　L'atelier Commont. Album de 188 dessins de Victor Commont avec une étude de l'atelier. *L'Anthropologie* 57:1–45.

Bordes, F., and Sonneville-Bordes, D. de.
1970　The Significance of Variability in Paleolithic Assemblages. *World Archaeology* 2:61–73.

Bosinski, G.
1963　Eine Mittelpaläolitische Formengruppe und das Problem ihrer geochronologischen Einordnung. *Gegenwart* 14:120–140.

Boucher de Perthes, J. de
1847–　*Antiquités celtiques et antédiluviennes.*
1864　*Mémoire sur l'industrie primitive et les arts à leur origine*, Vol. 1 (1847), Vol. 2 (1857), Vol. 3 (1864). Paris: Treuttel and Wurtz.

Bourgon, M.
1957　*Les industries moustériennes et prémoustériennes du Périgord.* Archives de l'Institut de Paléontologie Humaine Mémoire 27. Paris: Masson.

Bourlon, M.
1907　Débitage des rognons en tranches paralléles. *Bulletin de la Société Préhistorique Française* 4:330–332.

Breuil, H.
1926　Palaeolithic Industries from the Beginning of the Würmian Glaciation. *Man* 26 no. 116.
1954　Prolégomènes à une classification préhistorique. *Bulletin de la Société Préhistorique Française* 51:7–15.

Brézillon, M.
1968　*La dénomination des objets de pierre taillée: matériaux pour un vocabulaire des péhistoriens de langue française.* Gallia préhistoire Supplément 4. Paris: Centre National de la Recherche Scientifique.

Callow, P.
1986　The Artefacts: Introductory Remarks. Pp. 199–201 in *La Cotte de St. Brelade 1961–1978 Excavations by C. B. M. McBurney*, eds. P. Callow and J. Cornford. Norwich: Geo Books.

Callow, P., and Cornford, J., eds.
1986　*La Cotte de St. Brelade 1961–1978 Excavations by C. B. M. McBurney.* Norwich: Geo Books.

Capitan, L.
1902　Un nouveau gisement chelléen, commune de Clérieux près Curson (Drôme). Pp. 755–757 in *Association Française pour l'Avancement des Sciences*, 31ème session, Montauban.

Chase, P.
1990　Tool-Making Tools and Middle Paleolithic Behavior. *Current Anthropology* 31:443–446.

Chavaillon, J.
1964　*Classification des pièces présentant un biseau terminal.* Laboratoire de Géologie du Quaternaire, Centre National de la Recherche Scientifique, Meudon.

Cheynier, A.
1954　Observations présentées en séance par le Dr. A. Cheynier sur F. Bordes: notules de typologie paléolithique. *Bulletin de la Société Préhistorique Française* 51:339.

Chmielewski, W.
1969　Ensembles micoquo-prondnikiens en Europe centrale. *Geographie polonica* 17:71–386.

Clark, J. D.
1970　*The Prehistory of Africa.* New York: Praeger.

Clark, J. D., and Kleindienst, M. R.
1974　The Stone Age Cultural Sequence: Terminology, Typology and Raw Material. Pp. 71–106 in *Kalambo Falls Prehistoric Site*, Vol. 2, ed. J. D. Clark. London: Cambridge University Press.

Collina-Girard, J.
1975　Les industries archaïques sur galets des terrasses quaternaires de la plaine du Roussillon (Pyrénées orientales, France). Thesis, Marseille.

Combier, J.
1955　Pointes levalloisiennes retouchées sur la face plane (pointes type Soyons). *Bulletin de la Société Préhistorique Française* 52:432–434.
1967　*Le Paléolithique de l'Ardèche dans son cadre paléoclimatique.* Bordeaux: Delmas.

Commont, V.
1906　Les découvertes récentes de Saint-Acheul. L'Acheuléen. *Revue de l'Ecole d'Anthropologie de Paris* 16:228–241.
1908　Les industries de l'ancien Saint-Acheul. *L'Anthropologie* 19:557–572.
1909　L'industrie moustérienne dans le Nord de la France. Pp. 115–197 in *Congrès Préhistorique de France*, 5ème session, Beauvais.

Coon, C.
1951   *Cave Explorations in Iran.* Philadelphia: University Museum, University of Pennsylvania.

Cotterell, B., and Kamminga, J.
1987   The Formation of Flakes. *American Antiquity* 52(4):675–708.

Crabtree, D. E.
1972   *An Introduction to Flintworking.* Occasional Papers 28. Pocatello: Idaho State University Museum.

Dalloni, M.
1948   *Matériaux pour l'étude du Sahara oriental. Région entre la Libye, le Tibesti et le Kaouar (Niger). Géologie et Préhistoire.* Mission Scientifique du Fezzan Vol. 6. Alger: Institut de Recherches Sahariennes.

Daniel, G. E.
1975   *A Hundred and Fifty Years of Archaeology,* 2nd ed. London: Duckworth.

Debénath A.
1968   Le Moustérien type "Quina" de la Vauzelle (Charente-maritime). *Bulletin de la Société Préhistorique Française* 65:259–268.
1970   Compte-rendu des fouilles éffectués en 1969 à Dar-es-Soltane (Maroc). *Bulletin et Memoires de la Société Archéologique et Historique de la Charente* pp. 15–16.
1974   Recherches sur les terrains quaternaires des Charentes et les industries qui leur sont associées. Thesis, Université de Bordeaux.
1983   Quelques particularités techniques et typologiques des industries de La Chaise de Vouthon (Charente). Pp. 239–247 in *Actes du 105ème Congrès National des Sociétés Savantes* (Caen 1980).
1984   Remarques sur les industries acheuléennes en France: stades evolutifs et facies. Pp. 227–232 in *Actes du 106ème Congrès National des Sociétés Savantes* (Perpignon 1981).
1990   A propos de typologie lithique: inutilité ou inéluctabilité? *Bulletin de la Société d'Anthropologie du Sud-Ouest* 25:191–200.

Debénath, A., and Duport, L.
1986   Le Moustérien de la grotte de Montgaudier (Charente), note preliminaire. *Bulletin de la Société d'Anthropologie du Sud-Ouest* 21:5–9.

Delagnes, A.
1992   Etude technologiques des industries lithiques de La Chaise de Vouthon, Charente. Thesis, Université de Nanterre.

Desbrosse, R.; Kozlowski, J. K.; and Zuate y Zuber, J.
1976   Prondniks de France et d'Europe centrale. *L'Anthropologie* 80:431–448.

Dibble, H.
1984a   Interpreting Typological Variation of Middle Paleolithic Scrapers: Function, Style, or Sequence of Reduction? *Journal of Field Archaeology* 11:431–436.
1984b   The Mousterian Industry from Bisitun Cave (Iran). *Paléorient* 10:23–34.
1987   Reduction Sequences in the Manufacture of Mousterian Implements of France. Pp. 33–45 in *The Pleistocene Old World: Regional Perspectives,* ed. O. Soffer. New York: Plenum Press.
1988   Typological Aspects of Reduction and Intensity of Utilization of Lithic Resources in the French Mousterian. Pp. 181–197 in *Upper Pleistocene Prehistory of Western Eurasia,* eds. H. Dibble and A. Montet-White. University Museum Monograph 54. Philadelphia: University Museum, University of Pennsylvania.
1989   The Implications of Stone Tool Types for the Presence of Language during the Middle Paleolithic Pp. 415–432 in *The Human Revolution: Behavioural and Biological Perspectives on the Origins of Modern Humans,* eds. P. Mellars and C. Stringer. Edinburgh: Edinburgh University Press.
1991   Mousterian Assemblage Variability on an Interregional Scale. *Journal of Anthropological Research* 47(2):239–258. Special issue on A Quarter Century of Paleoanthropology: Views from the U.S.A., ed. L. G. Straus.

Dibble, H., and Bernard, M.
1980   A Comparison of Basic Edge Angle Measurement Techniques. *American Antiquity* 45:857–865.

Dibble, H., and Debénath, A.
1991   When a Problem is not a Problem: Paradigmatic Differences in a Collaborative Research Project. Pp. 217–226 in *Paradigmatic Biases in Circum-Mediterranean Hunter-Gatherer Research,* ed. G. Clark. Philadelphia: University of Pennsylvania Press.

Dibble, H., and Whittaker, J.
1981   New Experimental Evidence on the Relation between Percussion Flaking and Flake Variation. *Journal of Archaeological Science* 6:283–296.

Eloy, E.
1950   Reconstitutions réalisées à la suite de la fouille d'un atelier de taille omalien à Dommartin (Belgique). Pp. 279–290 in *Congrès Préhistorique de France*, 13ème session, Paris.

Ferry, H. de
1870   *Le Maconnais préhistorique*. Paris: Reinwald.

Fish, P.
1979   *The Interpretive Potential of Mousterian Debitage*. Arizona State University Anthropological Research Papers 16. Tempe.
1981   Beyond Tools: Middle Paleolithic Debitage Analysis and Cultural Inference. *Journal of Anthropological Research* 38:374–386.

Ford, J.
1954   On the Concept of Types. *American Anthropologist* 56:42–54.

Gábori-Csánk, V.
1968   L'industrie moustérienne d'Erd (Hongrie). Pp. 191–202 in *La Préhistoire, problemes et tendances*. Paris: Centre National de la Recherche Scientifique.

Geneste, M.
1985   Analyse lithique d'industries moustériennes du Périgord: une approche technologique du comportement des groupes humains au Paléolithique moyen. Thesis, Université de Bordeaux.

Gobert, E. G.
1950   Le gisement paléolithique de Sidi Zin, avec notice sur la faune de Sidi Zin de R. Vaufrey. *Karthago* 1:1–64.

Gould, R.
1977   Ethno-archaeology; or Where do Models Come From? Pp. 162–168 in *Stone Tools as Cultural Markers*, ed. R. V. S. Wright. Australian Institute of Aboriginal Studies. Canberra: Humanities Press.

Goury, G.
1931   *L'homme des cités lacustres*, Vol. 1. Paris: Picard.

Gruet, M.
1945   Etude sur le mot biface. *Bulletin de la Société Préhistorique Française* 42:97–199.
1959   Le gisement d'el Guettar et sa flore. *Libyca* 6–7:79–126.

Guichard, G.
1976   Les civilisations du Paléolithique inférieur en Périgord. Pp. 909–928 in *La préhistoire française*, ed. H. de Lumley. Paris: Centre National de la Recherche Scientifique.

Guichard, J.
1965   Un faciès original de l'Acheuléen: Cantalouette (commune de Creyssac, Dordogne). *L'Anthropologie* 69:413–464.

Guichard, J., and Guichard, G.
1966   A propos d'un site acheuléen du Bergeracois (Les Pendus, commune de Creysse); bifaces-hachereaux et hachereaux sur éclats, apperçu typologique. *Actes de la Société Linnéenne de Bordeaux* 103, série B (5).

Hayden, B.
1977   Stone Tool Functions in the Western Desert. Pp. 178–188 in *Stone Tools as Cultural Markers*, ed. R. V. S. Wright. Australian Institute of Aboriginal Studies. Canberra: Humanities Press.
1979   *Lithic Use-wear Analysis*. New York: Academic Press.

Hayden, B., and Hutchings, W.
1989   Whither the Billet Flake? Pp. 235–258 in *Experiments in Lithic Technology*, eds. D. Amick and R. Mauldin. British Archaeological Reports International Series 528. Oxford.

Heinzelin de Braucourt, J. de
1962   Manuel de typologie des industries lithiques. *Sciences* (Brussels) 14:1–72.

Holdaway, S.
1989   Were There Hafted Projectile Points in the Mousterian? *Journal of Field Archaeology* 16:79–85.

Jelinek, A.
1976   Form, Function and Style in Lithic Analysis. Pp. 19–33 in *Cultural Change and Continuity: Essays in Honor of James Bennett Griffin*, ed. C. E. Cleland. New York: Academic Press.
1977   A Preliminary Study of Flakes from the Tabun Cave, Israel. *Eretz-Israel* 13:87–96.
1990   The Amudian in the Context of the Mugharan Traditions at the Tabun Cave (Mount Carmel), Israel. Pp. 81–90 in *The Emergence of Modern Humans: An Archaeological Perspective*, ed. P. Mellars. Ithaca: Cornell University Press.

Jequier, J. P.
1975   *Le Moustérien alpin, révision critique.*
        Eburodunum II. Cahiers d'Archéologie
        Romande No. 2. Yverdon.

Kantman, S.
1970a   Esquisse d'un procédé analytique pour
        l'étude macrographiques des "encoches."
        Quaternaria 13:269–280.
1970b   Essai d'une méthode d'étude des "denticu-
        lés" moustériens par discrimination des
        variables morpho-fonctionnelles. *Quaterna-
        ria* 13:281–294.
1970c   "Raclettes moustériennes": une étude expéri-
        mental sur la distinction de retouche inten-
        tionelle et les modifications au tranchant par
        utilisation. *Quaternaria* 13:295–304.

Keeley, L.
1980   *Experimental Determination of Stone Tool
        Uses.* Chicago: University of Chicago Press.

Kelley, H.
1954   Burins levalloisiens. *Bulletin de la Société
        Préhistorique Française* 51:419–428.
1955   Burins acheuléens. *Bulletin de la Société
        Préhistorique Française* 52:278–283.

Kleindienst, M. R.
1961   Variability within the Late Acheulian
        Assemblage in Eastern Africa. *South African
        Archaeological Bulletin* 16:35–52.
1962   Components of the East African Acheulian
        Assemblage: An Analytical Approach. Pp.
        81–104 in *Actes du IVe Congrès Panafricain
        de Préhistoire et de l'Etude du Quaternaire.*

Krieger, A.
1944   The Typological Concept. *American
        Antiquity* 3:271–288.

Krukoqaki, S.
1924   Osobliwosci przyrody doliny Pradnika ze
        stanawiska ochrony przyrody. *Ochrona
        Przyrody* 4:85–92.

Kuhn, S. L.
1990   A Geometric Index of Reduction for
        Unifacial Stone Tools. *Journal of
        Archaeological Science* 17:583–593.
1992   Blank Form and Reduction as Determinants
        of Mousterian Scraper Morphology.
        American Antiquity 57:115–128.

Laplace-Jauretche, G.
1957   Typologie analytique. Application d'une
        nouvelle méthode d'étude des formes et des
        structures aux industries à lames et à
        lamelles. *Quaternaria* 4:133–164.
1964   Essai de typologie systématique. *Annali dell
        Universata di Ferrara,* Sezione 15, 1, suppl.
        2.

Leach, B.
1969   *Concept of Similarity in Prehistoric Studies.*
        Studies in Prehistoric Anthropology 1.
        Anthropology Department of Otago.

Leakey, L. S. B.
1935   *The Stone Age Races of Kenya.* Oxford:
        Oxford University Press.

Leakey, M. D.
1966   A Review of the Oldowan Culture from
        Olduvai Gorge, Tanzania. *Nature*
        210:462–466.
1971   *Olduvai Gorge.* Vol. III: *Excavations in Beds
        II and III, 1960–1963.* Cambridge:
        Cambridge University Press.

Lenoir, M.
1973   Obtention expérimentale de la retouche de
        type Quina. *Bulletin de la Société
        Préhistorique Française* 70:10–11.
1983   Le Paléolithique des basses vallées de la
        Dordogne et de la Garonne. Thesis,
        Université de Bordeaux.
1986   Un mode d'obtention de la retouche "Quina"
        dans le Moustérien de Combe-Grenal
        (Domme, Dordogne). *Bulletin de la Société
        d'Anthropologie du Sud-Ouest* 21:153–160.

Leroi-Gourhan, A.
        Le geste et la parole, I: *Technique et lan-
        gage.* Paris: Albin Michel.

Luedtke, B.
1984   Lithic Material Demand and Quarry
        Production. Pp. 65–76 in *Prehistoric
        Quarries and Lithic Production,* eds. J.
        Ericons and B. Purdy. Cambridge:
        Cambridge University Press.

Lumley, H. de
1971   *Le Paléolithique inférieur et moyen du Midi
        méditerranéen dans son cadre géologique.*
        Vol. 1: *Ligurie, Provence*; Vol. 2: *Bas-
        Languedoc, Roussillon, Catalogne.* Gallia
        préhistoire Supplément 5. Paris: Centre
        National de la Recherche Scientifique.

Lumley, H. de, and Bottet, B.
1960   Sur l'évolution des climats et des industries
        au Riss et au Würm d'aprés le remplissage
        de la Baume Bonne (Quinson, Basses Alpes).
        Pp. 271–301 in *Festschrift für Lothar Zotz.
        Steinzeitfragen der Alten und Neuen Welt.*
        Bonn: Ludwig Röhrscheid Verlag.

Martin, H.
1923   *Recherches sur l'évolution du Moustérien
        dans le gisement de la Quina (Charente).
        Industrie lithique.* Mémoires de la Société
        Archéologique et Historique de la Charente
        2. Paris.

Meignen, L., and Bar-Yosef, O.
1991   Les outillages lithiques moustériens de Kébara (Fouilles 1982–1985). Pp. 49–76 in *Le squelette moustérien de Kébara 2*, eds. O. Bar-Yosef and B. Vandermeersch. Cahiers de Paléontologie. Paris: Centre National de la Recherche Scientifique.

Mellars, P.
1974   The Paleolithic and Mesolithic. Pp. 41–49 and 268–279 in *British Prehistory: A New Outline*, ed. A. C. Renfrew. London: Duckworth.

Moisan, L.
1978   Recherche sur les terrasses alluvial de Libournais et leurs industries préhistoriques. Thesis, Université de Bordeaux.

Mortillet, G. de
1883   *Le préhistorique: antiquité de l'homme*. Paris: Reinwald.

Movius, H. L., Jr.
1957   Pebble-tool Terminology in India and Pakistan. *Man in India* 37(2):149–156.

Neuville, R.
1931   L'Acheuléen supérieur de la grotte d'Oumm-Qatafa (Palestine). *L'Anthropologie* 41:13–51.

Newcomer, H. M.
1976   Spontaneous Retouch. Pp. 62–64 in *Second International Symposium on Flint* (Maastricht 1975). *Staringia* 3.

Newcomer, H. M., and Hivernel-Guerre, F.
1974   Nucleus sur éclat: technologie et utilisation par différentes cultures préhistoriques. *Bulletin de la Société Préhistorique Française* 71:119–128.

Nishiaki, Y.
1985   Truncated-faceted Flakes from Levantine Mousterian Assemblages. *Department of Anthropology, University of Tokyo Bulletin* 4:215–226.

Pautrat, Y.
1985   Le Moustérien de Genay (Côte d'Or). *Bulletin de la Société Préhistorique Française* 82:138–142.

Perpère, M.
1986   Apport de la typometrie a la definition des eclats Levallois: l'exemple d'Ault. *Bulletin de la Société Préhistorique Française* 83:115–118.

Peyrony, D.
1932   Station préhistorique de la Gare de Couze ou de Saint-Sulpice-des-Magnats, commune de Lalinde (Dordogne). *Bulletin de la Société Historique et Archéologique du Périgord* 51:81–101.
1934   La Ferrassie. Moustérien, Périgordien, Aurignacien. *Préhistoire* 3:1–92.

Peyrony, D.; Bourrinet, P.; and Darpeix, A.
1930   Le burin moustérien. Pp. 310–315 in *Congrès International d'Anthropologie et d'Archéologie Préhistorique*, 15ème session, Portugal.

Pittard, E., and Montandon, R.
1914   L'outillage en silex de la station moustérienne "les Rebières I" (Dordogne). Les racloirs (coupoirs). *Archives Suisses d'Anthropologie Générale* 1:43–53.

Pradel, L.
1952   Les gisements moustériens de Fontmaure. Pp. 459–462 in *Congrès Préhistorique de France*, 13ème session, Paris.
1953   Précisions sur les burins d'angle et sur les burins plans. Pp. 545–552 in *Congrès Préhistorique de France*, 14ème session, Strasbourg-Metz.
1963   La pointe moustérienne. *Bulletin de la Société Préhistorique Française* 60:569–581.

Pradel, L., and Pradel, S.
1970   La Station Paléolithique de Fontmaure, Commune de Vellèches (Vienne). *L'Anthropologie* 74(7–8):481–526.

Ramendo, L.
1963   Les galets aménagés de Reggan, Sahara. *Libyca* 2:43–73.

Ricard, J.
1989   Gisement de Champ-Paillard (Commune de Saint l'Eger de Monbrun, Deux Sevres). Thesis, l'Ecole Protique de Hautes Etudes.

Rigaud, J.-P., and Texier, J.-P.
1981   A propos des particularités techniques et typologiques du gisement des Tares, commune de Sourzac (Dordogne). *Bulletin de la Société Préhistorique Française* 78:109–117.

Roe, D.
1968   British Lower and Middle Palaeolithic Handaxe Groups. *Proceedings of the Prehistoric Society* 34:1–82.

Rutot, A.
1909   Un homme de science peut-il, raisonnablement, admettre l'existence des industries primitives, dites éolithiques? *Bulletin et Mémoires de la Société d'Anthropologie de Paris*, 5ème série, 10:447–473.

Sackett, J.
1982   From de Mortillet to Bordes: A Century of French Palaeolithic Research. Pp. 85–99 in *Toward a History of Archaeology*, ed. G. Daniel. London: Thames and Hudson.

Schild, R., and Wendorf, F.
1977   *The Prehistory of Dakhla Oasis and Adjacent Desert*. Wroclaw: Ossolineum.

Semenov, S. A.
1964   *Prehistoric Technology*. London: Cory, Adams and Mackay.
1970   The Forms and Funktions of the Oldest Tools. *Quartär* 21:1–20.

Shea, J.
1989a A Functional Study of the Lithic Industries Associated with Hominid Fossils in the Kebara and Qafzeh Caves, Israel. Pp. 611–625 in *The Human Revolution: Behavioural and Biological Perspectives on the Origins of Modern Humans*, eds. P. Mellars and C. Stringer. Edinburgh: Edinburgh University Press.
1989b Spear Points from the Middle Paleolithic of the Levant. *Journal of Field Archaeology* 15:441–450.

Singer, R., and Wymer, J.
1982   *The Middle Stone Age at Klasies River Mouth in South Africa*. Chicago: University of Chicago Press.

Siret, L.
1933   Le coup de burin moustérien. *Bulletin de la Société Préhistorique Française* 30:120–127.

Solecki, R.
1992   More on Hafted Projectile Points in the Mousterian. *Journal of Field Archaeology* 19:207–212.

Solecki, R., and Solecki, R.
1970   Secondary Flaking Technique at the Nahr Ibrahim Cave Site, Lebanon. *Bulletin de Musée de Beyrouth* 23:137–142.

Sonneville-Bordes, D. de
1960   *Le Paléolithique supérieur en Périgord*. 2 vols. Bordeaux: Delmas.

Spaulding, A.
1953   Statistical Techiques for the Discovery of Artifact Types. *American Antiquity* 18:305–313.

Taschini, M., and Bietti, A.
1979   L'industrie lithique de Grota Guattari au Mont Circe (Latium): définition culturelle, typologique et chronologique du Pontinien. *Quaternaria* 21:179–247.

Tavoso, A.
1978   Le Paléolithique inférieur et moyen du Haut-Languedoc. *Etudes quaternaires* 5. Paris: Institut de Paléontologie Humaine.

Terrade, A.
1912   Le burin-ciseau de la station moustérienne de Catigny (Oise). *Bulletin de la Société Préhistorique Française* 2:185–192.

Thibault, C.
1970   Recherches sur les terrains quaternaires du Bassin de l'Adour. Thesis, Université de Bordeaux.

Tixier, J.
1956   Le hachereau dans l'Acheuléen nord-africain. Notes typologiques. Pp. 914–923 in *Congrès Préhistorique de France*, 15ème session, Poitiers-Angouléme.
1960   Les industries lithiques d' Aïn Fritissa (Maroc oriental). *Bulletin d'archéologie marocaine* 3:107–244.
1963   *Typologie de l'Epipaléolithique du Maghreb*. Mémoires du Centre de Recherches Anthropologiques, Préhistoriques et Ethnographiques 2. Alger, Paris: AMG.

Tixier, J.; Inizan, M. L.; and Roche, H.
1980   *Préhistoire de la pierre taillé*. Vol. 1: *Terminologie et technologie*. Antibes: Cercle de Recherches et d'Etudes Préhistoriques.

Tuffreau, A.
1984   Le débitage de lames dans le Paléolithique inférieur et moyen de la France septentrionale. Pp. 53–54 in *Préhistoire de la pierre taillée*. Vol. 2: *Economie du débitage laminaire*, ed. J. Tixier. Paris: Cercle de Recherches et d'Etudes Préhistoriques.

Turq, A.
1979   L'évolution du Moustérien de type Quina au Roc de Marsal et en Périgord. Thesis, l'Ecole des Hautes Etudes en Sciences Sociales, Bordeaux.
1989   Approche technologique et économique du faciès Moustérien de type Quina. *Bulletin de la Société Préhistorique Française* 86:244–256.

Turq, A., and Marcillaud, J. M.
1973   Les racloirs à amincissement de type "Kostienki" de La Plane, commune de Mazeyrolles (Dordogne). *Bulletin de la Société Préhistorique Française* 73:75–82.

Tyldesley, J. A.
1987   *The bout coupé Handaxe: A Typological Problem*. British Archaeological Reports British Series 170. Oxford.

Ulrix-Closset, M.
1975   *Le Paléolithique moyen dans le bassin mosan en Belgique*. Faculté de Philosophie et Lettres de l'Université de Liège, Publications Exceptionnelles 3. Liège: Éditions Universa.

Van Peer, P.
1991   Interassemblage Variability and Levallois Styles: The Case of the Northern African Middle Paleolithic. *Journal of Anthropological Archaeology* 10:107–51.

Van Riet Lowe, C.
1952   The Pleistocene Geology and Prehistory of Uganda, Part 1: Prehistory. *Geological Survey of Uganda* 6.

Vaufrey, R.
1955   *Préhistoire de l'Afrique*. Vol. I: *Maghreb*. Publications de l'Institut des Hautes Etudes de Tunis 4. Paris: Masson.

Vayson de Pradenne, A.
1920   La plus ancienne industrie de Saint-Acheul. *L'Anthropologie* 30:441–496.

Verjux, C.
1988   Les denticulés moustériens. Pp. 197–204 in *L'homme de Neandertal*. Vol. 4: *La technique*, eds. L. Binford and J.-P. Rigaud. Liège: Université de Liège.

Vertes, L.
1964   *Tata—Eine Mittelpaläolithische Travertinsiedlung in Ungarin*. Archeologia Hungarica 43. Budapest: Akadémiai Kiadó.

Wagner, E.
1983   *Die Mittelpaläolithikum der Grossen Grotte bei Blaubeuren (Alb-Donau-Kreis)*. Forshungen und Berichte zur Vor- und Frühgeschichte in Baden-Württemberg 16. Stuttgart: Konrad Theiss Verlag.

Whallon, R., and Brown, J.
1982   *Essays on Archaeological Typology*. Evanston, IL: Center for American Archaeology Press.

INDEX
OF TOOL TYPES